DATE DUE

DEMCO 38-296

Economic Crisis and
State Reform in Brazil

❖❖

K,

Economic Crisis and State Reform in Brazil

Toward a New Interpretation of Latin America

❖❖

Luiz Carlos Bresser Pereira

LYNNE
RIENNER
PUBLISHERS

BOULDER
LONDON

Published in the United States of America in 1996 by
Lynne Rienner Publishers, Inc.
1800 30th Street, Boulder, Colorado 80301

and in the United Kingdom by
Lynne Rienner Publishers, Inc.
3 Henrietta Street, Covent Garden, London WC2E 8LU

Library of Congress Cataloging-in-Publication Data
Bresser Pereira, Luiz Carlos.
    Economic crisis and state reform in Brazil   :   toward a new
  interpretation of Latin America   /   Luiz Carlos Bresser Pereira.
      p.   cm.
    Includes bibliographical references and index.
    ISBN 1-55587-532-7
    1. Latin America—Economic policy. 2. Latin America—Economic
  conditions—1982– 3. Brazil—Economic policy. 4. Brazil—Economic
  conditions—1985– I. Title.
  HC125.P4379   1994
  338.98—dc20   94-28296
                                                            CIP

British Cataloguing in Publication Data
A Cataloguing in Publication record for this book
is available from the British Library.

Printed and bound in the United States of America

      The paper used in this publication meets the requirements
  ∞ of the American National Standard for Permanence of
      Paper for Printed Library Materials Z39.48-1984.

      5   4   3   2   1

Contents

Tables and Figures

❖❖❖

TABLES

Introduction: The Search for a New Interpretation

◇◇

This book describes the economic crisis that seized Brazil and the rest of Latin America in the 1980s, its political consequences, and the economic reforms that were instituted in the mid-1980s but remain incomplete. This is foremost a book about Brazil, but analysis of the significant changes Latin America underwent from 1982, when the debt crisis broke, until the mid-1990s is present throughout. The crisis of the 1980s was essentially a Latin American crisis; it is impossible to understand this crisis in the context of only one country. Thus I had to study the economies of several Latin American countries, particularly Mexico and Argentina, but my focus is particularly on Brazil, the country I know best.

I speak about interpretations of Brazil and Latin America, corresponding economic development strategies, and corresponding class coalitions and broad political pacts. An interpretation of or approach to the causes of the Latin American crisis has a corresponding development strategy, which can be implemented only if a class coalition is able to informally celebrate an informal political pact to sustain it.

I begin from an interpretation of the Latin American crisis as a crisis of the state and propose that the strategy that will overcome it is market-oriented, but also a pragmatic and social-democratic strategy rather than a neoliberal one. Market orientation and fiscal discipline remain priorities, but the objective is not the minimal state but rather the reconstruction of state capacity and governance. However, in addition to being market-oriented—oriented toward domestic and international competition—reforms will have to carefully consider the national interest. Old-time nationalism—the nationalism that was tied to the import substitution strategy—lost ground in Latin America, but a new form of nationalism, in which the national interest is defended in a case-by-case approach, remains extremely relevant. In Brazil economic reforms were undertaken more slowly because they were consistently not only market-oriented but also Brazil-oriented. They were particularly concerned not with building confidence in Washington and New York but with protecting the national interest and the macroeconomic fundamentals, and they had as their basic objective reforming the state. After all, fiscal adjustment, privitization, and liberalization are essentially state reforms.

1

M y interpretation of the Latin American crisis can be extended to Eastern Europe and, with some caveats, to most developed countries. The 1980s were years of crisis for both Latin America and Eastern Europe. In the developed countries the crisis was less severe, but they, too, have faced a slowdown in economic growth since the early 1970s, and unemployment has emerged as a major problem. In the last twenty years, GDP growth in the OECD countries was half that of the previous twenty years. Brazil and Latin America are just emerging from this crisis, but they are far from achieving sustained growth. In Eastern Europe the transition from statism to capitalism has been extremely painful. In most countries per capita income today is 25 percent below 1989 levels.

Whereas the crisis of the 1930s was a Keynesian crisis, defined by chronic insufficiency of demand, my hypothesis is that the crisis of the 1980s and 1990s is a crisis of the state, of its mode of intervention, and a fiscal crisis.

The collapse of communism was the conclusion of a long-term crisis that started in the 1970s. Many people thought it the triumph of capitalism, but it was only the failure of a radical mode of state intervention that coincided with capitalism's own crisis. The first oil shock, in 1973, was a turning point for the world economy, but there were earlier signs of economic malaise, well expressed in the 1971 suspension of the dollar convertibility. Since that time the growth rates of the developed countries have slowed down, and a neoconservative wave has begun. The United States lost its world economic hegemony. Its growth rates have been particularly unsatisfactory, productivity has increased slowly, the wage rate has stalled, income has become increasingly concentrated, and the number of people below the poverty line has continued to grow.

On the other hand, the United States has retained its military and ideological hegemony. The major U.S. universities are still outstanding centers of excellence. They, together with a decreasing number of other industries, constitute an export industry, attracting students from all over the world. They remain a domineering force in the scientific and ideological realms, having originated the theoretical concepts, the economic and political models that served as a basis for the neoconservative or neoliberal wave that swept the United States and, subsequently, the world. This wave, which in the United States was represented by monetarist macroeconomics, the neoclassical rational expectations school, and the public choice or rational choice school, was, on one hand, a response to the slowdown of the developed economies since the 1970s and to the crisis of the state that was at that slowdown's origin. On the other hand, it signaled the failure of Keynesian economic policy to assure full employment, price stability, and growth.

In the First World the new conservatism—modern, intellectually sophisticated, pessimistic about humankind, and individualistic—materialized in the neoliberal interpretation. *Neoliberal,* as used here, is not to be confused with *American liberalism*—the form by which the moderate left, the U.S. social democrats, express and define themselves. Neoliberalism is a radical and utopian form of European (and Latin American) liberalism. Neoliberalism brought back and radicalized the old bourgeois liberalism, asking for the absolute rule of the market and a minimum state, which would only protect property rights and enforce contracts.

Neoliberalism emerged in the United States and Europe when, beginning in the 1970s, Keynesian policies proved unable to control the economy; when inflation accelerated, unemployment increased, and growth rates slowed. In Latin America the same economic crisis took place ten years later, in the 1980s, but it was more severe than was realized in the neoliberal interpretation, the "Washington consensus," which became dominant in the region only in the late 1980s. The economic reforms of the neoliberal credo were obviously radical and utopian, but they were correct in their intent. After many years of state expansion, the state had become distorted, the fiscal crisis had paralyzed governments, economies were clearly overprotected and overregulated. A pragmatic synthesis between the old development strategies and the dogmatic neoliberal critique was required.

These reforms took place in Latin America in the shape of fiscal adjustment, trade liberalization, privatization, deregulation—all reforms of the state—and the restructuring of business enterprises. Some of these reforms were well developed and were both Latin America–oriented and market-oriented. Others were designed to build confidence. In the 1990s, following substantial economic reforms that reduced the state apparatus and deregulated the economy, Latin American countries have gradually resumed growth.

The crisis was caused by the excessive and distorted growth of the state: the developmentalist state in the Third World; the communist state in the Second World; and the welfare state in the First World. The potential of the market as a resource-allocating mechanism and as a coordinator of the economy was badly overlooked. The state became too big; although it was apparently too strong, it was increasingly weak, expensive, and inefficient. It was a victim of special interest groups and dominated by fiscal indiscipline or economic populism.

The neoliberal critique points out that the solution to this crisis is to reduce the state, aiming at the minimum state; to destroy not only the communist state but also the developmentalist and even the welfare state. The state would not perform any economic role except to guarantee property rights and the national currency. According to the "rhetoric of reaction" that Hirschman (1991) so strongly denounced, even social functions should be eliminated or reduced, given their "perverse effects." Market failures could occur, but even worse would be government failures.

M y reaction to this neoconservative wave was critical, although respectful. It became clear to me that the new conservatism offered a useful critique of the problems the world faces, particularly of the distortions that befell the state; this conservatism, however, provides only a partial solution to the problems, given its ideological and dogmatic nature and its lack of pragmatism. The market is a wonderful mechanism, and I agree that all economic reforms should be market-oriented and even market-biased. By this I mean that we should always start from the assumption that the market will do its job in coordinating the economy. But reforms should not be market-blinded or oriented toward building confidence. They should not transform the market, which is only an institution created by society and regulated by the state, into a sort of myth. They should not assume that confidence building is good per se. Building confidence in Washington or in New York may stimulate investments in the short run. But neither the bureaucrats and politicians in Washington nor the bankers and financial operators in New York can be viewed as depositaries of universal economic rationality, much less as people concerned with the national interests of Latin American countries. In fact, a confidence-building strategy may well be implemented at the expense of national interests and macroeconomic fundamentals, as happened in Salinas's Mexico.

It is a mistake to identify market orientation with market coordination. To be efficient, all economies should be market-oriented. All economic reforms should aim to spur competition. A market-oriented economy is strongly competitive in both domestic and international terms. Even within firms competition is a basic management and motivation principle. But the coordination of an economic system involves more than competition; it also follows from cooperation. And for cooperation to occur at the national and international levels, society needs the supplementary coordinating role of the state. Every economic system includes not one but two coordinating principles or mechanisms: the market and the state. Successful economic systems are usually those that combine, in a balanced and dynamic way, the role of the market and the role of the state. Some European social democracies, as well as Japan and the East Asian countries, are good examples.

Starting from these very broad observations, I come to what I call the "crisis of the state approach." This approach may eventually become a third paradigmatic moment of interpretation of Latin America.

I began my work in the context of the first paradigmatic moment: the national-bourgeois and structuralist interpretation of Latin America that originated in the ideas of Raúl Prebisch (1949). Following the economic crisis of the 1960s, I actively participated in formulating a second paradigmatic moment of interpretation of the region: the new dependency theory. Both interpretations can be combined under a more general denomination—the national-developmentalist interpretation—which was the outcome of Latin American structuralism and Keynesianism, both loosely combined with the Marxist and the Weberian traditions. The national-developmentalist interpretation soon became the victim of populism of all sorts. Keynes was supposed to support chronic budget deficits. The argument favoring protection of infant industries led to permanent protectionism. Bureaucratic interests were confused with the interests of labor and the left. Since the 1960s this approach has faced increasing difficulties in its attempt to offer sensible policies to the region, whereas the corresponding industrializing strategy—import substitution—proved to be exhausted. In the early 1980s, when the debt crisis erupted and inflation exploded in Latin America, I became increasingly interested in short-term macroeconomic issues, particularly with inflation and balance-of-payments adjustments. I was turning from structuralism, which was mainly concerned with long-term development strategies, to a more short-term approach in which scarcity and efficient allocation of resources, public savings, and a balanced budget receive full attention, without renouncing my structuralist origins.

On the other hand, the neoliberal approach—although correct when it proposes market-oriented state reforms and fiscal discipline—is dogmatic and lacks pragmatism or operationality. Thus an alternative, some kind of synthesis between the old developmentalism and the new neoliberalism, is required. In broad theoretical terms, the neostructuralist approach may be this alternative. I suggest that perceiving a crisis of the state, the approach I discuss in the next section and throughout the book, provides a new interpretation of the region. This interpretation, or approach, is market-oriented but also Latin America–oriented, and corresponds to a social-democratic and pragmatic development strategy. This book, in addition to analyzing crises and reforms in Brazil, can be thought of as a search for a new interpretation of and new development strategies for Latin America.[1]

The crisis of the state approach is an attempt to synthesize the old paradigms, which reserved a decisive role for the state, and the neoliberal paradigm. It views the crisis of the state as having two aspects: a fiscal crisis and a crisis of the mode of intervention. The fiscal crisis is defined by the loss of public credit. It may also be defined by the fact that a large public debt—coupled with high inflation, chronic public deficits, high domestic interest rates, and decreasing rates of growth—renders explosive expectations that the public debt might increase. The crisis of the mode of intervention is defined by the exhaustion of protectionist forms of intervention and by the multiplication of subsidies and regulations in an economy where rent seeking becomes the norm.

The crisis of the state is the basic cause of the economic crisis in the Third World and Eastern Europe and also of the slowdown affecting the developed countries since the 1970s. The countries able to overcome the crisis were essentially those that conserved (Japan, Germany, Korea, Colombia) or recovered (Chile) fiscal solvency. The choice of this variable to explain the crisis is crucial because it implies that other causes are either ancillary or complementary. The basic cause of the crisis will not be found in excessively capital-intensive (or capital-saving) technological progress nor in the weariness of capital-labor relations based on Taylorist techniques. These two causes, particularly the latter, may help to explain the crisis but do not constitute the essential explanation. Chronic insufficiency of demand, correctly used by Keynes to explain the crisis in the 1930s, is not a good explanation for the present crisis. The collapse of the Keynesian consensus in the 1970s, which economists usually attribute to the failure of the Phillips curve to explain stagflation, was actually caused by the fact that demand management no longer constituted an answer to the problems in economies in which the state had grown too large and faced serious financial problems.

The crisis of the state approach borrows the neoliberal paradigm's market orientation and belief that the functions of the state were severely distorted. It affirms, however, that, if the basic cause of the economic crisis is the crisis of the state, then the state has an important economic role. If other explanations were adopted—if the crisis were associated with, for instance, insufficiency of demand or technological problems, implying an increasing capital-output ratio—other consequences would need to be derived. But if we acknowledge that the crisis of the state is the main explanation, we have no alternative but to admit that the first and primary task is to reform the state, recover its solvency, and redefine its mode of intervention in such a way that the market and the state complement each other, that together they assure an adequate rate of savings and investments, an efficient allocation of resources, and a fair distribution of income.

Historically the state's economic role has been constantly changing, but it has always been essential. In addition to guaranteeing property rights and contracts and ameliorating market failures, the state has positive economic roles that are particularly important to economic development. An essential condition is the recovery of public finances, making public savings positive again so they can finance public investment in the infrastructure, in industrial and technological policies, and in new social and environmental protection expenditures. A state that is bankrupt, that does not dispose of public savings, and that is chronically the victim of a public deficit is a weak state. It may be large, but it is also sick. In cases where hyperinflation is nearly reached, the state's government—the top politicians and bureaucrats who directly control the state apparatus—is unable to govern. Public policies become endogenous because the government does not effectively command the fiscal resources required to formulate and implement policies.

According to the crisis of the state approach, the objective, after streamlining the state apparatus, is to create a leaner but stronger, more flexible state. Market-oriented reforms, privatization, deregulation, and trade liberalization, as well as fiscal discipline, monetary reforms, and tight monetary policies, are means to strengthen the state rather than weaken it. One can picture the reformed state as a sleek young tiger, instead of an ailing old elephant.

T o understand this approach, how I came to it, and the structure of this book, a short story is in order. In the mid-1980s it became clear to me that the dependency interpretation and the import substitution strategy, which had been useful tools, no longer offered a sensible explanation for the Latin American crisis or effective policies to overcome it. For decades the Brazilian state had been strong and powerful, financing and subsidizing the private sector. But in 1983, just after the Latin American debt crisis erupted, I realized that the state had become poor and increasingly bankrupt, whereas the private sector was now rich and was providing financing for the state.

In the early 1980s Yoshiaki Nakano and I were involved in the analysis of the high and chronic rates of inflation then prevailing in Brazil. We formulated the theory of inertial inflation (see Bresser Pereira and Nakano 1983), which provided an alternative not only to monetarism but also to Keynesianism. Keynes was the most important and creative economist this century has produced, but his ideas on inflation did not explain inertial inflation because they were unable to explain stagflation.

Yet in addition to the macroeconomic view in the theory of inertial inflation, we needed a more structural or microeconomic explanation for the crisis Brazil and Latin America were facing, which had as one of its symptoms inertial inflation. The answer began to form in the mid-1980s, when I read some extremely insightful articles on the state and state-owned corporations written by Rogério Werneck (1983, 1985, 1986). Werneck was already suggesting a crisis of the state, although he did not relate it to the larger Brazilian economic crisis. I was invited to participate in a conference on Latin America at Cambridge University, and I wrote my first paper on the crisis of the state (1987). Chapter 4 of this book is based on that work.

I presented the paper in Cambridge in April 1987. Three weeks later I was invited to become finance minister of Brazil. The long-term economic crisis, which had prevailed since the early 1980s, had been aggravated by an acute economic and financial crisis originating in the Cruzado Plan's collapse. Immediately after taking office, I asked my economic team to formulate a macroeconomic consistency plan, using as their parameters the ideas in my Cambridge paper. The staff did an outstanding job. The Macroeconomic Control Plan was probably the first systematic assessment of the Brazilian fiscal crisis. On the structural or microeconomic level, however, it was clear that the import substitution strategy—that is, the mode of state intervention—had lost functionality, making privatization and particularly trade liberalization urgent. Members of my staff, economists from the World Bank, and Juan Sourrouile—Argentina's minister of the economy at the time—helped me to reach this conclusion. Two months later I made my first trip to the United States as finance minister, met Jeffrey Sachs, and read his work on trade reforms and the debt crisis in Latin America (1987). I learned from Sachs that the debt crisis was essentially a fiscal crisis, which led me to recollect James O'Connor's extraordinary book *The Fiscal Crisis of the State* (1973).

I had learned a great deal from putting all these ideas together and completing an assessment of the Brazilian crisis, but the country had not. A populist mood still fully dominated Brazilian politics, making impossible economic policies aimed at fiscal discipline and market-oriented reforms. I resigned as finance minister in December 1987 and returned to academic life. In the next years I dedicated myself to further developing ideas on Brazil and Latin America that were consistent with the crisis of the state approach. I wrote numerous articles, participated in national and international conferences, talked to people, and followed the new ideas that were emerging. The outcome is this book.

An important factor in developing the crisis of the state approach was my participation in the East-South System Transformations Project, led by Adam Przeworski. In this context I wrote, with Przeworski and José Maria Maravall, *Economic Reforms in New Democracies* (1993), in which I was first able to shape this interpretation. I initially called it "the fiscal crisis approach," but I later realized that it was actually a global crisis of the state; it was not only a fiscal crisis but also a crisis of the mode of intervention. "The crisis of the state approach" is a good name for an interpretation of the crisis rather than an indication of the policies designed to solve it.

This book is divided into four parts. Part 1 deals with conflicting interpretations of Brazil and their respective development strategies. Chapter 2, in which the crisis of the state interpretation is outlined, is the central chapter. The approach to the crisis as a crisis of the state started with an intuition that Brazil and Latin America faced a fiscal crisis connected to the debt crisis and to economic populism. But it was also based on another intuition. I observed that the state's role was changing and that this fact was related to the "cyclical and ever-changing character of state intervention," which is the title of a paper I wrote in 1988. This cyclical process explains how the state, which had performed a strategic role in development between the 1930s and the 1970s, fell into a deep crisis in the 1980s, and why, after that time, fiscal discipline, privatization, and trade liberalization became mandatory. It also explains why the conservative, neoliberal wave was so strong. Chapter 3 summarizes my views on the cyclical character of state intervention and applies those views to Brazil. It is the basic model behind the role and concept of the state I adopt in this book.

Part 2 examines the economic crisis of the 1980s: the historical process that led to the crisis; its perverse macroeconomics; and the debt crisis.

Part 3 is centered on the political dimension of the crisis. All of the chapters in this book have a political as well as an economic dimension, but the four chapters in this part are specifically political. In them I examine the crisis and the renovation of the left, the political obstacles to economic reforms, the contradictory aspects of the short but significative Collor administration, and what I call "the citizenship contradiction": a very large number of citizens with the right to vote in a radically heterogeneous society in which governments face a permanent legitimacy crisis as long as the classical social contract is insufficient, requiring additionally a development-oriented political pact. Brazil is a dual society. Income distribution is extremely uneven. The gap between the elites and the masses is enormous. If a modern society is not only market-oriented, one in which resource allocation is efficient and technological change dynamic, but is also a democratic and socially balanced society, this social gap is a major obstacle to its modernization. Forming a democratic political coalition able to consolidate democracy, reduce economic inequalities, and promote growth becomes extremely difficult.

Finally, Part 4 is an analysis of the economic reforms undertaken in Brazil, particularly since 1987 with the collapse of the Cruzado Plan, that were accelerated in 1990 during the Collor administration and crowned by the Real Plan in 1994, which stabilized prices. Thus this is a book on crisis, but it also addresses the changes and reforms that have been taking place in Brazil since the early 1980s but that have been concealed or shadowed by the prevailing high and inertial inflation. In this part I first discuss the failed attempts to stabilize, proposing that the causes behind the failures were also, but not mainly, political. The incompetence of policymakers, who were unable to understand the abnormal times Brazil and Latin America were experiencing, and particularly the nature of inertial inflation, were also major causes of the failures. Second, I discuss the successful reforms. I conclude with an analysis of the social and political changes in the direction of the formation of a new, development-oriented political pact. In Chapter 16 I discuss the international strategy of Brazil. It is clear to me that the Initiative for the Americas (1991) and NAFTA opened a new phase in Latin American–U.S. relations. These initiatives are a response to the crisis in Latin America but also to the end of U.S. world economic hegemony. In this part of the book I discuss the difference between the old nationalism, tied to the import substitution strategy, and international policy based on national interest. And I propose that economic reforms should not be only market-oriented but also national-oriented—Brazil-oriented, for instance. The alternative is for economic reforms to be oriented toward building confidence, as occurred in Salinas's Mexico. Such confidence, while comforting to Washington and New York, is often precarious and bought at the expense of the reforming country's national interest and macroeconomic fundamentals.

Some sections of this book have been published in other versions, as individual articles; they have been updated and revised in several ways.

For the development of the ideas presented here, my experience as finance minister, my role as a professor of economics at Getúlio Vargas Foundation, São Paulo, and my participation in debates on Latin America and Brazil in many domestic and international seminars were essential. I am indebted to many friends, but I would like to mention four economists—Jeffrey Sachs, Roberto Frenkel, Rogério Werneck, and Yoshiaki Nakano—with whom I wrote Chapters 7 and 13—and two political scientists, Adam Przeworski and José Maria Maravall. To them I indeed owe a great deal.

❈ Part 1 ❈
Interpreting the Crisis

✠ 1 ✠

Interpretations and Strategies

Latin America was in deep crisis in the 1980s. Incomes per capita decreased around 10 percent during the decade. In the 1990s, after a serious effort to stabilize their economies, to promote fiscal adjustment, and to adopt market-oriented reforms, countries have timidly resumed growth, although the problems that gave rise to the crisis are far from being fully solved. In 1994 income for the entire region increased around 3 percent. Since 1991 the average annual rate of growth has been moderate, a little above 3 percent, which means income per capita is at last increasing, but only around 1 percent each year. The last Latin American country to stabilize high inflation was Brazil, in 1994. Inflation, which was around 900 percent for the entire region in 1990, fell to around 16 percent in 1994 if we exclude Brazil. In Brazil inflation remained very high in the first half of 1994 but fell dramatically beginning July 1, when the Real Plan was enacted.

Yet it is too early to say that Latin America has overcome its crisis. Capital is flooding in, depressing the exchange rate and stimulating consumption rather than promoting savings and investments. Wage rates have only recently recovered to 1980 levels. The debt crisis, although no longer a dramatic problem, has not been satisfactorily solved. Manufacturing industries in the countries that liberalized trade and stabilized prices, such as Mexico and Argentina, are facing difficult times—evidence that an industrialization strategy to replace the exhausted import substitution one is still to be found. In most countries the fiscal crisis of the state, although less acute, remains a major problem.

All Latin American countries faced serious difficulties in the 1980s. Some, particularly Colombia, did not experience a real crisis. Others fully overcame their crisis, as Chile did. Other countries—particularly Mexico, Costa Rica, and Bolivia—have nearly overcome it. Argentina is a question mark, despite four years of successful stabilization. Brazil underwent substantial economic reforms and only recently stabilized prices. Peru stabilized its economy in 1991 and is engaged in economic reforms. Venezuela, where a radical stabilization plan politically destabilized the country, continues to face difficult times.

Since 1991, when countries in Latin America started showing good results (whereas reform in Eastern Europe proved to be harder than initially expected), the continent again began to be viewed positively by the First World. Gross domestic product (GDP) for the entire region grew 3.8 percent in 1991. This and the very low interest rates prevailing in the developed countries vis-à-vis the very high rates in Latin America triggered large capital flows not only to Mexico and Chile but also to Venezuela, Brazil, and Argentina, whose economies were far from adjusted. Net transfers of resources, which were extremely negative throughout the 1980s, again turned positive in 1991 and increased further in the following years.[1]

The new optimism that swept Washington is based on the assumption that Latin American countries had finally adopted necessary economic reforms, signed debt agreements according to the Brady Plan, stabilized their economies, and returned to economic growth. Yet this optimism does not seem to be well grounded. Countries such as Venezuela and Peru, which in 1991 were viewed as having adopted neoliberal economic reforms and on the way to recovery, face serious political troubles. In Peru a new authoritarian government was established in 1992. Argentina's stabilization remains based on a serious overvaluation of the peso. To a lesser extent, the same is true of Mexico and Brazil. In fact, most Latin American countries still face a fiscal crisis.

Given these facts, some questions are obvious. Why was the crisis so profound? Why is the performance Table 1.1 reflects so poor? Why did per capita income in Latin America fall 9.06 percent during the 1980s, and the share of investment in GDP plunge from 23.2 to 15.6 percent in the same period? Why was per capita income in 1991 on the level of that of 1977? Why did inflation, which in 1980 averaged 54.9 percent, climb to 1,185 percent in 1990? Why did some countries escape the crisis and others manage to overcome it? Which interpretations of Latin America are relevant in understanding the crisis and helpful in the development of strategies to defeat it? Are the politicians' populist practices and immoderate state intervention, as is frequently said, sufficient to explain the crisis?

Table 1.1   Macroeconomic Variables, 1980–1992

	1980	1990	1991	1992
GDP growth (individual)	100.0	112.0	116.0	118.8
GDP per capita (individual)	100.0	90.6	92.2	92.7
Investment/GDP (%)	23.2	15.6	–	–
Debt/exports (%)	2.2	2.9	2.9	2.8
Net transfer (US$ billion)	–	–14.4	8.4	27.4
Inflation (%)	54.9	1,185.0	198.7	410.7

Sources: Economic Commission for Latin America, *Panorama Económico de América Latina,* 1990 and 1991; World Bank, several *World Development Reports;* Inter-American Development Bank, *Economic and Social Progress in Latin America: 1990 Report.*

Otherwise, what is necessary to overcome this crisis? Is it enough to achieve stabilization, to privatize and liberalize, for growth to automatically resume? Could the relative success some of these economies are experiencing be attributed to market-oriented economic reforms and to the dominance of a neoliberal approach to Latin America's problems? Or are the challenges the region faces still immense, requiring a new interpretation of the Latin American crisis and the definition of a new growth strategy? This is what I call the crisis of the state approach, or the social-democratic and pragmatic strategy. Are privatization, trade liberalization, and deregulation only conservative reforms, or can they also be adopted by progressive or moderate-left politicians and policymakers?

The Latin American crisis was triggered by the debt crisis. Its basic cause was the fiscal crisis of the state—the fact that the state went bankrupt, lost its credit, and was immobilized. A complementary cause was the exhaustion of a formerly successful development strategy and a corresponding interpretation of Latin America's problems: the national-developmentalist approach, based on import substitution and on active state intervention in the productive sector of the economy.

Two competing approaches presently attempt to define this crisis and offer solutions to it: the neoliberal, or Washington consensus, approach; and the crisis of the state interpretation, or the social-democratic and pragmatic strategy. These approaches agree on some of the causes of the crisis and how to solve it. In particular, both criticize the populism and national developmentalism that long prevailed in Latin America, and they agree that the state grew too much in the region. Yet they have an essentially different view of the basic cause of the crisis and how to remedy it. Whereas the neoliberal approach attributes the crisis only to domestic problems, the crisis of the state approach also emphasizes the role played by the debt crisis; whereas one approach states that the basic cause of the crisis is the excessive strength of a state that grew too much, the other says the basic cause is the increasing weakness of a state that grew in a distorted way and went bankrupt. Both agree that it is necessary to reduce the size of the state, to privatize and liberalize, and to adopt market-oriented reforms, but the objective of the neoliberal approach is to reduce the coordinating role of the state—aiming at the minimal state—whereas the objective of the fiscal approach is to rebuild the state and recover state capacity.

The crisis of the state approach gives a more realistic view of the Latin American crisis. It is less dogmatic with regard to the policies to be followed. It uses the positive aspects of the neoliberal interpretation but is not contaminated by the radical and utopian neoconservatism lying behind neoliberal ideas. Nevertheless, since the neoliberal approach emanates from Washington—the dominant source of foreign political power for the region—actual policy will likely consist of a mixture of both approaches.

And the rhetoric of Latin American elites will be that the Washington consensus is being adopted.

The crisis of the state interpretation is central to this book. Yet in this first chapter I discuss the previous interpretations of Latin America, which serve as a background for the current ideas. In Chapter 2 I discuss the neoliberal and the crisis of the state approaches.

W hen we think about Latin American economic development, it is useful to refer to interpretations and strategies. For each basic interpretation of the causes of the region's relative underdevelopment, there is a corresponding strategy. Sometimes this strategy is clear, other times it is implicit. Conversely, because interpretations and strategies are ideologically prone, for each leftist approach there is a competing rightist one, and for each nationalist approach there is a competing internationalist approach. For simplicity we can call the union of interpretation and strategy approaches to Latin America.[2]

The adoption of a historical perspective is important because it illuminates the present. In addition, the remnants of some of these old interpretations—particularly of the national-developmentalist approach, which is charged with a strong populist content—are still strongly felt in Latin America today. Economic and political approaches are always ideological. They reflect clashes of class interests, which are particularly salient in Latin America where class differences are so accentuated.

The interpretations of Latin America's underdevelopment and their corresponding development strategies can be presented according to historical and ideological criteria. They can be enumerated as follows, with the decades during which they dominated:

- The agrarian destiny or liberal-oligarchic approach (up to 1930), competing with:
- The national-developmentalist approach, subdivided into the national-bourgeois approach (1930–1964) and the new dependency approach (1970s–mid-1980s)
- The modernizing-authoritarian approach (1964–mid-1970s), also competing with the new dependency approach
- The neoliberal approach (mid-1970s–today), competing with:
- The crisis of the state or social-democratic approach (mid-1980s–today)

These interpretations and development strategies sometimes succeeded and sometimes conflicted with each other. When they dominated, they corresponded to a development-oriented political pact or class coalition (I examine these pacts in Chapter 17).

The liberal-oligarchic interpretation and the corresponding agrarian destiny strategy ruled until the 1930s. The national-developmentalist approach, which originated in the left and in the nationalist bourgeoisie, and the corresponding import substitution strategy were dominant in the 1950s, when Getúlio Vargas's populist pact prevailed. After the crisis during the 1960s, national developmentalism assumed a more sophisticated form—the new dependency interpretation—which, in spite of its name, criticized the view that imperialism was a major cause of underdevelopment in Latin America. Yet it underlined the distorting consequences—income concentration and authoritarianism—of the alliance of the United States and the multinational corporations (MNCs) with the local bourgeoisie and the military. It also criticized the populist views that had distorted the national-bourgeois approach. This critique, however, was not strong enough to prevent the reappearance in Brazil of populism, a shadow from the past, in the form of the Democratic Populist Political Pact, which was in force during the transition to democracy from 1977 to 1984 and the first two years of the new democratic government (1985–1986).[3] Populism also reappeared in Argentina after the transition to democracy.

The modernizing-authoritarian interpretation was a feature of Brazil's technobureaucratic-capitalist regime from 1964 to 1984. It, too, corresponded to an excluding political pact involving the local bourgeoisie, the bureaucratic middle class, and the MNCs. It rose as a critique of the national-developmentalist approach yet it favored the import substitution strategy.

From the mid-1970s, when the local bourgeoisie broke its alliance with the military, to 1986, when the Cruzado Plan failed, a populist and democratic political pact involving the bourgeoisie, the democratic salaried middle class, and the workers commanded the Brazilian transition to democracy.

The neoliberal interpretation, a product of the right, began to gain ground in the 1970s when the dominant international ideology was neoliberalism, but it gained strength only after the final collapse of the modernizing-authoritarian pact (1984) and the subsequent inability of the populist democratic pact of the Diretas Já to face the emerging problems (1986). The crisis of the state approach—which can also be called pragmatic interpretation, because it rejects any dogmatism and shares East Asian pragmatism; or social democratic, because it also has as its model the European social democracies—began to assert itself among the moderate left after the Cruzado Plan's failure (1986) demonstrated the definitive exhaustion of the national-developmentalist strategy. At present, it is the real alternative to neoliberalism.

The neoliberal and the crisis of the state interpretations and their respective strategies are internationalist, but the first is based on the assumption of common international interests, whereas the latter is based on the national-interest principle.[4] The neoliberal and social-democratic interpretations are discussed in Chapter 2.

The old agrarian destiny or liberal-oligarchic interpretation is distinguished from the neoliberal interpretation as follows: (1) the former's liberalism and individualism were more rhetorical than real; (2) its criticism of state intervention was based only on the disadvantages of intervention for the market and not on a pessimistic philosophical denial of the possibility of collective action; (3) its conservatism was based more on authoritarianism and tradition than on a definite identification of modernity with the market; and (4) its development strategy was based on export agriculture rather than on modern industry and a sophisticated and increasingly internationalized financial market.

The agrarian destiny interpretation recognized Brazil's underdevelopment and its economic and cultural dependence on the industrialized countries. It saw Brazil as being in the process of modernization, changing from a traditional society to a modern, capitalist one. This transition should have been based on Brazil's comparative advantages, which resided for the most part in agriculture. Industrialization was rejected because it would be "artificial." The central countries were seen as superior entities whose interests pretty much coincided with those of Brazil. Any kind of nationalism was rejected in the name of an internationalism that believed it was always possible to count on the goodwill of the developed world.

The agrarian destiny approach lost ground beginning in the early 1930s as successful industrialization proved the export agriculture strategy was wrong. The national-developmentalist approach then became dominant. Conservatives, who had adopted the agrarian destiny approach, slowly began to adhere to the industrializing strategy, particularly to its protectionist and developmentalist aspects. After the 1964 coup d'état this kind of rightist developmentalism—internationalist and modernizing but also protectionist—dominated Brazil. The political regime, which Guillermo O'Donnell called bureaucratic-authoritarian, had a corresponding industrialization strategy—the modernizing-authoritarian economic strategy—which was very similar to the populist nationalist one because it was based on protection of local industry and on active state intervention.

National populism became dominant in Brazil and generally in Latin America in the 1950s, although the situation that gave rise to it—import substitution industrialization—had existed since the 1930s. Populist national developmentalism in Latin America had been formulated mostly by the left, but it was never fully and authentically a left-wing strategy because it was based on the realistic recognition of both the weakness of the left and the unlikelihood of a socialist revolution. This double recognition led to a proposed alliance of workers, technobureaucrats, and industrialists around an industrialization project.

The national-developmentalist interpretation was essentially nationalistic and moderately in favor of state intervention because it saw the protection of national industry as essential to growth. It also saw Brazil as an underdeveloped country in transition from mercantile to industrial capitalism, in which infant industry was permanently threatened by imperialist competition from the industrialized countries, which wanted Brazil to remain an exporter of raw materials. Given these threats, Brazil's only alternative was to protect itself and to protect the internal market that had grown during the primary export period, reserving it for national industry. The import substitution industrialization model thus naturally imposed itself. For the country to resign itself to an agrarian vocation would have been suicide, given the unequal trade between producers of primary and industrial products and the tendency toward deterioration in the terms of trade for primary products.

This interpretation and the corresponding development strategy effectively promoted Brazilian industrialization until the 1950s. The approach was essentially but not entirely correct; the notion that the core countries would oppose Brazilian industrialization was disproved by the facts. Beginning in the 1950s MNCs began to play an increasingly important role in Brazil's industrialization, leading to the first schism among those who had taken part in the populist pact: between those who began to admit a positive role for MNCs and those who remained nationalistic.

Import substitution is essentially a transitory strategy for industrialization. It is effective in protecting industry in its infancy. This model of industrialization is limited by the size of a country's internal market because tradable goods are produced below international standards of efficiency and quality. Once this limit has been reached, the model has exhausted itself, and industrialization becomes exclusively dependent on the growth of the internal market, which in turn grows slowly because of low productivity or the lack of competitiveness of the excessively protected industry.

In the early 1960s, when the Brazilian economy went into crisis, the exhaustion of the import substitution model was perceived by the economists who had helped to formulate and justify it but who had also understood its transitory nature. As Celso Furtado (1964:119) noted, "We must recognize [that] the dynamic possibilities of import substitution have been exhausted." The 1964 coup d'état, in great part an outcome of this crisis, was interpreted by many of these authors—myself included—as marking the end of the populist pact and the industrialization model peculiar to it. The authoritarian military regime did in fact represent the end of Getúlio Vargas–style populism because it excluded workers and the left. The new, authoritarian political pact was restricted to civilian and military technobureaucrats and local and international capitalists. But when it came to development strategy, the regime resumed the same national-developmentalist strategy based on import substitution—that is, on protectionism. Now, how-

ever, it was under the exclusive command of the right and had an internationalist rather than a nationalist character. Protectionism was no longer
national, taking on an international character as belief in the goodwill of
international partners returned. It was assumed that common interests clearly transcended any conflict of interest between Brazil and other countries.

Yet there was an important modification of strategy. It was recognized
that Brazil could and should export industrial goods. Export promotion of
manufactured goods received special attention. Emphasis, however, continued to be given to the protection of national industry and to import substitution. The laws preventing the import of goods similar to those produced
locally and the complex system of quantitative import control were maintained. Beginning in 1974 with the PND II, an ambitious import substitution
program was set up for capital and basic intermediate goods, based on a typically autarkic perspective of the national economy that took for granted the
need to "complete" the import substitution process. Through FINEP, the
organ that finances Brazilian technology, technological development began
to receive the attention it needed. The orientation of technological policy,
however, was the same as that of the industrial policy: import substitution
aimed at technical proficiency in all sectors rather than seeking international competitiveness in some selected sectors.[5]

In addition to being protectionist, this strategy was strongly interventionist, heavily subsidizing local capital goods and export industries and at
the same time reserving a growing share of the intermediate inputs market
and energy for state corporations. The state thus continued the strategy introduced in the 1930s, which had been based on protecting and subsidizing
local industry and on directly investing in strategic sectors whenever national or multinational capital was not capable of or interested in doing the job.

This curious survival of the protectionist development strategy when it
was no longer economically justifiable because it only defended the interests of industrial sectors that were incapable of competing internationally
was possible in the 1970s thanks to foreign borrowing. The strategy's survival was nevertheless clearly artificial and very expensive. In the 1980s this
same foreign debt threw Brazil into a deep fiscal crisis that disorganized and
paralyzed the state, leading the economy to stagnation and hyperinflation.

The economic crisis of the 1980s led the left and the right, the
progressives or social democrats and the conservatives, to reformulate
their interpretations. The right had little difficulty. It took advantage of the
conservative and neoliberal wave that had gained momentum in the 1970s
all over the world as a consequence of the slowdown in the growth rates of
the central countries, the crisis of the welfare state, the collapse of the
Keynesian consensus, and the fiscal crisis of the state, which had become
the major problem in all countries—developed and underdeveloped, capitalist and statist alike. The right rapidly and rhetorically abandoned its

authoritarian interventionist strategy, which it had consolidated following its alliance with the military technobureaucracy in 1964, to adopt a neoliberal stand in defense of the minimal state, deregulation, and opening up the Brazilian economy. In practice, however, a significant segment of the right continued to support protectionism and to benefit from state intervention. In a way, this restored in a different historical context the classical contradiction between rhetoric and practice that, during the entire nineteenth century and the first half of the twentieth, had characterized the Brazilian conservative (free-market) ideology. At that time, what today is called neoliberalism was the banner of the oligarchic landowners.

For the left or progressive sectors, the abandonment of the national-developmentalist interpretation was and still is painful. The general crisis of the left worldwide was added to the crisis of Latin American national populism, whose industrialization strategy was viewed by the left as part of its way of being. When they came into power in 1985 following the victorious process of redemocratization, the progressive sectors—or at least those sectors that were supposed to be progressive by the mere fact of having opposed the military regime—tried to resume the populist and developmentalist policies that had been successful many years before.

The 1985–1986 economic policy, which ended with the failure of the Cruzado Plan, is an example of a populist economic policy. Populism was not part of the Cruzado Plan as originally conceived; rather, the plan was based on the innovative theory of inertial inflation. Its failure was the result of the disastrous way it was administered.

Economic populism, the economic practice behind the national-developmentalist approach—including its authoritarian version[6]—can be summarized in a few rules: (1) development should be oriented to the internal market; (2) protection of national industry should continue as the basic industrial strategy; (3) technological development complements the more general policy of import substitution; (4) a policy oriented toward exports is conservative because it concentrates income; (5) a public deficit is justified as long as unemployment and idle capacity exist, so that any fiscal adjustment should be viewed as "orthodox" economic policy; (6) high interest rates are a result of the machinations of finance capital and speculators; (7) nominal wage increases do not cause inflation in Brazil because they always lag behind inflation; (8) real wage increases may not be inflationary, given the high degree of income concentration; (9) state corporations are basically efficient, but they are not more profitable because their prices are artificially depressed; and (10) economic regulation through the state tends to perform better than the market.

These views dominated the democratic opposition's economic criticism of the military regime. They were adopted by the PMDB and the PFL, the two leading political parties, when they assumed command of the government in 1985. The economic populism that characterized the first two years of the Sarney administration was the consequence of this economic view, as well as of the optimistic economic hopes that flowered in Brazil with rede-mocratization.

These populist ideas are deeply entrenched in Brazilian politics. They are found not only in the left-wing parties, such as the PT, and the center-left parties, such as the PDT, the PMDB, and the PSDB, but also in the center-right and right-wing parties, such as the PFL and the PDS, recently renamed Partido Popular Republicano (PPR).[7] The right, however, only adopted these ideas for opportunistic reasons, whereas many in the left believed and still believe them an essential part of their parties' programs, that left-wing politics necessarily includes these ideas.

Opposed to these ideas are the neoliberal and the social-democratic interpretations, which I examine in Chapter 2. These two interpretations share a common rejection of populism and nationalism, but they diverge on the causes of the crisis and the role of the state in promoting growth and welfare in Latin America.

⭐ 2 ⭐

The Crisis of
the State Approach

The import substitution, state-led strategy that dominated Latin America from the 1930s to the 1970s was opposed rhetorically by conservatives and by Washington, but in practice businesspeople and governments supported it as long as it was successful. In Washington, the U.S. government and multilateral agencies, as well as businesses and commercial banks, mildly criticized the import substitution strategy, but in practice they financed it. The World Bank, until the end of the 1970s, was devoted to development economics and to an industrializing strategy very similar to national developmentalism. Yet this industrialization strategy had exhausted its potentialities in Latin America by the 1960s. Its life span was artificially extended in the 1970s by the availability of foreign capital. But real prices were increasingly dissociated from market-clearing prices by the distortions involved in the state intervention process. Subsidies to private enterprises and, less often, to consumption were maintained long after they had lost their original justification, aggravating the inefficient allocation of resources. The state paid the account. Public savings, which had been high in the 1970s, began to disappear. In the early 1980s a growing external public debt, which financed increasing public deficits, turned into a fiscal crisis of the state.[1]

This Latin American crisis was essentially the consequence of two decisions made in the early 1970s: on the Latin American side, the decision to persist in a growth strategy and in a mode of state intervention (import substitution) that no longer worked; and on the creditor countries' side, the decision to finance this strategy, thus ensuring its artificial survival. These two decisions increased Latin American indebtedness; and then, in each Latin American country they led the state to bankruptcy. A fiscal crisis ensued as the foreign debt increased and was nationalized, the increase in the interest burden plus renewed populist policies augmented the public deficit and reduced public savings, the public debt soared, and public credit evaporated. Initially, the foreign debt was not primarily public. In the 1970s state borrowing represented about 50 percent of the debt. In the early 1980s, however, it became nationalized as private firms paid their debts in local currency to their respective central banks, usually at an overvalued exchange

rate. This practice, in addition to shifting the foreign debt to the state, subsidized the private sector and induced deficit spending. Foreign savings
were used by Latin American governments, particularly Brazil, to finance
heavy import substitution projects and consumption (economic populism).

By the mid-1980s, when the transmutation of the foreign debt into state
debt ended, around 90 percent of the debt had become the state's responsibility. The private sector remained capable of generating a foreign surplus,
but only the state was supposed to pay the foreign debt. The nationalization
of the foreign debt was a perverse form of financing public deficits and
spurring the fiscal crisis. In the 1970s the public deficit was financed primarily by foreign borrowing; in the first half of the 1980s it was financed by
private firms that paid their debts (usually in privileged conditions) in local
currency to the state, which in turn had too little foreign currency to pay the
banks. In the late 1980s countries either drastically reduced their public
deficit by lowering wages and internal consumption, as was the case in Chile
and Mexico, or their fiscal crisis deepened, as happened in most other Latin
American countries.

Nearly all Latin American countries were committed to tight fiscal
adjustment policies. But the fiscal deficit was so high, and the interest component related to the public debt so heavy, that countries were unable to adequately adjust their economies. In addition, the possibility of transmuting
the old foreign debt into government debt offered an easy way to finance
current deficits. Thus, foreign borrowing, which in the 1970s had backed the
state-led import substitution strategy and fiscal indiscipline, continued to
indirectly and negatively affect public finances in the first half of the 1980s
as the nationalization of the debt fostered fiscal indiscipline and laid the
foundation for a deep fiscal crisis.

James O'Connor (1973) introduced the concept of the fiscal crisis of the
state, explaining it as the state's increasing difficulty in coping with the
growing demands of several sectors of the economy and corresponding
social groups. The concept I am using here is based on his ideas. The expression *fiscal crisis of the state* is redundant because all fiscal crisis is related
to the state; but, in 1987, when I clearly comprehended this crisis, I decided
to use the term to explain the Latin American crisis because it clarifies the
central role of the state in that crisis. We could also refer to a "financial crisis of the state" because all fiscal crises have as their outcome the state's
increased difficulty in financing itself.[2]

In the 1980s the fiscal crisis of the state in Latin America had five ingredients: (1) a budget deficit; (2) negative or very small public savings; (3) an
excessive foreign and domestic debt; (4) poor creditworthiness of the state,
expressed in the lack of confidence in national currency and in the short-
term maturity of the domestic debt (the Brazilian overnight market for
Treasury bonds);[3] and (5) a lack of government credibility.[4] Public deficit

and insufficient, if not negative, public savings are, to use an economist's jargon, a flow characteristic of the fiscal crisis, whereas the size of the public debt—be it internal or external—is a stock property. Actually, the lack of public credit is the fundamental feature of a fiscal crisis of the state. A country may have a high public deficit and a high public debt, but the state does not need to lose credit or the government its credibility. This is the present case in the United States and Italy, where in spite of the deficit and the public debt there is no fiscal crisis, or the one that prevails is much milder than those existing in Latin America. The state's loss of credit—its inability to finance itself except through seigniorage (money creation)—is the quintessential characteristic of fiscal crises. When this loss of credit becomes absolute, or in other words when the fiscal crisis becomes acute and out of control, the state loses its capacity to guarantee its money, and hyperinflation is the likely outcome.

Most characteristics of the fiscal crisis are self-explanatory. Yet I believe it is important to stress the issue of insufficiency of public savings. The fundamental flow characteristic of a fiscal crisis is not the budget deficit but rather negative public savings. Particularly in a developing country this factor has a strategic role. Negative public savings tend to be a direct cause of low investment rates and the stagnation of per capita incomes.

Public savings, S_G, are equal to current revenue, T, less current expenditure, C_G, where interest is included.[5]

$$S_G = T - C_G$$

Public savings represent a different concept from public deficit, D_G, which is equal to current state revenue less all expenditures including investments, I_G, and corresponds to the increase in the public debt:

$$D_G = T - C_G - I_G$$

Given these definitions, and not considering real seigniorage, public investments are financed by either public savings or public deficit.

$$I_G = S_G + D_G$$

These distinctions are important. They are part of the standard national accounts system but with a shortcoming: state-owned enterprises are excluded from the calculation of public savings. Yet few economists include public savings among their tools.[6] Under the fiscal and monetary adjustment approach adopted by the IMF, the stabilization literature refers almost exclusively to the public deficit. I believe, however, that in analyzing the economy of any country, public savings are at least as important as the concept of public deficit.

Public savings become particularly important if we adopt a broad concept of public investment. According to this concept, public investments cover not only investments proper, which include investments in projects in which the private sector has shown no interest (usually infrastructure), social investments (education and health), and investments in security (police and prisons). Public investments also include free public expenditures—"free" because they are not committed to public officers' salaries or to current state services, which improve the country's competitiveness; these investments include subsidies or incentives to private investment (agricultural and industrial policy) and expenditures on technological development to be provided for the private sector.

When public savings are near zero, the state has only one alternative: to finance investment through the public deficit. However, if the objective is to reduce the public deficit—an intrinsic part of any program to resolve a fiscal crisis—a likely outcome is a cut in public investments and the consequent reduction of GDP growth. Thus, with zero public savings, if the state invests, its indebtedness will increase and its creditworthiness will further diminish; if the public deficit is eliminated, investment will be cut. If public savings are negative, the state will have a deficit even if public investments are zero. The deficit will finance current expenditures, the bulk of which is typically interest on loans. In any event, the state will be paralyzed, unable to formulate and implement policies that promote growth. And this paralysis, more than anything else, reveals the relation between fiscal crises and economic stagnation.

When the Latin American crisis broke out, the creditor countries' interpretation of its causes and remedies underwent two phases. At first, between 1982 and 1984, the crisis was minimized and was viewed as only a liquidity crisis. Beginning around 1985, however, the crisis started to be taken more seriously. In addition to fiscal and balance-of-payments adjustments, "structural," market-oriented reforms were viewed as essential.[7] The Washington consensus was at last emerging, pushed by a conservative, neoliberal wave extant in the First World since the mid-1970s.

In the Washington consensus, the crisis was admitted to but in a limited way. Its causes were defined: fiscal indiscipline (or economic populism), resulting in public deficit; and excessive state intervention—particularly through state-owned enterprises, trade restrictions, and several types of subsidies to investment and consumption. The remedies were listed: fiscal adjustment aimed at eliminating the public deficit; structural or market-oriented reforms (particularly trade liberalization and privatization) aimed at deregulating and reducing the state apparatus; and limited debt reduction, according to the 1989 Brady Plan.

The debt crisis was not viewed as the single most important cause of the overall crisis. The internal causes received much more attention. When the

Brady Plan was formulated in February 1989, analysis demonstrated that it was correct overall but that the debt reduction it implied was insufficient. The burden of adjustment and reforms would fall almost exclusively on the shoulders of the debtor countries. Yet soon after Mexico signed the first debt agreement according to the plan, capital flows increased, and Mexico's economy steadily improved. A spurious correlation between the Brady Plan and these capital flows was immediately established. "Hot" money was going to the region, not because Latin America had solved its problems and was growing again but because it was attracting high interest rates, a perverse result of the lack of confidence provoked by the debt crisis. Yet Washington and the banks convinced themselves that the debt crisis had been solved. The motivation for an effective solution vanished.[8] Since 1990 the standard phrase in Washington—which is essential to the neoliberal approach—has been that "the debt crisis was grossly overestimated."

Fanelli, Frenkel, and Rozenwurcel (1990:1), in their critique of the Washington consensus, observed that the Latin American crisis

> did not originate in the weaknesses of the import substitution strategy but rather in the dynamics of the adjustment to the external shock that took place in the beginning of the 1980s. In fact, the principal constraints to growth today originate in the long-lasting features of the external and fiscal imbalances induced by the debt crisis that has still not reversed after ten years of adjustment.

The three Argentine economists underestimated the exhaustion of the import substitution strategy, but their definition of the origins and nature of the crisis is an excellent example of the crisis of the state approach.[9]

Additionally, the political origins of this crisis did not primarily stem from economic populism, as is usually thought in Washington.[10] Populist economic policies undoubtedly played a role, but populism has always existed in Latin America, and before the 1980s did not throw up an obstacle to reasonable price stability and growth. The new historical event that led Latin American economies to their first ever fiscal crisis was a nonpopulist decision made in the 1970s, mostly by the military regimes, to underwrite an enormous foreign debt and, subsequently, to turn it into a state responsibility. Populism is blamed by the neoliberal approach for something that was not primarily its fault (Bresser Pereira and Dall'Acqua 1991; Cardoso and Helwege 1990). It was not by chance that the only country in Latin America that experienced satisfactory rates of growth in the 1980s was Colombia, which had not previously run up a large foreign debt.

The inability to finance the state through taxes, particularly income taxes, is an essential trait of the Latin American countries now enduring a fiscal crisis. Wealthy people do not pay their fair share of taxes in Latin America. The tax burden tends to be systematically low, not only when compared with developed countries but also in contrast to Asian countries at about the same level of development (Kagami 1990). Tax systems tend systematically to be regressive in Latin America because they are based primarily on indirect taxes.

The state in Latin America was originally financed through export taxes. Later, when rents from primary products exports had been reduced, state investments were financed by indirect taxes, by specific taxes matching expenditures in a given sector,[11] by the reinvestment of profits of monopolist state-owned enterprises,[12] and by security funds—which, by definition, tend to present a surplus in the first years after they are created. In the 1970s, when for several reasons these sources of state revenue had been exhausted or were insufficient, foreign debt proved an easy alternative to finance the state. With the suspension of this source of financing, inflationary tax increased as a means of financing the state.[13] The typical way of financing the state—through taxes, particularly income taxes—was never typical in Latin America. As Przeworski (1990:20–21) observed, "The crucial question is whether the particular state is capable, politically and administratively, of collecting tax revenue from those who can afford it: in several Latin American countries, Argentina notably, the state is so bankrupt that the only way it can survive day-to-day is by borrowing money from those who could be tax-payers." This feature could be attributed to populism, but I would rather identify it with the authoritarian, limited democratic character of the Latin American capitalist state, which entails subjecting the state to the rich.

The fact that governments in Latin America usually tax insufficiently while incurring budget deficits, initially financed through borrowing and later by an inflationary tax, may have a third explanation in addition to populism and authoritarian rule. Some authors, involved in a "new political economy," relate this phenomenon to political instability and polarization. The perspective of political alternance (instability) and the highly conflicting social systems (polarization) existing in Latin America as a consequence of the extremely uneven distribution of income induce governments to incur deficits today that will be paid in the future by another government probably representing other interest groups (Alesina and Edwards 1989; Alesina and Tabellini 1988; Edwards and Tabellini 1990).

The Washington consensus was defined by Williamson (1990) and immediately became identified with neoliberal ideas. In fact, it is a milder form of neoliberalism because the Washington bureaucrats who formulated it lacked the dogmatism that characterizes neoliberal or neoconservative ideas. Neoliberals, for instance, aim at the minimum state, whereas Washington—even in its more conservative phase in the late 1980s, when the consensus was formulated—always attributed a positive role to the state in social expenditures (education and health) and infrastructure investments. Williamson himself is not a neoliberal but a classical liberal.[14] Since the

Democratic Party won the presidential elections in 1992, the neoliberal wave has clearly receded in Washington.

This milder form assumed by the Washington consensus, in comparison with neoliberal ideas, combined with the changes that have taken place since the consensus was formed in the late 1980s, has led some to ask whether there really is a difference between it and the crisis of the state approach. There is. First, we are not considering the intentions of *A* or *B* but the statements, as they were made by the leading figures in Washington. Second, we are not taking into consideration the changes that have occurred. These changes did occur, and reveal that soon after the consensus was formed it began to disintegrate, but this does not alter the basic neoliberal roots of the original consensus.[15]

The Washington consensus views itself as the only alternative to the import substitution strategy and to the national-developmentalist interpretation of Latin America. This is not the case. New facts demand new approaches. The national-developmentalist approach can be considered the generic designation of two interpretations of Latin America: the national-bourgeois and the new dependency interpretations. The national-bourgeois (or center-periphery) approach, which Prebisch (1949) formulated in Santiago, Chile, as executive director of the United Nations' ECLA (now ECLAC), was the first paradigmatic moment of self-interpretation of Latin American development. Celso Furtado (1950) was the Brazilian pioneer of this vision of Latin American development. The new dependency theory, first comprehensively analyzed by Cardoso and Faletto (1969), was a second paradigmatic moment of interpretation of Latin America. It prevailed in the 1970s, following the economic crisis of the 1960s. These two approaches were closely connected. They lost their capacity to explain Latin American development as the crisis expanded in the 1980s.[16] The neoliberal critique emerged and prospered in the void left by the failure of the two previous interpretations. But as is the case with all ideological interpretations, it, too, was soon revealed as dogmatic and unrealistic.[17] A new synthesis is on the way as the 1980s crisis is being overcome. It may constitute the third paradigmatic moment of interpretation of Latin American development once it is in fact under way. I call it the crisis of the state or the social-democratic approach.

The crisis of the state approach, whose immediate origins are found in the new dependency theory, takes us a step forward in the direction of more market-oriented and market-state–coordinated reforms. It acknowledges that there is a populist, fiscal indiscipline problem and that the public deficit is also a major problem, but it adds that the problem is more serious than merely one of fiscal indiscipline. In fact, most Latin American countries face a fiscal crisis.

The fiscal crisis approach defines the fiscal crisis as the consequence not only of the public deficit but also of excessive public debt, negative public savings, and—following on the lack of state credit (its incapacity to finance itself except through seigniorage)—the government's lack of credibility and immobilization. It acknowledges that the state has become too big, that state-owned enterprises tend to be inefficient, that regulation has been distorted (protecting the special interests of bureaucrats and industries), and that national developmentalism became distorted by populism. Thus it supports market-oriented reforms, particularly outward-oriented, export-led industrialization. But it does not confuse market-oriented with market-coordinated reforms. The economy must be strongly market-oriented—that is, it must be as competitive as possible, both inwardly and outwardly. Economic coordination, nevertheless, must be mixed. This approach assigns to the market the basic role of resource allocation, but the state, after being reformed and fiscally adjusted, must assume new and important coordinating functions not only in the social realm but also in the fields of technology and international trade, as well as maintaining primary responsibility for infrastructure investments.

The crux of the fiscal crisis approach is the idea that the crisis is the outgrowth of a state that is too weak. The state did not become too big and too strong, but too big and too weak—unable to carry out its specific functions and to complement the market as it should. The state is weakened and immobilized by the fiscal crisis that was the outcome of the disordered and distorted growth of the state apparatus. The objective of structural reforms should not be to reach the minimum state but rather to strengthen the state and to define a new strategy of development consistent with new and limited forms of state intervention. Given the cyclical and ever-changing character of state intervention (Bresser Pereira 1993d), the new sectors in which the state will have to invest, in addition to the social sector and infrastructure, are high technology and the environment.

The assumption that it is enough to stabilize and to reduce state intervention to achieve growth is false. Although liberalizing reforms do foster market coordination and improve resource allocation, creating a more efficient economic system is insufficient for growth. If growth is to resume, it is necessary to combat the fiscal crisis, recover the public savings capacity, and define a new strategy of development. The national-developmentalist approach has stressed the role of the state but, supposedly following a Keynesian view, has accepted and even advocated chronic public deficits. This populist view is contradictory in itself. Its sponsors have weakened the very state they intended to make stronger. In public savings lies the difference between current state revenue and expenditures. A state can only be strong and capable of playing a strategic role in the development process if it is able to finance its investments and its social and economic policies with public savings, rather than incurring increasing debts.

The crisis of the state or social-democratic approach assigns the blame for Latin America's economic difficulties to the debt problem as much as to economic populism. A consequence of both was a fiscal crisis of the state, which expressed itself in high rates of inflation. As prices and wages tend to be informally indexed, this high inflation often has a chronic or an inertial character. This was particularly true in Brazil. In this approach, stabilization programs, in addition to adopting orthodox fiscal and monetary policies, should include income policies and reduce the outstanding public debt. Once stabilization has been achieved, market-oriented reforms should ensue, but the state that emerges from these reforms—although smaller and reorganized—should have not only a political and a welfare role but an economic role as well, particularly in the area of targeted industrial policy oriented toward export promotion.[18]

Although the fiscal crisis or social-democratic approach has as its antecedent the national-developmentalist and dependency approaches that dominated the 1970s, it differs from them somewhat. The major difference between it and the national-developmentalist approach lies in the fact that the latter interpretation took the causes of underdevelopment to be structural and directly related to imperialism, whereas the social-democratic approach assumes that the causes are to some extent strategic and have major domestic origins. To proponents of the crisis of the state approach, underdevelopment is not ordained by fate and cannot be explained mainly by imperialistic exploitation; it can be overcome when correct domestic strategies are adopted, particularly when a fiscally sound state aligns itself with the private sector and together they define a development strategy. Also, proponents of the social-democratic approach criticize the populism that often distorted national developmentalism. As with the previous approaches, the crisis of the state interpretation denies the thesis of the minimum state. It is also concerned with the importance of international variables, which were manifested in the 1980s through the debt crisis and the protectionist policies of the developed countries. It is critical of the standard diagnoses and recipes, which ignore the specificities of Latin American countries.

Since the onset of the debt crisis, the adjustment programs sponsored by Washington have called for balancing budgets through current expenditure and investment reductions. The alternative—eliminating the budget deficit through an increase in taxes and a reduction of the public debt—has received less attention.[19] In practical terms, balance-of-payment and price adjustments are considered to be so important that the quality of fiscal adjustment is not taken into account. A fiscal adjustment that hurts investments is considered to be as good as one that cuts current expenditures. Expenditure cuts are treated as superior to tax increases, ignoring the fact that expenditure cuts will usually be regressive whereas tax increases can be a tool of income distribution.[20] Debt reduction is systematically left as a last resort. And the idea that the recovery of public savings is an essential part of reforms is usually disregarded.

In contrast, the fiscal crisis approach starts from the hypothesis that growth does not automatically resume following stabilization, either because stabilization is achieved at the cost of public investment or because reform does not tackle the public savings issue. This approach asserts that growth will be resumed only if stabilization and market-oriented reforms are combined with the recovery of the public savings capacity and with policies that define a new strategic role for the state. For the fiscal crisis means not only that the state has no credit and is unable to finance its activities but also that it has lost the capacity to invest in and propel long-range policies oriented toward industrial, agricultural, and technological development. Once the fiscal crisis has been overcome, public savings will have to be restored to finance a growth program.[21]

The neoliberal approach assumes that private savings and investments will substitute for public investment. True, historically this has been the trend of investments in manufacturing and infrastructure. The state played a decisive role in both Germany and Japan at the end of the nineteenth century, directly investing in the productive sector. Since the beginning of the twentieth century, this role has continually been reduced and transformed. In both countries, however, the state continues to play a fundamental role in the social field and in promoting economic development through industrial and trade policy. The privatization that started in the 1980s is a second historical wave of substituting private for state ownership. It is being induced not only by ideological but also, if not mainly, by fiscal reasons. It is a form of overcoming the fiscal crisis of the state. Through selling state-owned enterprises the state reduces—or should reduce—its debt to the private sector.

As has happened in the developed countries, the state in the developing ones will continue to play a fundamental role in the social field and in development promotion. According to the crisis of the state or social-democratic interpretation, the state in Latin America will have to perform a supplementary but nevertheless strategic role in coordinating the economy and promoting economic growth, as Japan did and East and Southeast Asia are now doing. These regions, where development has been extraordinary, are made up of fiscally balanced states that use public savings to promote development.

The social-democratic approach supports trade liberalization but not as a magic formula. As Colin Bradford, Jr. (1991:88) observed, the recent literature on development strategies presents two alternatives to achieving international competitiveness: (1) "structural reform of the national economy for domestic competitiveness which results in dynamic growth and an increased supply of exports"; and (2) "trade policy reform for international competitiveness which allows the economy to respond to external demand."

The second alternative is characteristic of Washington's approach. Its representatives enumerate several prerequisites for a successful outward-oriented strategy (Krueger 1985), but it is fairly clear that the essential prerequisite in their view is to liberalize trade and open the economy. The first alternative is preferable in the social-democratic approach. Whereas trade liberalization alone may be an appropriate strategy for small countries like Singapore, Hong Kong, or Uruguay, for the large countries of Latin America trade liberalization should be only one ingredient in a development strategy that encompasses public savings, investments in education and technology, and export promotion.

The import substitution strategy exhausted its potential a long time ago. This strategy does not assure international competitiveness. But it makes little sense to believe it is enough for the state to stabilize, liberalize trade, and promote public education for growth to resume automatically. In Bradford's words (1991:93):

> The export-led growth [neoliberal] idea is based on the notion that if conditions are right, exports will occur, but the theory does not specify the agents of dynamic export growth beyond the efficiency gains from the static allocative effects of getting prices right. The growth-led export [pragmatic] idea is based on a richer range of elements which activate the growth process. These focus on the knowledge generation process both domestically through education, training, literacy, R&D [research and development] support and the like as well as the crucial absorption of technologies from abroad through open economic policies.

The social-democratic approach should be viewed not as a rejection of but as an alternative to the Washington consensus, with which it shares many views. Both are opposed to the national-populist posture still alive in Latin America, although with progressively less credibility and support.[22] The social-democratic approach accepts the need for reducing the size of the state, which grew exorbitantly over the past fifty years, and agrees that this expansion has generated serious distortions because the state has tended to be captured by the special interests of rent seekers. It emphasizes, however, that the crisis of the Latin American state is a result of the fiscal crisis, which weakened the state, and the fact that the form of state intervention—the import substitution strategy of industrialization—is exhausted. This approach does not accept the neoliberal axiom that says "since state failures are worse than market failures, the solution is to reduce state intervention to a minimum." In fact, state failures are dependent upon the state's own cyclical growth movement. When the state is dominated by the interests of special groups and falls victim to fiscal crisis, its failures will be overwhelming. At that point market-oriented reforms will be nothing more than required reforms of the state. Once the state has achieved that reform, which is similar to a business enterprise's restructuring, public policies will recover efficiency and effectiveness, and the state will be able once again to play a complementary but strategic role in coordinating the economy.

Hence, market-oriented reforms are not the monopoly of neoconservatism. A social-democratic approach will support them provided they are not radical or dogmatic, aiming at an unrealistic minimal state. This approach stresses, however, that the neoliberal assessment of the causes of the crisis is incomplete and partially mistaken—for instance, when it confuses a deep fiscal crisis with a voluntaristic conception of fiscal "indiscipline," when it underplays the role of the debt crisis, and when it ignores the fact that there are conflicting as well as mutual interests between both Latin America and the First World and Latin America and other developing countries.

According to the social-democratic approach, the Latin American crisis can be explained by the cumulative distortions provoked by years of populism and national developmentalism, the excessive and distorted growth of the state, the burden of the foreign debt, the exhaustion of the import substitution strategy, and the basic consequence of all of these accumulated trends: the financial crisis of the state—a crisis that immobilizes the state, transforming it into an obstacle to rather than an effective agent of growth.

The concept of the fiscal crisis of the state should be clearly distinguished from mere fiscal laxity or budget deficits. The fiscal crisis is a structural phenomenon rather than a short-run, circumstantial one. Persistent public deficits certainly engender a fiscal crisis, but once the deficits have been eliminated, the country confronts a more serious problem: potential public savings are being used to pay interest on domestic and foreign debts instead of being used to promote growth.

A two-entries matrix (Figure 2.1) helps to summarize the differences among the social-democratic or crisis of the state approach, the neoliberal or orthodox approach, and the populist version of the national-developmentalist approach. On one axis we have fiscal discipline (low or high), on the other market-state coordination (mixed or market). The first cell (fiscal indiscipline–mixed coordination) corresponds to the populist national-developmentalist approach. The second cell (high fiscal discipline–mixed coordination) corresponds to the social-democratic approach; it is typical of the European social democracy. It could also be called the East Asian approach because fiscal discipline and state intervention have been the cornerstones of Japanese, Korean, and Taiwanese economic policy. The difference between the social-democratic and the East Asian approaches is that the first accentuates the income distribution role of the state and the second does not.[23] The third cell (high fiscal discipline–exclusive market coordination) corresponds to the neoliberal approach or orthodox economic views. Finally, the fourth cell (low fiscal discipline–exclusive market coordination) corresponds to populist neoconservatism, whose best example was

Figure 2.1   Four Approaches to Crisis

		Fiscal Discipline	
		Low	High
Market-State Coordination	Mixed	Populist	Social-Democratic
	Market	Reaganomics	Neoliberal

Reaganomics—the economic policies that characterized the Reagan administration in the United States (1981–1989). There is no example of this kind of approach in Latin America.

With this general framework in mind, let us examine the eight largest countries in Latin America (see Table 2.1). Two—Chile and Columbia—have had strong development for some time. Colombia never experienced a real fiscal crisis or high rates of inflation. Chile was able to solve its fiscal crisis and to stabilize in the 1970s, adopting orthodox, costly, and inefficient—but eventually effective—economic policies. Colombia did not undertake modernizing or liberalizing economic reforms. Chile did, although it did not privatize its copper mines. Both countries show large public savings. One country—Mexico—adopted a strict fiscal adjustment program in 1985; implemented bold economic reforms in 1987; and liberalized and privatized its economy, and stabilized its inflation in December 1987, when prices and wages were frozen and the government mediated a social agreement—the Pacto de Solidariedad Social—between businesses and workers. Mexico did not actually solve its debt crisis because the negotiation of its foreign debt according to the Brady Plan produced a limited reduction of the debt (around 15 percent). The internal fiscal effort, however, was enormous. The heterodox shock in December 1987 was well prepared, well negotiated, and well implemented. And the structural reforms were radical. This internal effort, the perspective that Mexico would be a part of NAFTA, and an increasing flow of foreign investments have created positive expectations regarding Mexico. Since 1991 Mexico has started to grow again but at modest rates that are not compatible with the high levels of foreign investments. A sign that its fiscal crisis has not been completely overcome is the heavy burden of the payments of interest on the public debt.

The other five countries are still dealing with fiscal crises. Bolivia's inflation was stabilized in 1985; the economy remained stagnant for some time but has recently begun to grow again. Venezuela and Peru adopted rad-

Table 2.1   Latin American Per Capita GDP Growth and Inflation in the
1980s (selected countries)

	GDP Per Capita (%)			Inflation (%)		
	1985–1989	1989	1990	1985–1989	1989	1990
Argentina	−2.1	−5.6	−1.8	468.6	4,923.8	1,344.4
Brazil	2.2	1.2	−5.9	489.4	2,337.6	1,585.2
Bolivia	−1.8	−0.1	−0.2	192.8	16.6	18.0
Chile	4.4	8.0	0.3	19.8	21.4	27.3
Colombia	2.7	1.5	2.1	24.5	26.1	32.4
Mexico	−1.3	0.9	1.7	73.8	19.7	29.9
Peru	−2.6	−13.2	−6.8	443.2	2,775.8	7,649.7
Venezuela	−1.1	−10.1	3.2	32.5	81.0	36.5

Source: Economic Commission for Latin America, *Panorama Económico de América Latina,*
1990 and 1991.

ical economic reforms in 1991 but were caught in serious political crises the
next year. In 1992 the democratic regime in Peru broke down, and the newly
elected president assumed dictatorial powers. In Venezuela, President
Andrés Perez and his orthodox economic reforms are under serious attack
from all sectors of society. In Argentina, which—like Bolivia, Peru, and
Brazil—experienced hyperinflation, the Cavallo Plan induced an exchange
rate shock (the adoption of the exchange rate as a nominal anchor) in April
1991, which combined with strong fiscal adjustment and economic reforms
to allow the economy to stabilize and resume growth. The overvaluation of
the peso, however, threatens the program.

It is useful to mention that the governments of the Latin American countries—mainly Chile and Colombia, which have enjoyed positive economic
outcomes—are far from following all of the neoliberal recipes. Chile's copper mines are still state-owned, and its public savings are around 10 percent
of GDP. Colombia has executed few liberalizing reforms. Mexico was stabilized as a consequence of a heterodox shock and still firmly controls the
prices of monopolistic sectors. In all of these countries the state, which is
slowly being restored, plays a central role.

Brazil has long been trying to implement fiscal adjustment and economic reforms. Early in 1990 a frontal attack on inflation—the Collor Plan
I—was undertaken but failed. In 1992, an orthodox and gradualist economic program monitored by the IMF pushed real interest rates to around 4 percent a month and led the economy into a deep recession without reducing
inflation. The program only succeeded in keeping the inflation rate stable at
a little above 20 percent a month. At the end of the year the president, who
had been charged with corruption, was impeached. Until March 1994 the

new president, Itamar Franco, showed no capacity to face the chronic or inertial inflation, which is currently over 30 percent a month.[24]

The two approaches to the Latin American crisis—the neoliberal strategy and the social-democratic one—are compatible with two alternative strategies of stabilization and reform: a frontal attack on the fiscal crisis and inflation; or a gradual confidence-building strategy. Both strategies involve fiscal discipline, balance-of-payments equilibrium, and market-oriented economic reforms—particularly trade liberalization and privatization. Both are concerned with eliminating subsidies and administrative controls, correcting prices, stimulating internal and foreign competition, assuring efficient resource allocation, and reducing the size of the state.

Depending upon the seriousness of the fiscal crisis, a frontal attack strategy or a gradual confidence-building one is recommended. If the fiscal crisis has become hyperinflation and, in practical terms, the state is destroyed, the only alternative is a risky frontal attack on the fiscal crisis. If the economic situation has not deteriorated so greatly, a gradual confidence-building strategy is feasible.

By frontal attack I mean canceling internal public debt through monetary reform and reducing foreign public debt unilaterally or quasi-unilaterally to levels consistent with balance-of-payments and fiscal constraints. All countries that face hyperinflation must adopt some combination of these two measures. The problem is that this strategy is risky. If it fails, the ensuing situation will be even worse than the previous one. This is why a gradual confidence-building strategy is used when possible.

Bolivia, Peru, and Argentina—which had the worst fiscal crises among the Latin American countries, achieving hyperinflation—had no alternative except frontal attack. Brazil tried a frontal attack strategy in 1990, but it failed. The classical case of a confidence-building strategy was used in Mexico, although inflation there was also eliminated by a shock. However, in Mexico, as in Venezuela, the public debt was not canceled, and the fiscal adjustment was based on expenditure and wage reduction rather than on tax increases. A conventional Brady Plan was signed in August 1989, six months after the plan was announced by the U.S. secretary of the treasury. Public savings recovery, however, was very limited. Market-oriented structural reforms were undertaken fully—in other words, the costs of adjustment and of overcoming the fiscal crisis were imposed on the workers and the middle class. Local and foreign creditors were exempted from substantial debt reduction, and wealthy local people were exonerated from paying higher taxes. As a trade-off, confidence was restored among investors. Foreign investment and repatriation of capital started to take place.

The realistic alternative for Latin America lies somewhere in between a frontal attack and a confidence-building strategy. A pragmatic strategy recognizes: (1) the weight of the fiscal crisis; (2) the need for market-oriented structural reforms and fiscal discipline; (3) the necessity of reducing internal and foreign public debt; (4) the hegemonic (and conservative) character of the United States in Latin America; and (5) the conflicting views of the Latin American elites, who are aware of the fiscal crisis but resist tackling it through fiscal discipline and debt reduction—including foreign debt reduction, given strong ties with the United States.

The national interests of the Latin American countries and of the United States have much in common. Clearly, the United States is more relevant to Latin America than Latin America is to the United States, but many opportunities are open to all of these countries if they are able to understand each other and manage their differences productively. Although U.S. economic hegemony was not limited to Latin America but extended all over the world, the possibilities for cooperation between the United States and Latin America were limited while that hegemony existed. At the moment, however, it seems this global hegemony has been ceded to Japan and Europe, and new possibilities for international alliances have emerged as a result (see Chapter 16). Conflicts between the United States or, more broadly, between the First World and Latin America may on some occasions have had a real or a factual basis. The debt crisis was one paradigmatic case; disputes over property rights may be another. But in most cases the national interests of the Latin American countries and the First World coincide. Yet in many cases ideological viewpoints and conflicting approaches to the problems and solutions to the Latin American crisis cloud these mutual interests.

The conflicting approaches I have analyzed here constitute a case in point. In practical terms, the crisis of the state approach to the origins of the crisis and the social-democratic or pragmatic approach to solving it are preferred by the Latin American countries. The First World, which in practice does not apply the neoliberal approach, uses it rhetorically as a standard recipe for Latin American problems. Yet as growth continues in Latin America in the 1990s, it will be the social-democratic approach—based on the European and the East Asian experience—rather than the Washington consensus that will prevail, if only because the neoliberal approach is an effective critique of the national-developmental and state-led strategies but not a practical or viable answer to Latin American problems.

⚛ 3 ⚛

The Cycles of the State

The crisis of the state approach is a tool for understanding the economic crisis in Latin America in the 1980s and the modest recovery in the 1990s. This theoretical tool, however, gains full explanatory power only if one adds the hypothesis of a cyclical pattern of state intervention. According to this hypothesis, throughout the world the state grew too much from the 1930s to the 1970s. The neoliberal critique was a reaction to this growth, which became increasingly distorted. Since the 1980s market-oriented reforms of the state—particularly privatization, deregulation, and trade liberalization—have reduced the state apparatus. Yet if the process is intrinsically cyclical, once the crisis has purged the state, new forms of regulation will soon relate the state and the market, and the state will again expand.

On certain occasions limited state intervention becomes an acceptable political practice. This was clearly the case from the 1930s to the 1960s, when a Keynesian consensus prevailed. At other times, as during the past twenty years, the conservative attack on state intervention predominates. After the economic depression of the 1930s, the failures of the market were contrasted with the advantages of policymaking and planning. Today the inverse type of reasoning seems to represent the truth for a neoliberal "new right," whose ideas are based on economic theory and the market rather than on political philosophy and the ideas about tradition and hierarchy that defined the "old right." Yet there are signs that this conservative wave is waning. An ideological downturn seems to be a real possibility.

In macroeconomics, the monetarism that surfaced in the 1960s and the "new classical" school based on rational expectations, which appeared in the 1970s, are the clearest manifestations of the conservative wave. What caused the rise of the new right in macroeconomic theory was the collapse of the Keynesian consensus. On the one hand, the state had become too large and inefficient and was plagued by a fiscal crisis; on the other, standard Keynesian economic policies, based on the assumption of chronic insufficiency of demand, failed to cope with rising unemployment and increasing rates of inflation that became stagflation. In development economics, the failure of the "big push" industrialization theories, which were behind the dominant import substitution model of industrialization in the 1950s and 1960s, gave rise in the 1970s to an export-led, market-oriented theory of growth, whose basic tenets were privatization and trade liberalization. The fact that countries adopting the export-led strategy, such as Korea and Taiwan, did so in combination with aggressive industrial policies rather than leaving the fate of the economy to the market did not hinder the followers of the new credo from using these countries as examples of their liberal neo-ideas. Finally, in comparative economics, the failure of statist economies during the 1970s and 1980s to maintain the high rates of growth achieved in the 1950s and 1960s served as a powerful ideological argument favoring the neoliberal approach. The subsequent collapse of communism was proffered as evidence of the triumph of neoliberal ideas. The fact that in the Soviet Union and Eastern Europe an extreme form of statism had been adopted was forgotten. The conservative strategy was to put support for limited state intervention and extreme state control of the economy in the same basket.

More recently this neoliberal wave has been coming under attack. The inadequacies of monetarism and rational expectations are becoming manifest. The status of state intervention in economic theory is again rising, although modestly, as the new international trade theory (Paul Krugman) and the new endogenous growth theory (Paul Rommer) provide new paths for mainstream economics. The simplistic idea held by the new right that market failures may exist but are always less damaging than government failures seems correct, but it cannot be sustained on theoretical or practical grounds.

Changes in the way market and state intervention is viewed are related to the recurrent successes and failures of such intervention. As long as state intervention is successful, theories that support limited intervention are in favor. When intervention ceases to be effective, the voices of conservatives and neoliberals become louder. This is a symptom of the cyclical and ever-changing nature of state intervention. In this chapter, after a review of the complementary roles of the market and the state in contemporary capitalism—a fascinating example of bureaucratic influence and market orientation—I apply the theory of the cycles of the state to the Brazilian case.

The state and the market are at the center of the recent upheavals throughout the world. It is very difficult to understand these events if we do not have a theory to explain the relationship between these two institutions. There are different interpretations of what the role of the state has been and what role it can still play on the economic level. Yet in recent years those on the right and on the left have criticized state action.

Neoliberals contend that collective action is impossible, that the state is necessarily inefficient because it is a hostage to private interests, that its protection discourages work, and that it tends to favor pressure groups. They also believe efficiency is synonymous with the market, that state failures are worse than market failures, and that it is better to live with market failures than to try to correct them using the state. Thus they propose, unrealistically, the minimal state as their basic policy objective.

The modern left also views state intervention as inefficient but not intrinsically so. Those on the left do not say intervention necessarily discourages work but rather that it favors oligopolistic capital. However, the state easily falls victim to inefficiency and private interests that "privatize" the state, turning it into the private property of various pressure groups. It is possible to elicit effective and efficient action from the state, but this requires that the state undergo a permanent process of reform because it lacks an automatic (if imperfect) system of correction like that found in the market. Administering bureaucratic organizations—among which the state is the most important—is a process that constantly needs correcting, that is in permanent need of reform.

When I speak of the state, I am referring only to the state apparatus, the state bureaucratic organization, and the legal system that constitutes it. I am not referring to the nation-state, which is identified with a country or a nation, or to a political regime (e.g., the authoritarian state), much less to an economic system (e.g., the capitalist state). The *state,* in the strict sense in which I am using the term here, is a special kind of bureaucratic organization formed on the one hand by a government, a public bureaucracy, and an armed force, and on the other by a complex legal or constitutional system that has the exclusive power to legislate and levy tributes on the inhabitants of a given geographic area: the nation-state.[1]

The market and the state are the two basic institutions that coordinate any contemporary economic system. In contemporary capitalism the state and the large corporations have a special role in complementing the market's resource allocation mechanism. We find, in the social system we call capitalism, important traits of a statist or a bureaucratic type of society. The economic system is basically coordinated by the market, particularly by the price system. But the state has a major role in regulating and institutionalizing the market. And in the major corporations, as in the state, bureaucrats play an extremely influential role in regulating and coordinating the economy.

If, in abstract terms, capitalism is an economic system coordinated by the market, statism is an economic system in which the state almost completely substitutes for the market in coordinating the economy. Although the demise of the Soviet type of economic system has demonstrated the infeasibility of pure bureaucratism or statism, as was found in Eastern Europe, "pure capitalism," in which small firms would be coordinated only by the market with no participation from the state, is equally infeasible.

In the twentieth century, bureaucratic capitalism has been characterized increasingly by social-democratic regulation of the market. This regulation is carried out by governments through a process of permanent intermediation between capitalists and workers, where the objective is to make the profit rate and investments consistent with an acceptable distribution of income. This intervention is indispensable because in the market for unskilled workers the wage rate of equilibrium is very low (Roemer 1990). This rate is in equilibrium economically because it clears the market, but it is not politically feasible. The welfare state's social-democratic regulation taxes the capitalists and the bureaucrats, the upper and middle classes, to finance the social expenditures that raise the equilibrium wage rate for unskilled workers.[2]

The market is an institution. It does not exist naturally. It is dependent on the laws and regulations issued by the state. Markets can perform their resource allocation role only if there is a strong state to sustain that allocation—and to correct it when the market alone is unable to do so. The state's corrective actions must be very limited because the distortions of an overgrown state are unavoidable. But it is utopian to believe that contemporary capitalism can work without a strong state and without a strong bureaucracy within the state and the large corporations. Contemporary capitalism is highly competitive, market-oriented, and bureaucratic. History demonstrates that an economy coordinated only by bureaucrats and the state is doomed to failure, but history also shows that successful economies controlled exclusively by capitalists and the market are pure fiction. Coordination is always the outcome of the joint operation of the market and state regulations, of the interaction of businesspeople and bureaucrats' decisions.

Thus it makes no sense to define economics as the study of the market and political science as the study of power and the state. In fact, without the state neither capital nor money would exist; therefore, neither production nor large-scale trade would be possible. It is impossible to consider coordinating the economy only with the market or only with the state.

S tate intervention in modern times has assumed three forms, corresponding to three historical models of development: (1) the state as a substitute for the market in the coordination of the economy (statist or Soviet model); (2) the state as a decisive agent in promoting capital accumulation and technological development (the historical German and Japanese model of industrialization, adopted in varying degrees by most developing countries during this century)—the developmentalist state; and (3) the state as macroeconomic policymaker, promoter of welfare, microeconomic regulator of business enterprises and the environment, fiscal stimulator of technological growth geared toward international competitiveness, and bargaining agent for international trade on behalf of its respective countries (the present OECD model)—the coordinating state. The first historical model of state intervention falls outside the scope of this book. I will discuss state intervention in Brazil, assuming that we are dealing with a capitalist, market-oriented economic system in transition from the second to the third model of intervention.

State intervention expands and contracts cyclically, and in each new cycle the mode of state intervention changes.[3] When intervention is expanding, the state assumes an increasing role in the coordination of the economic system, the microallocation of resources, the macrodefinition of the level of savings and investments (or of the equilibrium between aggregate demand and supply), and the micro-macro determination of income distribution among social classes and sectors of the economy. Intervention increases because the state is performing a role the market is unable to perform or performs inefficiently. It also increases because the state responds in a fairly effective way to the demands of society.

But as state intervention increases, whether in terms of its share of GDP or of the degree of regulation the economy is subjected to, it begins to become disfunctional. The three basic symptoms indicating that the state's expansion has gone too far are excesses in regulation (which hinder rather than stimulate economic activity), huge public deficits that crowd out private investments, and negative public savings that reduce total savings. This is the point at which the cycle reverts, when state control contracts and market control expands. This is the time for some deregulation and denationalization.

This hypothesis of the cyclical nature of state intervention conflicts with both the static theories, which assume a given level of state intervention as ideal, and the historical theories, which claim there has been a long-term tendency toward the statization of the economy. For neoliberals, the ideal level of state intervention is very low; for statists it is very high; and for pragmatists it is intermediate. Although I am closer to the pragmatists, I would say these three positions are unacceptable as long as they assume a given relation between market and state control as ideal or optimum. My hypothesis is that this ideal relation will necessarily vary historically and according to the cyclical pattern of state intervention just described.

Thus, rather than falling into an endless discussion about a doubtful optimum, I propose that there is a cyclical and ever-changing pattern of state intervention. If I am even minimally successful in demonstrating this hypothesis, I hope the ideological content of the debate over the economic intervention of the state will to some degree be reduced.

There are economic and political limits to the state's growth. Relations between the state and civil society or between the state and the market are not arbitrary. The market and the state are the two mechanisms that are responsible for the coordination of an economy. Although they are not parallel institutions, because the state existed previous to the market and is responsible for its institutionalization and regulation, it is possible to think they fill complementary roles in coordinating the economy. These roles have to be performed in a balanced way. A state that grows too much in relation to the market may cause economic and political problems that, sooner or later, will limit its expansion. In this book I suggest that the state grows cyclically. I propose that, in the same way that in the strictly economic realm there are business cycles and Kondratieff cycles and in the private–public interest alternative there is the Hirschman cycle, in the economic-political realm there are cycles of state intervention.

The present historical process of a relative reduction of the economic role of the state, which started in the mid-1970s, must be viewed as a phase of the cyclical pattern of state intervention. The slowdown of the capitalist economies since that time is, in part, the consequence of the distortions and inefficiencies provoked by the previous growth of the state. As these distortions were perceived by society, they gave rise to the conservative or neoliberal wave. State failures were blamed for all of the major problems that arose, market failures were ignored, and the objective became the minimal state. The proposed instruments for reduction are trade liberalization, privatization and regulation, and market-oriented reforms.

Yet there is no reason to identify market-oriented reforms with neoliberalism; nor should we identify market orientation with market coordination. Japan and the Asian tigers are market-oriented economies—that is, strongly competitive within the country and abroad—but they are not particularly market-coordinated economies—that is, resource allocation is not the exclusive role of the market. On the contrary, in this respect the state plays an important part. Economic reforms that liberalize trade, privatize, and deregulate may merely be sensible economic policy, provided they do not aim at the minimal state, disregard market failures, or ignore the potentialities of collective action. If the pattern of state intervention is cyclical, it tends to change. In each cycle or historical moment it will assume a different form. Following liberalization and privatization, the state will perform new roles—institutionalizing markets, investing in infrastructure and education, stimulating science and technology, protecting the environment, and promoting welfare.

To say that state intervention is, in principle, efficient or inefficient makes no sense. State intervention may be efficient or inefficient, necessary or unnecessary, in need of expansion or reduction depending on each specific situation. In general terms, state intervention will be necessary and efficient in the initial phase of the intervention cycle and excessive and inefficient in the final phase. In this phase the state will probably be inflated and will have become increasingly unable to act, given the interests of external (lobbying) and internal (technobureaucratic) constituencies, which lead the state into fiscal trouble if not crisis.

In the Brazilian case the cyclical and changing character of state intervention is fairly clear. From the 1930s to the 1970s the state played a decisive role in promoting economic growth; in the 1980s, given the fiscal crisis, the state lost its capacity to promote economic growth and, in fact, became a basic obstacle to such growth.[4]

Some economists and political scientists in Brazil, who had previously supported state intervention for the protection of local industry and the creation and development of state-owned enterprises in those sectors private capital was unable or unwilling to enter, currently favor trade liberalization and privatization. This does not mean that they have become conservative. It only means Brazil is in a different phase of the state intervention cycle— one in which it is necessary to streamline and tighten the state's structure to overcome the fiscal crisis and create the conditions for a new stage of economic development. In this new phase the state will have a different but necessarily important economic role to play.

Between the 1930s and the 1970s the pattern of state intervention in Brazil changed continually; nevertheless, it was effective in promoting economic development. Data on the growth of GDP during this period demonstrate this. In the 1930s the state began a long-term and initially successful industrial policy of import substitution. In the 1940s and 1950s state-owned enterprises were established in the basic sectors of the economy: steel; oil; electrical power; and transportation.

The 1960s were a period of transition and fiscal adjustment, but changes in industrial policy were quite limited. The basic innovation of the technobureaucratic, authoritarian government was a clear export-oriented policy. The objective was to export manufactured goods. But protection of local industry, a key characteristic of import substitution industrialization, was maintained. And direct investment by the state was resumed; the state nationalized the telephone industry and completed the nationalization of the electrical power industry.

The 1970s were the decade of the economic miracle (1968–1978) and the PND II (1974–1979). This plan was characterized by the promotion of a new wave of import substitution in the basic sectors of the economy (steel, nonferrous metals, oil, petrochemicals) under the direct control of state-owned enterprises, and also by the decision to promote full import substitution in the private, mostly nationally owned capital goods industry. The 1970s were also when Brazil acquired its huge international debt and began to run up a large (state) domestic debt.

During these fifty years we can distinguish two cycles. The first ended in the mid-1960s, when the military government that triumphed in the 1964 coup was able to overcome the fiscal crisis and the recession that followed the excesses of President Kubistchek's Plano de Metas. Between 1964 and 1967 the Brazilian state underwent a fiscal macroeconomic adjustment and structural reforms (an indexation system, tax reform, financial reform, housing–bank system reform) that recovered the state's capacity to promote forced savings and to channel them to direct state investments or subsidized private investments. The second cycle is not yet complete because the country has not yet overcome the fiscal and economic crisis of the 1980s.

The conservative wave that has inundated the world since the 1970s and Brazil since the late 1980s becomes easier to understand if we accept the idea of a cyclical pattern of state intervention. As soon as the state begins to show clear signs that it has grown too much and in a distorted way—the welfare state in the developed countries, the developmental state in the developing countries, and the command state in the statist countries— the opportunity arises for the neoliberal critique of collective action. This critique—particularly the one that came from the public choice school— correctly viewed the public deficit as the outcome of demands from special interest groups. It was unacceptable for its radicalism and conservatism, but it was correct in pointing to the excessive growth of the state and the need for market-oriented reforms.

Furthermore, we can infer that the cyclical upturns of state growth give rise to ideological waves. This seems to be supported by the facts. In the 1930s an upturn gave rise to a successful critique of economic liberalism; in the 1970s state growth led to an also successful (although pessimistic) evaluation of state intervention. One reason the ideological mood changes is that many people tend to adopt the pragmatic approach, which, in my opinion, is the correct thing to do. Technocratic economists exemplify this tendency. In the short run, given that the ongoing economic crisis is essentially a fiscal crisis, pragmatic economists—who in the past had argued in favor of demand-stimulating economic policies—begin to ask for fiscal discipline, for an effective fiscal adjustment that will eliminate the public deficit, and, in extreme cases, for some form of public debt cancellation. However, given that the origin of the fiscal crisis is the foreign debt crisis and that it is practically impossible to eliminate the public deficit while honoring all interests related to that debt, the approach I have been calling social-democratic would demand debt reduction—the securing of a substantial part of the debt. Privatization of as many state-owned enterprises as possible and trade liberalization would be important parts of this type of policy, but the objective— in contrast to that of the neoliberals—would not be the minimal state but the reform of the state so it once again becomes capable of formulating and implementing effective economic policy.

The new strategy adopted by pragmatic economists does not propose direct state investment, much less protection for inefficient import substitution industries, but rather the support of technological development for international competitiveness. Income distribution through increased expenditures for education and health is also important. It is becoming increasingly plain that the high degree of income concentration in Brazil is a major barrier to economic growth and price stability because it permanently feeds a high level of distributive conflict and reduces the government's legitimacy.

In addition to being pragmatic, this approach to state intervention in Brazil is dialectical: it simultaneously supports a strong market-oriented economy and state intervention in the critical areas the market is unable to coordinate; and it acknowledges the cyclical nature of state intervention. Sometimes, as at present, it is necessary to reduce and reshape the state to render it more effective (able to implement public policies) and efficient (able to implement those policies at low cost).

Technocratic economists all over the world tend to be pragmatic, but those from the Far East seem to be particularly so. I saw this clearly when I took part in an international seminar in Tokyo in summer 1989. At this seminar most of the Asian economists were members of their respective governments, and they defined themselves without embarrassment—on the contrary, they seemed fairly proud—as pragmatic technocrats in opposition to theoretical and ideological economists.[5]

The role the state has played in the development of the East and Southeast Asian countries is well known, starting with Japan and then Korea, Taiwan, Singapore, Malaysia, and, more recently, Thailand and Indonesia.[6] Whereas the Latin American countries are stagnant, the East and Southeast Asian nations are booming. Whereas per capita income in the Latin American countries decreased in the 1980s, it grew about 4 percent annually in the Asian countries.

One explanation for this difference in economic performance is that Asian pragmatic economists combine very strong fiscal discipline with a high degree of state intervention. But their discourse carefully avoids reference to state intervention while strongly praising their market-oriented economies. They believe in a market-oriented economy, but they also believe in and practice permanent state intervention. A good example of this general attitude was expressed by Seiji Naya (1989:5, 7).

> The NIEs [newly industrialized economies] and the ASEAN-4 countries have largely allowed the market to work and have adopted a private sector approach to economic development. . . . This does not mean that they are laissez-faire economies; in fact, governments intervene strongly. . . . In East Asia there is a hierarchical relationship under which the government may directly influence the conduct of private enterprises for the benefit of the public good and in turn is expected to assist and protect them.

This Asian economic pragmatism includes a certain degree of pragmatic dissimulation. The dominant capitalist class wants to hear that Asian economies are market-oriented, and the Asian countries insistently repeat that as fact. In Japan, for instance, government economists say the government's economic role is currently very small. Only after much questioning will they admit that the Japanese state presently dispenses large sums of money to subsidize technological development. Rather than dissimulated, however, this attitude is dialectical. Asians do believe in the benefits of a market-oriented economy, and at the same time they know very well that the state continues to play a decisive role in economic development and income distribution—income distribution that, by the way, is far more equal in their countries than is the case in Latin America.

Technocratic economists have long existed in Brazil. Yet many of them compromised with the authoritarian regime and failed to face the economic crisis when it arose in the late 1970s; thus they have come under attack.[7] As a defense mechanism, they have tended to disguise themselves and to make their existence as inconspicuous as possible. With democratization, they lost power over both the bourgeoisie and the professional politicians. There is no doubt, however, that if the solution to the Brazilian crisis involves the formation of a new and broader political coalition—broader than the one that existed under the bureaucratic-authoritarian regime—this coalition will have to encompass businesspeople, workers, and the private and state bureaucratic class. Fernando Henrique Cardoso's election to the presidency points toward such a coalition and, to a certain extent, signals the new political pact that will probably be formed.

✳ Part 2 ✳
The Fiscal Crisis

✖ 4 ✖

Crisis and Change

The pattern of financing investment in Brazil changed in the 1980s as an outcome of the fiscal crisis of the state. During the 1970s investment was based on the classical pattern that usually prevails in the early stages of development—that is, on state and foreign savings. In the 1990s, as growth has resumed, the role of the private sector has become strategic. In this chapter I deal with the crisis of the 1980s and this changing pattern of financing investment. My main concern is with the funding of investments. The basic assumption is that the stage of primitive accumulation, when the rate of investment grows from precapitalist levels to around 20 percent of GDP, definitely ended in the 1970s. Brazil is a mature, although unevenly developed, capitalist economy facing a deep cyclical crisis—a crisis that is also a transition to a new form of financing capital accumulation.

This chapter is divided into eight sections. In section 1, I build a model to show that, in the early stages of development, in addition to external finance, forced saving is imposed by the state, and the resulting resources are used to finance either private investment or state investment. In a second phase, after the basic stock of capital has been built up, the private sector—through regular increases in productivity and profits—assumes a more important role in investment. In section 2, I analyze the decline in the state's capacity to save and to invest. Section 3 demonstrates that during the 1970s total investment was a function of both external and state savings. The state not only invested directly but was also responsible for financing and subsidizing private investment. Section 4 analyzes how external financing as a source of funds for investment ended beginning in 1979. Section 5 analyzes the deterioration of public finance or the increasing decline in the state's capacity to impose forced savings. The reduction of the fiscal burden, the artificial price controls of the state-owned corporations, the increase in the state's indebtedness—which was aggravated by higher interest rates—the pressure to reduce the public deficit, and the political weakening of the state technobureaucracy are also examined.

Section 6 is an analysis of the falling rate of profit of state-owned and private national and multinational corporations. This fall is related to the adjustment process, the loss of the state's capacity to subsidize the private sector, and an increase in capital intensity or a reduction in the marginal output-capital relation as a result of capital-intensive import-substituting

51

investments. Section 7 presents a short analysis of the relationship between wages and productivity. Finally, in section 8, I discuss the likely patterns of financing investment in the second half of the 1990s. Two questions are posed: what will the new pattern of investment be, and what will be its results? Rogério Furquim Werneck's article on the subject is reviewed. Although there is a clear need to recover the state's savings and investment capacity, it is not reasonable to try to return to the 1970s pattern of financing investments. The indebtedness of the state, the new strength of the private sector, and the existence of a new financial market and a much bigger stock of capital suggest a new strategy based on exporting manufactured goods and increasing the marginal output-capital relation.

The basic variable in any process of industrialization is the rate of investment. Given the productivity of investment, which is the consequence of technological innovation and can be measured by the marginal product-capital relation, the rate of growth in the long run will depend on the rate of investment.

Investment is the result of decisions of private business firms, multinational corporations, state-owned corporations, and the state itself. Depending on the stage of development and the industrialization strategy adopted, investment will be undertaken predominantly by one or two of these economic agents. In the early periods of development the state and state-owned corporations frequently assume a dominant role. This was the case with Japan and Germany and is presently the case in Korea and Taiwan. In other instances local business enterprises start the process, and the state and the multinationals become involved later. In any case the interplay among these agents—entrepreneurs, the state, and state-owned and multinational enterprises—is essential for understanding a given pattern of industrial development.

The rate of investment is defined by the ratio of total investment to GDP. It depends in the long run on: (1) business enterprises' capacity to finance themselves through their profit rates; (2) their ability to obtain internal and external financing, including new capital; and (3) exclusively for the state, the capacity to promote forced saving. In the short run the rate of investment also depends on the cyclical fluctuations of the expected rate of profit, which is directly tied to the relation between aggregate supply and aggregate demand. The laws that govern short-run economic processes are not the same as those that explain the long-run processes, but short-run investment decisions necessarily influence the long run. So although I will not give priority to short-run analysis, I must consider it. Although the decision to invest depends essentially on profit expectations, it also depends on the fear of losing market shares and on the danger of being defeated by technological competition. If expectations of positive profits or negative fears related to the market share and technological competition are strong, investment may be sustained in the face of relatively high interest rates.

It could be said that, in the long run, investment capacity depends on savings. Under conditions of full employment this is true. In the more common situation of unemployment it will be investment, through the multiplier, that will determine income and aggregate savings. But even when full employment exists I prefer to put savings in a subordinate position—dependent on business enterprises' capacity to self-finance, the availability of internal and external financing, and the state's capacity to impose forced saving.

The capacity of business enterprises to finance their investments depends on the size of their capital and the rate of profit. Given the assumption that investment, I, is equal to profits, R, a high rate of profit, $R{:}K$, will mean a high rate of accumulation, $I{:}Y$, unless the capital-output ratio, $K{:}Y$, is considerably higher than 1. The higher the capital-output ratio—that is, the more inefficient or capital-expending technical progress is—the lower the accumulation rate, given the rate of profit. This can be clearly seen by dividing the numerator and the denominator of the accumulation rate by K:

$$\frac{I/K}{Y/X}$$

In the first stages of development the total stock of capital is small in relation to current production—that is, the capital-output ratio tends to be small. Thus the average rate of profit would have to be exceptionally high to permit a high rate of accumulation. The problem, however, is that the average rate of profit will also tend to be small. Thus, even if the marginal rate of profit on new investments is high, the average rate of accumulation will not be high.

The rate of profit depends on: (1) the rate and type of technological progress; (2) the profit-wage ratio, which is based on the rate of surplus value; and (3) the role of primitive accumulation.[1] Primitive accumulation encompasses all forms of appropriation of surplus or realization of profits by capitalists outside the regular market process. Karl Marx (1867:ch. 24) said that in the early stages of development primitive accumulation is essential for building the basic stock of capital. Only in a later stage does the surplus value mechanism—which presupposes an existing stock of capital—work as a means of appropriation of a surplus through market mechanisms. Primitive accumulation is obtained in modern times through monopoly practices, particularly through state protection and subsidies.

The availability of funds for the accumulation of capital depends internally on the existence of a rentier class and a financial system to transfer savings from rentiers to business enterprises.[2] Externally it depends on the availability of international credit and on the country's creditworthiness.

Since in the early stages of development the rentier class tends to be small, the state's forced savings, imposed through either taxes or inflation, are usually an important substitute.

Forced savings imposed by the state can be channeled to private business enterprises through loans made by state-owned banks or through several kinds of subsidies (primitive accumulation). They can also be invested directly by the state or transferred to state-owned enterprises. In any circumstance, forced savings and primitive accumulation will play a decisive role in financing investment in the early stages of development because the stock of capital in the hands of business enterprises and rentiers will necessarily be small in relation to production. After a certain period of development, given the increase in the total capital-output relation, these extra-market mechanisms will have less importance, and capital accumulation will be able to proceed based on technical progress and the surplus value mechanism, with supernormal profits being derived from innovation, speculation, and monopoly power.

T he pattern of investment financing changed markedly in the 1980s compared with the 1970s. During the 1980s the rate of savings and investment declined, and the rate of growth of output fluctuated sharply (see Table 4.1).

The reduction in the savings rate is clearly related to the decline of external savings and particularly of public savings. From a high of 31.7 percent of GDP in 1975, total savings fell to 15.7 percent in 1984; in this period external savings fell from 5.3 to minus 0.1 percent, and state savings declined from 8.2 percent of GDP to 0.8 percent whereas private savings remained relatively stable. Investment fell correspondingly from 31.7 percent of the GDP in 1975 to 16.7 percent in 1983. In this period private investment fell sharply, whereas public investment suffered a small decline. Since this behavior is not compatible with that of savings, it indicates a strong increase in the indebtedness of the public sector. In fact, since 1976 the rate of investment of the public sector has been consistently higher than its rate of savings, further indicating the increasing indebtedness of the public sector.

This increasing indebtedness can be seen in the increase of state-owned corporations' ratio of financial costs to operational revenue, which went from an index of 100 in 1980 to an index of 237.39 in 1983 (see Werneck 1985:12). It can also be seen in the relation of the real or operational public deficit (the variation in PSBR during the year, excluding monetary correction) to the GDP. PSBR averaged 7 percent of GDP between 1979 and 1982 and fell to an average of 4 percent of GDP in the following four years. The internal public debt, according to the Central Bank definition, increased 81 percent in real terms from December 1981 to December 1985, and the total debt—including the external debt—increased 78 percent.

Table 4.1   Growth, Savings, and Investment (percentage of GDP)

	GDP (growth rate)	Internal Savings[a]			External Savings[a]	Investment[a]		
		Private	State	Total		Private	State	Total
1970	8.3	–	–	24.1	1.4	–	–	25.5
1971	11.3	–	–	23.3	2.7	–	–	26.0
1972	12.1	–	–	23.5	2.6	–	–	26.1
1973	14.0	15.7	9.5	25.2	2.0	19.7	5.7	27.2
1974	9.0	15.4	8.1	23.5	6.7	19.6	8.0	30.2
1975	5.2	18.2	8.2	26.4	5.3	20.9	8.6	31.7
1976	10.1	16.2	7.1	23.3	3.8	16.1	10.5	27.1
1977	4.5	15.9	7.6	23.5	2.2	15.7	9.4	25.7
1978	4.7	15.6	7.6	23.2	3.3	13.6	10.7	26.5
1979	7.2	15.1	3.8	18.9	3.1	8.2	14.0	22.0
1980	9.1	15.6	2.2	17.8	4.5	12.6	9.0	22.3
1981	–3.1	16.3	2.3	18.6	4.5	13.0	10.1	23.1
1982	1.1	13.5	1.8	15.3	5.8	12.2	8.9	21.1
1983	–2.8	12.7	0.6	13.3	3.4	9.6	7.1	16.7
1984	5.7	15.0	0.8	15.8	–0.1	8.3	7.4	15.7
1985	8.4	18.8	0.3	19.1	0.1	9.8	9.4	19.2
1986	8.0	15.2	1.9	17.1	2.0	7.3	11.8	19.1
1987	2.9	23.0	–1.2	21.8	0.5	12.6	9.7	22.3
1988	–1.0	26.5	–2.4	24.1	–1.3	14.1	8.7	22.8
1989	3.3	30.4	–5.3	25.1	–0.2	17.6	7.3	24.9
1990	–4.0	20.4	0.8	21.2	0.5	6.9	14.8	21.7

Source: Central Bank, *Brazil Economic Program,* several issues.
Note: a. Gross formation of fixed capital includes savings, uses, and investment.

The basic question now is whether a reasonable GDP growth of, say, 6 percent a year is compatible with this reduction of savings and investment, as well as with this increase in public debt. If it is not, an additional question is whether this decrease in savings and investment is reversible. To answer these questions, I examine the pattern of investment financing in Brazil in the 1970s and 1980s.

In Brazil during the 1970s financing investment followed the classical pattern of the early stages of development. Total investment during those years was a direct function of external indebtedness and state investment. If one takes, for instance, the period 1974–1976, external savings accounted for 32 percent of total savings, and state investment accounted for 30 percent of total investments.

In fact, the state's contribution to investment was greater than 30 percent, given the process of primitive accumulation. In addition to investing directly or through state-owned corporations, the state strongly subsidized private investment. No precise figures exist for these subsidies. During the 1970s there were many kinds of subsidies: export, credit, fiscal subsidies (tax incentives) for industrial sectors and regions, and artificially low prices of goods and services produced by state-owned corporations. The cost of credit subsidies alone averaged 3.5 percent of GDP during the period 1980–1982 (World Bank 1984a:52). If one adds to this value the fiscal subsidies to, and the artificially low prices of, the products of the state-owned corporations, particularly the prices of steel and electric energy, this figure would probably be doubled, or around 7 percent of GDP for subsidies to the private sector. These subsidies as a whole represent primitive accumulation (I am not considering consumption subsidies). They represent an addition to the profits of the private sector, and an indeterminate part—say, 5 percent—represents additional investment. Thus, in addition to the 30 percent share of investments directly conducted by the state and state-owned corporations, around 20 percent of total investments were financed by primitive accumulation, that is, by state subsidies.

State participation in promoting (financing, in the broad sense of the expression) investment is, however, even greater because it is necessary to include the specific financing of investments that in Brazil was done through the state and, in the 1970s, also occurred through foreign borrowing. It is well known that the private financial system is, or was, unable to finance long-term investment. Long-term industrial lending was carried out almost entirely through the BNDES system. According to a World Bank report (1984b:xix) on the Brazilian financial system, in 1978 BNDES disbursements were equivalent to 40 percent of the industrial fixed capital formation. Most of this credit was either explicitly subsidized or carried low real interest rates when fully corrected for inflation.

This pattern of investment—based on external and state financing, direct state investment, and subsidized private investment—which prevailed during the 1970s, entered a deep crisis when the flow of net external financing dried up in 1982 at the same time the state began to lose its ability to impose forced saving. In fact, the process of foreign indebtedness stopped being a source of funds for new investments early in 1979, when the increase in the total external debt became approximately equal to the interest payments that were being made, as can be seen by comparing columns 3 and 4 of Table 4.2. From that point on, new loans were made only to roll over the interest. On the other hand, the inflow of real resources, which during the 1970s had averaged 2.1 percent of GDP per year, turned into an outflow in 1983 when the country started attaining high trade surpluses.

To the real resources transfers, which reached around 5 percent of GDP in 1984 and 1985, should be added the net outflow of foreign money represented by the excess of remittances of profits and dividends in relation to

Table 4.2 External Debt and Transfer of Resources (US$ million)

	External Debt	External Debt Increase	Interest	Transfer of Real Resources[a] (% GDP)
1970	6.049	–	–	(0.5)
1971	7.947	1.898	302	(2.2)
1972	11.026	3.079	359	(2.0)
1973	13.962	2.936	514	(1.8)
1974	18.871	4.909	652	(8.3)
1975	24.186	5.315	1.498	(6.5)
1976	30.970	6.784	1.809	(4.1)
1977	32.037	1.067	2.103	(1.2)
1978	43.511	11.474	2.696	(2.1)
1979	49.904	6.393	4.185	(3.5)
1980	53.848	3.944	6.311	(3.3)
1981	61.411	7.563	9.161	(0.6)
1982	69.654	8.243	11.353	(1.0)
1983	81.319	11.665	9.555	2.7
1984	91.091	9.772	10.203	5.9
1985	95.857	4.766	9.589	5.2
1986	101.759	5.902	9.300	2.7
1987	107.514	5.755	8.792	3.6
1988	102.555	(4.959)	9.900	6.2
1989	99.285	(3.270)	9.633	4.9
1990	96.546	(2.739)	8.906	2.8

Sources: Central Bank, *Brazil Economic Program,* several issues; Paulo N. Batista, Jr. (1987) for column 4 (until 1985).
Note: a. Transfer of real resources equals surplus on trade account, including real service.

Table 4.3   Foreign Investment Balance (US$ million)

Discrimination	1983	1984	1985	1986	1987	1988	1989	1990
1. Direct investment(net)	664	1,077	710	70	531	2,267	125	68
2. Conversion of loans into investment	425	731	537	176	336	2,087	946	283
3. New investment (3=1–2)	239	346	173	–106	195	180	–821	215
4. Remittance of profits and dividends	758	796	1,059	1,100	–909	1,539	2,383	1,614
5. Net inflow of money (5=3–4)	–519	–450	–886	–1,206	1,104	–1,359	–3,204	–1,399

Sources: Central Bank, *Brazil Economic Program,* several issues; Paulo N. Batista, Jr. (1987).

direct foreign investment (see Table 4.3). This net outflow of foreign money
reached $1,430 million in 1986 and represented 0.5 percent of GDP.

The deterioration of public finance, or the state's increasing incapacity
to impose forced savings, is the second negative factor contributing to
the decrease in the rate of investment during the 1980s. A clear picture of
this deterioration of public finances emerges from an analysis of the fiscal
burden. The net fiscal burden fell from 17.4 percent of GDP in 1970 to 9.5
percent in 1984 (see Table 4.4). In 1975 the gross fiscal burden reached a
high of 26.3 percent and fell after that. Recovery started only after the

Table 4.4 Fiscal Burden (percentage of GDP)

			Transferences				
	Gross Fiscal Burden (1)	Interest on Internal Public Debt (2)	Social Security and Assistance (3)	Fiscal Subsidies (4)	Other (5)	Total (6)	Net Fiscal Burden[a] (7)
1970	26.0	0.7	8.2	0.8	−1.1	8.6	17.4
1971	25.1	0.5	7.0	0.8	−0.8	7.5	17.6
1972	25.9	0.5	7.3	0.7	0.2	8.7	17.2
1973	26.3	0.5	7.0	1.2	1.6	10.3	16.0
1974	26.2	0.5	6.3	2.3	2.2	11.3	14.9
1975	26.3	0.4	7.0	2.8	0.8	11.0	15.3
1976	25.3	0.5	7.2	1.6	0.2	9.5	15.8
1977	25.6	0.5	7.3	1.5	1.6	10.9	14.7
1978	25.7	0.5	8.1	1.9	1.5	12.0	13.7
1979	24.3	0.5	7.7	1.9	0.6	10.7	13.6
1980	24.2	0.7	7.6	3.6	0.9	12.8	11.4
1981	24.6	1.1	8.2	2.7	1.1	13.1	11.5
1982	26.2	1.2	9.0	2.6	1.3	14.1	12.1
1983	24.7	1.7	8.3	2.6	1.5	14.1	10.6
1984	21.6	2.1	7.7	1.6	0.7	12.1	9.5
1985	22.0	2.2	7.1	1.6	0.9	11.8	10.2
1986	24.3	1.1	8.0	1.5	1.4	12.0	12.3
1987	22.6	1.1	7.5	1.6	1.4	11.6	11.0
1988	21.9	1.6	7.2	1.2	0.2	10.2	11.7
1989	21.9	1.4	7.5	1.9	−1.7	9.1	12.8
1990	27.4	1.1	8.3	1.7	5.3	16.4	11.0

Sources: Secretaria de Planejamento da Presidencia da República, unpublished reports; Central
Bank, *Brazil Economic Program,* several issues.
Note: a. Column (1) less Column (6).

decrease in the fiscal burden accelerated in 1984 and 1985, when recession, monetarist policies, and the acceleration of inflation caused, respectively, an increase of transfers to the private sector, an increase in the interest rate on the internal debt, and a loss in tax revenues. On the other hand, fiscal subsidies, which reached 3.6 percent of GDP in 1980, fell to 1.6 percent in 1984. The general explanation for this consistent fall in the fiscal burden is the acceleration of inflation. The inflationary tax is actually smaller than the loss of taxes because of the inflation that occurs between the moment the tax is incurred and the moment it is paid (the Olivera-Tanzi effect). The indexation devices developed in Brazil were unable to avoid this financial loss for the state.

Since 1979 the real public deficit has had a tendency to fall. The decrease in the deficit in 1981, 1983, and 1984 was clearly related to the country's adjustment process (see Table 4.5). Since the public deficit—or the increase in the public-sector borrowing requirements—decreased, it could be said that public finances improved. But it can also be said that the investment capacity of the state diminished. As can be seen in Table 4.4, the fiscal burden started decreasing in 1975; Table 4.1 shows that the state's saving capacity suffered a great decline in the 1980s.

Table 4.5   Operational Public Deficit (percentage of GDP)

1979	1980	1981	1982	1983	1984	1985	1986	1987	1988	1989	1990
8.3	6.7	6.0	7.3	4.4	2.7	4.3	3.6	5.5	4.8	6.9	−1.2

Source: Central Bank, *Brazil Economic Program,* several issues.

In fact, the deterioration of the savings and investment capacities of the state began in 1975, when the bourgeoisie initiated a vociferous campaign against state interventionism. Although the bourgeoisie was the main beneficiary of the authoritarian regime and of state interventionism, it began to be afraid of, or at least unhappy with, the power of the state technobureaucracy. The campaign against state interventionism was the first sign of the rupture of the alliance between the bourgeoisie and the state bureaucracy, particularly the military (see Bresser Pereira 1978, 1984). The basic economic reason for the fracture of the class coalition was the end of the economic miracle (1967–1974); that is, the start of a slowdown or of a relative diminution of the economic surplus, to be divided among the bourgeoisie and the technobureaucracy. This process was begun after the PND II had been launched and was instrumental in its partial suspension beginning in 1976. The extremely ambitious targets of this plan depended on an increase in the savings capacity of the state—including an increase in the prices and profits of state-owned corporations—that the bourgeoisie was not ready to sustain.

The deterioration of the savings and investment capacities of the state was accentuated by the change in priorities following democratization. The democratic government that took power in March 1985 established social expenditures as its top priority. Several social programs aimed at the distribution of income were started. Although the government assured that these social expenditures would not substitute for investments, maintaining a reasonable level of public investment in 1985 was possible only because of an increase in the public deficit.

As the state lost part of its ability to impose forced savings, it diminished its subsidies to the private sector. In others words, the process of financing private investment through primitive accumulation began to lose importance. As can be seen in Table 4.4, fiscal subsidies, which had reached 3.6 percent of GDP in 1980, were down to 1.6 percent in 1984.

An explanation for the deterioration of the state's savings capacity in the long run can be found in the price controls imposed on state-owned corporations. These price controls on large corporations—mainly state-owned and multinational corporations—had been a constant in Brazil during the 1970s, but they were accentuated beginning in August 1979.[3] The only exception occurred in 1981 when prices were liberalized. The CIP, used as a device to control inflation, was in fact a powerful instrument for reducing the profits of state-owned and multinational corporations. Private national corporations were also subjected to price controls, but because they were smaller and politically more influential, they suffered less.

The decreasing profitability of the state-owned corporations between 1978 and 1987 is both a consequence and a cause of the deterioration of the savings and investment capacities of the state. The profit rate for all corporations decreased sharply during this period (see Table 4.6). There is a clear relationship between corporations' loss of profitability and the economic cycle. The profit rate of the thousand largest corporations was lowest in 1983, the year of the deepest recession in Brazil's industrial history. The recovery of the profit rate in 1984 and 1985 was clearly insufficient. In 1985, a year of great economic expansion, the general rate of profit was almost one-third that of 1978 and less than half that of 1979. For the state-owned and multinational corporations, this fall was related to price controls. For the private national corporations, the influence of price controls was less important, whereas the reduction of subsidies played a decisive role. The 1989 share increase of the market rate was the perverse outcome of excess demand that prevailed that year. It anticipated hyperinflation in the first months of 1990.

Table 4.6   Rate of Profit of the 1,000 Largest Brazilian Corporations (percentage of net worth)

	Private	State-Owned	Multinational	Total[a]
1978	30.9	11.0	23.6	17.6
1979	23.2	8.8	12.6	13.4
1980	22.1	6.0	15.8	12.0
1981	13.6	7.1	11.8	10.8
1982	10.7	6.4	12.8	8.3
1983	7.6	2.6	9.1	4.7
1984	10.1	6.0	12.1	7.8
1985	11.7	(4.3)	6.5	7.0
1986	9.3	8.5	8.1	8.9
1987	11.4	(9.4)	5.0	6.0
1988	13.0	1.3	11.4	9.1
1989	20.2	8.9	19.9	17.7
1990	(0.7)	(29.0)	(3.2)	(8.4)

Source: Getúlio Vargas Foundation, Grupo de Análise Contábil, in *Conjuntura Econômica,* November 1985 and 1991.
Note: a. Weighted average.

For all corporations, this fall in profitability can probably be explained by an increase in the organic composition of capital or a reduction of the marginal output-capital rate. This reduction was particularly accentuated in the case of state-owned corporations, but it can be generalized for all corporations. The strategy of the PND II was basically to complete the import substitution process of basic inputs and capital goods. These large import substitution investments in the areas of oil, electric energy, steel, nonferrous metals, petrochemicals, paper, and cellulose, as well as the export-oriented mining investments (particularly iron), were highly capital-intensive and thus led to an increase in the organic composition of capital. This kind of investment is usually associated with capital-using technical progress—a progress defined by the reduction of the marginal output-capital relationship—that makes the rate of profit decline. Only in the second stage, after these import substitution projects have been carried out, can export-oriented manufacturing investments be undertaken. Then technical progress tends to become neutral or even capital-saving, and the output-capital relation and the rate of profit increase again. Antonio Barros de Castro and Pires de Souza (1985) and Jorge Chami Batista (1987) demonstrated that the PND II, launched in 1974, was—contrary to many superficial analyses—a bold and successful strategy to consolidate Brazilian industrial development at a time of worldwide economic recession and crisis. The large trade surpluses after 1983 are in large part a result of the great investment projects of the PND II.

But the cost entailed not only the increase of the external debt and the deterioration of public finance but also an increase in the organic composition of capital and a fall in the rate of profit.

F inally, to understand the deterioration of the savings and investment capacities not only of the state but also of the entire economy, it is appropriate to consider the relation between the behavior of the real average wage and productivity. Per capita income is taken as a proxy for productivity.

As can be seen in Table 4.7, and more easily in Figure 4.1, during the economic miracle between 1970 and 1974 productivity increased very rapidly, and wages increased at a much slower pace. The consequent increase in the rate of surplus value resulted in an increasing rate of profits. From 1974 to 1978 the rate of increase in productivity slowed down, and the rate of growth of wages increased. As a consequence, both increased at approximately the same rate. The years 1979 and 1980 were a transition

Table 4.7   Wages and Productivity

	Average Real Wage	Productivity[a]
1970	100[b]	100
1971	102	109
1972	106	118
1973	111	130
1974	111	139
1975	120	143
1976	127	152
1977	129	157
1978	139	160
1979	142	165
1980	137	176
1981	133	171
1982	152	169
1983	134	159
1984	115	162
1985	129	173
1986	145	182
1987	133	185
1988	149	181
1989	172	183
1990	135	173

Sources: Domingo Zurron Ocio (1986) for average real wage (until 1984); Getúlio Vargas Foundation for productivity.
Notes: a. Productivity equals increase in income per capita.
b. 1970 = 100.

Figure 4.1   Wages and Productivity

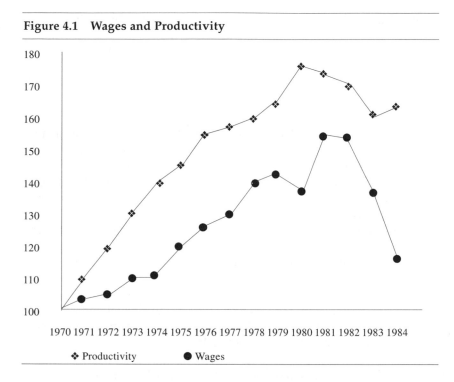

period. After 1980 productivity decreased until 1983, and wages followed with a one-year lag.

Therefore, during the fifteen years examined here, only in the first four years (1970–1974) were the profit-wage ratio and the correlate productivity-wage ratio highly favorable to capital. Since 1975 the relation between capital and labor has been more or less balanced. The decrease in the rate of profit since 1978 cannot be explained by wage increases above productivity.

Since the end of the 1970s the Brazilian economy has faced a serious deterioration in its capacities to save and invest. The deterioration in the capacity to save is related to: (1) the loss of the state's ability to impose forced savings and to subsidize the private sector; (2) the decrease of the fiscal burden; and (3) the decrease of the profit rate, caused by the slowdown of the growth rate, the imposition of price controls to fight inflation, and the increase of the organic composition of capital derived from the huge PND II import substitution investments. The first two variables indicated a serious deterioration in the finances of the state and pointed to the need for a fiscal adjustment aimed at reducing the size of the public deficit. The last factor was a signal of the imbalances the import substitution strategy had imposed on the Brazilian economy. The deterioration of the economy's investment capacity is also clearly related to the end of the inflow of net external resources aimed at effectively financing new investments, which occurred in 1979.

The task now is to know, first, what the new pattern of investments will be, and, second, whether this new pattern will be able to produce an acceptable rate of growth.

Werneck (1986) developed a model for analyzing the various alternatives conducive to increasing the country's total rate of saving from the 16 percent of GDP prevailing in 1984 to 24 percent. This rate would be necessary to ensure a growth rate of 7 percent of GDP in the following year (marginal output-capital relation of 0.3). He showed that, in theory, an increase in the rate of savings can originate from: (1) an increase in the capitalists' and workers' propensity to save and a concentration of income benefiting the capitalists; (2) an increase in the fiscal burden and in the investment-consumption relation of the state; (3) an increase in the profit rate of state-owned corporations; and (4) a reduction in the interest rates on the external debt and the internal public debt, including the debt of the state-owned corporations (Werneck 1986:11). After making several simulations with these variables and partially dismissing the Keynesian proposition that investment creates its own savings, Werneck (1986:29) concluded that

> The recovery of the average rate of growth observed between the end of World War II and the end of the 1970s will necessarily require that the public sector assume again its historical role as an important gatherer of resources for financing investments. The lack of realism implicit in the idea that the increase in the saving effort can be the basic responsibility of the private sector has been demonstrated.

Werneck's conclusions are essentially correct. There is no doubt that it is unrealistic to base the Brazilian strategy of development exclusively on an increase in the private sector's propensity to save. Given the impossibility of resorting to external finance, an increase in the state's savings and investment capacities—through an increase of the fiscal burden, the control of consumption expenditures (wages of the civil servants), and the setting of realistic prices for state-owned corporations—is a more efficient and more socially equitable strategy for assuring the required increase in savings.

Yet it is important not to try to return to the pattern of investment that prevailed between the 1950s and the PND II. This idea, which is almost explicit in Werneck's analysis, is also unrealistic.

Brazil in the 1980s was very different from Brazil in the 1950s, 1960s, and 1970s. State indebtedness was very high. The internal debt of the state, including state-owned corporations, represented 48.1 percent of GDP in 1985. The private sector, however, was capitalized. For the 550 corporations studied in "Melhores e Maiores" (*Exame,* São Paulo, April, September

1986), the ratio of general indebtedness decreased from 57.1 percent of total assets in 1981 to 46.3 percent in 1985. Since the end of the 1970s Ignácio Rangel (1978) has insisted that it is essential to transfer the excess savings existing in the private sector, where idle capacity prevails, to the public sector, where there are great opportunities for investment. To achieve this objective, he could have proposed an increase in the fiscal burden, but instead he insisted on the privatization of public utilities. This strategy may also be unrealistic, but it emphasizes the existence of unused savings capacity in the private sector that could be put to work either through an increase in the fiscal burden or by opening new profitable opportunities for investment in the private sector.

On the other hand, it is not acceptable to dismiss an improvement in the marginal output-capital ratio as easily as Werneck did (1986:3). The large import substitution investments of the 1970s lowered this ratio. To establish a basic stock of capital, it is necessary to lower this relation or to increase the marginal capital-output ratio. The resulting increase in the total capital-output ratio cannot always be detected in the national accounts, not only because the measurements of the stock of capital are imprecise but also because the depreciation of capital made by accountants is larger than the real depreciation. As the more important, highly capital-intensive import substitution investments are made, it is reasonable to admit that the marginal output-capital relation will increase. It is true that large investments will have to be made in hydroelectric energy, steel, and nonferrous metals, but it is also reasonable to expect that the emphasis of the new investments—particularly in the private sector—will be on export-oriented industries with low capital intensity and a high output-capital relation.

In the past twenty-five years Brazil has developed an internationally competitive manufacturing industry. In 1967 this industry accounted for around 6 percent of total Brazilian exports; today it accounts for ten times that amount. Brazilian exports of manufactured goods—which accounted for 0.35 percent of world exports of manufactured goods, 5.03 percent of the exports of developing countries, and 33.34 percent of exports of the ALADI countries in 1973—increased their share to 0.69, 6.33, and 54.88 percent, respectively, in 1982 (Chami Batista 1987). This extraordinary increase in the export of manufactured goods in relation to other Latin American countries is a fundamental explanation for the Brazilian economy's superior long-term performance compared with these countries. The more modest increase in relation to the exports of all developing countries results from the successful export strategies of countries like Korea, Taiwan, Singapore, and Hong Kong.

Simultaneous to the recovery of the saving capacity of the state—a basic strategy for the Brazilian economy that will increase private savings, especially the output-capital relation—is the stimulation of the export of manufactured goods. The usual argument that this strategy leads to concentration of income is incorrect. Several studies have demonstrated that, because they are less capital-intensive, investments in export-oriented manufacturing industries are compatible with a more equitable distribution of income than are import substitution investments (see Little 1982:142).

Brazil must face its large external debt objectively. Since the debt cannot increase forever by the amount of interest due each year, a given transfer of real resources is unavoidable. What is important is for Brazil to negotiate a reduction in the interest rate—specifically a reduction in the spreads—and to be able to obtain large trade surpluses, which would be consistent with the payment of part of the interest on the external debt and with an expansion of GDP. Only an export-oriented strategy will be able to achieve this goal.

Finally, we should consider that international trade will probably continue to grow at a higher rate than the growth rate of the industrialized countries. Brazil, which pays lower wages than many countries, presumably has a competitive advantage that could and should be used to increase internal employment and obtain external surpluses. As the demand for more-specialized labor increases, real wages will tend to increase internally. The pressure to increase productivity, essential for economic growth, will be stronger because the Brazilian manufacturing industry's profits depend on its international competitiveness.

The state-owned corporations will continue to play an important role in conducting investment, but the role of the private national and multinational corporations will likely increase as well. The state, which initially financed and subsidized private investment, is now in debt and is being financed by the private sector through open market operations. An adequate objective of economic policy would be to recover the capacity of the state and state-owned corporations to generate funds internally for their investments, whereas the private national and multinational corporations should have a profit rate sufficiently attractive to stimulate their investments. The financial system that finances the state today would have to give priority to financing private investment. As long as private business enterprises feel stimulated to invest, savings will appear to finance investments.

In conclusion, an adequate rate of growth for the Brazilian economy will be possible as long as the state recovers part of its saving and investment capacity and as long as private businesses have profitable opportunities for investing and their investments are oriented toward sectors with a higher output-capital relation. Primitive accumulation—that is, the complex system of subsidies that was essential in the first stages of Brazilian industrial development—can now play only a secondary role. Brazil already possesses a basic stock of capital that allows investment and growth to be based on profits regularly achieved in the market by the private sector and that systematically incorporates technical progress.

⚘ 5 ⚘

Perverse Macroeconomics

S tagnation and high rates of inflation were the main characteristics of the Brazilian economy in the 1980s. Growth in a country that had expanded rapidly during the last century stopped suddenly in 1981. In 1990 income per capita was below what it had been in 1980. In that first moment—between 1981 and 1983—the slowdown was correctly attributed to the adjustment effort imposed by the debt crisis; in a second moment— 1984 to 1986—the crisis seemed to have been overcome and the adjustment process to have been successful. In 1987, however, the crisis returned. In 1988 and 1990 GDP growth was negative; in the years since, it has been very small (see Table 5.1).

This crisis can be explained in several ways. Its connection with the external debt is clear. The fiscal crisis that developed from the debt is obviously at the core of this economic stagnation. The acceleration of the inflationary process that occurred during the 1980s can be partially

Table 5.1   Internal Macroeconomic Variables (percentages)

	GDP	Investment/ GDP (current prices)	Investment/ GDP (constant prices)	Gross Savings/ GDP (current prices)
1979	7.2	22.0	22.9	18.9
1980	9.1	22.3	22.9	17.8
1981	(3.1)	23.1	21.0	18.6
1982	1.1	21.1	19.5	15.3
1983	(2.8)	16.7	16.9	13.3
1984	5.7	15.7	16.2	15.8
1985	8.4	19.2	16.7	19.1
1986	8.0	19.1	19.0	17.1
1987	2.9	22.3	18.3	21.8
1988	(1.0)	22.8	17.0	24.1
1989	3.3	24.9	16.7	25.1
1990	(4.0)	21.7	16.0	21.2

Source: Instituto Brasileiro de Geografia e Estatística, *Anuário Estatístico,* several years.

67

explained by the fiscal crisis, but it can definitely be explained by distributive conflict, which characterizes an economy in which income is as unevenly distributed as is the case in Brazil and which is the fundamental cause of inflation and its acceleration. The foreign debt, so far as it either directly or indirectly caused the distributive conflict to worsen, played an important role in the acceleration of inflation. Inflation, in turn, fed the real sector crisis because it increased the public deficit, hindered investments, and lowered the productivity of capital.

All of these factors are interrelated. There is a dictum that nothing succeeds like success; the reverse is also true—the vicious circle of a crisis is or seems to be endless. There is a perverse logic in the stagnation of the Brazilian economy. In this chapter I will try to describe and formalize this logic and to define the perverse macroeconomics of Brazilian stagnation. To begin, I discuss the external debt, which is the origin of the crisis—a crisis defined by the fiscal crisis of the state, the fall in the rate of investment, and the loss in efficiency of the stock of capital. I then define this crisis as both a stock and a flow crisis, and I analyze the perverse character of adjustment in these circumstances. I next discuss the fiscal crisis in terms of the public deficit and the reduction in public savings; the relation between the two phenomena is presented. I then examine how a debt crisis turns into a fiscal crisis. An analysis of the high rates of inflation that prevail in these circumstances follows; inflation becomes inertial or autonomous, tending to accelerate slowly but firmly. In this process money plays a passive role, which I describe. The paralysis of the state as a result of the fiscal crisis is discussed, followed by a description of the overall logic of stagnation in a country plagued by debt, deficit, and inflation. But we do not expect stagnation to be a permanent situation; thus I conclude with a discussion of the pattern for financing investments that will be consistent with growth in Brazil. The requirements for overcoming the crisis and resuming growth are briefly presented.

T he fundamental cause of the Brazilian economic crisis is the country's fiscal crisis—a structural, financial imbalance of the public sector—which, in turn, has as one of its fundamental causes the excessive size of the external public debt. I stated above that the fiscal crisis is one of the assumptions of this analysis; the topic has been widely discussed.[1] However, it is mistaken to suppose that this crisis is limited to a large public deficit, as if it were possible to separate it from the current discussion of the Brazilian economy. In point of fact, the fiscal crisis has three dimensions: (1) a flow dimension (the public deficit and reduced public savings); (2) a stock dimension (the internal and foreign public debts); and (3) a psychosocial dimension—the lack of confidence in the state, defined in objective terms by its inability to finance its deficit except on the overnight market.

The flow dimension of the fiscal crisis is the most commonly analyzed.

It can be measured in two ways, as shown in Table 5.2: by the operational public deficit and by the ability of the public sector to save. The first includes the state corporations and corresponds to an increase in borrowing or an increase in the public sector's need for financing. In addition to measuring the financial imbalance of the state, it could also be an indication of excess demand. Because the public deficit has a substantial financial component and often occurs at the same time the private sector is reducing investments and financing the public sector at high interest rates, the result is insufficient aggregate demand (see Dall'Acqua and Bresser Pereira 1987). The Brazilian public deficit was very high in the early 1980s. Beginning in 1983, it was reduced by severe cuts in public investment and social spending. Yet with the adoption of populist economic policies in the Sarney administration (1985–1989), it increased once again.

Table 5.2 Public-Sector Accounts (percentage of GDP)

	Tax Revenue	Personnel Expenditures	Interest on Internal Debt	Interest on External Debt	Public Savings	Public Deficit
1979	24.3	6.9	0.55	0.29	3.8	8.3
1980	24.2	6.2	0.74	0.36	2.2	6.7
1981	24.6	6.5	1.08	0.29	2.3	6.0
1982	26.2	7.3	1.21	1.18	1.8	7.3
1983	24.7	6.5	1.65	1.57	0.6	4.4
1984	21.6	5.6	2.05	1.83	0.8	2.7
1985	22.0	6.8	2.24	1.51	0.3	4.3
1986	24.3	7.0	1.14	1.35	1.9	3.6
1987	22.6	7.7	1.15	1.44	(1.2)	5.5
1988	21.9	7.9	1.58	1.72	(2.4)	4.8
1989	21.9	9.7	1.44	2.03	(5.3)	6.5
1990	27.4	10.5	1.09	2.12	0.8	(1.2)

Sources: First four columns, Instituto de Pesquisas Econômicas Aplicadas; last two columns, Central Bank.
Note: The first five columns refer to the public sector in the strict sense; the last includes state corporations.

A second flow imbalance is also related to the state's financial incapacity to save. Public savings cannot be directly compared with the public-sector deficit because Brazil's national accounts do not include state corporations in the public sector. However, these two measurements are related. Public savings, which were around 5 percent of GDP in the mid-1970s, dropped to 3.8 percent in 1979 and then to –1.2 percent in 1987. This means that in the 1970s the public sector was able to collect forced savings and invest them; that is, to carry out the role of the state par excellence in the development process. In the 1980s, however, although the state was forced to invest because it was still responsible for a good part of the country's productive infrastructure, it did not save. The only form of financing public investment was to borrow from the private sector, increasing the public deficit.

These two flow imbalances result in a growing stock imbalance, that is, public debt. In the 1970s public debt was mainly foreign. Since 1979, however, when international banks began to reduce the rollover of the foreign debt, and particularly since 1982, when they definitively stopped the rollover, internal debt began to grow explosively. The foreign public debt continued to grow because the private sector paid or prepaid its foreign commitments to the Central Bank in cruzados, changing those commitments into foreign public debt. In 1988, with a GDP of nearly $320 billion, Brazil had a foreign public debt of approximately $100 billion (almost 85 percent of the total foreign debt), which, added to the Treasury's short-term internal debt of $41 billion and to approximately $30 billion in other internal debts, totaled about $170 billion in public debt—corresponding to more than half of GDP.

Both the flow imbalance and the stock imbalance are very high in relation to GDP. However, this does not necessarily imply a fiscal crisis. To take an extreme case, Italy has a public deficit of almost 10 percent of its GDP and a public debt almost equal to its GDP, but one cannot say the Italian state is bankrupt. The most we could say is that it is undergoing a potentially serious fiscal crisis. In Japan, where in the late 1970s the public deficit was around 6 percent of GDP and has recently fallen to 2 percent of GDP, fiscal crisis is out of the question. Why is it, then, that in the case of Brazil but not in other countries, the public sector is insolvent, even though in Italy the quantitative indices of fiscal imbalance are higher than those in Brazil? The reason is that in these other countries the state still has credit. It is able to obtain financing from the private sector—for one or two years in the case of Italy and for at least ten years in the case of Japan—whereas the Brazilian state has almost no credit. Almost all of its internal financing takes place on the overnight market. In such a situation there is almost no difference between financing through the emission of money and through the sale of Central Bank bonds on the overnight market.

The financial imbalance of the public sector originated in the 1970s through a policy of promoting growth through foreign borrowing. This strategy was justified until 1978, when the debt:export ratio for Brazil was near the limit of 2. It became totally unjustifiable in 1979 and 1980, not only because the debt was already very high but also because four external shocks had forced Brazil to adjust its economy immediately: (1) the second oil shock, which increased import costs; (2) the recession in the United States, which reduced exports; (3) the increase in the nominal interest rate because of inflation in the United States; and (4) the increase in the real interest rate as a result of the U.S. monetarist adjustment policy. The last two shocks raised the amount of interest Brazil had to pay to its creditors.

The crisis of the Brazilian economy started in 1979, when Brazil—as with all of the highly indebted countries—should have engaged in a strong adjustment process. The second oil shock, the rate of interest shock, and the U.S. recession were clear indications that this was the line to follow. Korea was one of the few highly indebted countries that decided to adjust at that time. Brazil and all of the other Latin American countries did not. When Brazil began to adjust in 1981, following two years of accelerated growth, it was too late. The debt had become too high to be paid.[2]

The perverse logic of the external debt appears when it becomes too high. But when does a debt become too high, and what is too high a debt?

A debt becomes too high from the standpoint of the creditors when they decide to suspend its rollover—to finance the interest to be paid. When the process of indebtedness begins, the country receives loans to finance real expenditures (consumption or, it is hoped, investment). After some time, however, the interest due becomes so high that the financing of interest is halted. In fact, the process of indebtedness undergoes consecutive phases: (1) loans finance additional expenditures; (2) they finance additional expenditures and interest; (3) they finance only interest; (4) they finance only part of the interest to be paid on the old loans; and (5) new loans are suspended.

The suspension of new loans to Brazil in 1982 was part of a more general decision by bankers following the Mexican default in August of that year. But it is also based on some objective considerations that caused bankers to consider the Brazilian debt to be too high. There are basically two parameters. First, there is a stock rule of thumb, which says that the relation between the external debt, DX, and exports, X, of a country should never exceed 2 (in Brazil the debt:export ratio achieved this limit in 1979). Second, there is a flow reasoning, which says that when this ratio is achieved, the rate of interest, j, should not exceed the rate of growth of exports, x'.

$$DX:X < 2$$

and

if

$$DX:X > 2$$

then

$$j < x'$$

Following the suspension of the market—that is, of voluntary loans to a debtor country—from the debtor country's point of view there are three situations in which a debt would be considered to be too high. Basically it is too high if, after a reasonable internal adjustment process, it remains impossible to serve the debt fully. In this case the external interests, J_x, to be fully paid, (1) have to be financed with additional loans, which in turn leads to an increase in total debt, dDX; and/or (2) can be paid only if too large a trade surplus, R, has to be produced. "Too large a trade surplus" means a trade surplus that implies a transfer of real resources to the creditor countries, which, to be achieved, depends on a reduction in imports, M, rather than an increase in exports, X. The reduction in imports is basically achieved by reducing investments, I, rather than consumption, C. In this case the actual trade surplus, R, is larger than the potential surplus, R^*, since we define potential surplus as the trade surplus that can be achieved while maintaining the "necessary" level of investments, I^*.

A third situation in which the debt would be seen as being too high is the one in which the debt is almost entirely a state responsibility, DXG_t, and the revenues from exports are private, X_{Pr}. In this case, the external debt becomes a basic reason for the crisis even if the country is producing a trade surplus. The interest paid on the external public debt becomes a root cause of the public deficit. When the public deficit can no longer be financed by an increase in the external debt, it is financed by increasing the internal debt or by printing money. Fiscal crisis and inflation are the obvious outcomes.

Thus an external debt is too high when, to pay fully the respective interests, we have:

$$DX_{t+1} > DX_t \tag{1}$$

and/or

$$R > R^* - I < I^* \tag{2}$$

and/or when

$$DXG_t \text{ versus } X_{Pr} \tag{3}$$

In Brazil during the 1980s these three conditions were present. Let us take 1980 as a starting point because it was at the end of that year that the adjustment process began in Brazil as a result of the debt crisis. Since that time, (1) total foreign debt has practically doubled; (2) the rate of investments has fallen by 5 percentage points below the previous level; and (3) the external public debt, which accounted for 68 percent of the nation's total foreign debt in 1979, currently makes up 87 percent, whereas exports and the trade surplus continue to be almost entirely private.

I begin the exploration of stock disequilibrium leading to flow disequilibrium using conventional or textbook models of stabilization. Suppose that in the first half of the 1970s the Brazilian macroeconomic variables were basically balanced—that is, aggregate demand was equal to aggregate supply—so that

$$I + G + X = S + T + M$$

where G is state expenditures, including expenditures of publicly owned enterprises, S is private savings, and T is state revenues (taxes and sales of publicly owned enterprises). This nice equilibrium, in which interests are disregarded, was completed by an equilibrium in each sector:

in the private sector
$$I = S$$
in the public sector
$$G = T$$
and in the foreign
trade sector $\qquad X = M$

External indebtedness during the 1970s disrupted these three equilibria. The external indebtedness of the public sector was synonymous with the public deficit $(G > T)$, which had as its counterpart a trade deficit $(X < M)$ financed by external savings, S_x. Following textbook or conventional economics of adjustment—so much used and misused by policymakers everywhere—the private sector remained in equilibrium. Finally, when the time of stabilization arrived (1981–1983), public-sector adjustment was given priority.

The basic objectives of the adjustment were, externally, to produce an equilibrium in the current account and, internally, to eliminate the public deficit, E. Both objectives were to be achieved simultaneously. By reducing and eventually eliminating the public deficit, the country would reach a current account balance.

$$E = G + J_x - T = 0$$

and so

$$M + J_x = X$$

where M now explicitly excludes interest and J_x represents net interest paid on the external debt.

We have seen that the reduction in the public deficit was achieved, although perversely, through the reduction of public-sector investments, given that reducing current public expenditures is always very difficult, even for an authoritarian government. Some results were achieved in this area by reducing salaries of public officials and employees of state-owned enterprises. After the end of the authoritarian regime, the new democratic government that took office in 1985 was unable to maintain this reduction of salaries, and the public deficit increased once again [3] However, the creditors' basic objective—to attain equilibrium in the current account—was achieved or nearly achieved starting in 1984.

It is interesting to observe, contrary to conventional adjustment models, that achieving current account equilibrium did not imply achieving budget equilibrium; in other words, the permanence of a large public deficit was consistent with a large trade surplus and an equilibrium in the current account. The explanation for this fact is simple. Conventional macroeconomic adjustment models are merely flow models. They take into account only the basic flows of an economy. This is a reasonable approach when the stock of debt (particularly the public debt and the external debt, which can largely intersect, as is the case in Brazil) is modest. When it is too high the conventional models simply do not apply. In addition to a flow model, one needs a stock model, or a flow model that takes into account the stock of debt. The imbalances in the economy are not just flow imbalances but are also stock imbalances. The economy may achieve a current account equilibrium, but because of the volume of interest paid by the state, the public deficit may remain high.

In these circumstances the basic macroeconomic equation must be rewritten by making explicit on the left side the interest paid by the state on its external debt, J_{gx} (assuming that the debt is fully nationalized and there is not yet any internal debt), and on the right side the interest paid on the foreign debt.

$$I + G + J_{gx} + X = S + T + M + J_x$$

Now we can no longer say that it is the nonfinancial public deficit $(G > T)$ that leads to excess demand and causes a trade deficit $(X < M)$. The trade balance, as well as the nonfinancial public accounts, may be balanced, but the country can still have a current account deficit $(X < M + J_x)$. And the more likely causal relation is just the opposite of conventional models. It is the current account deficit caused by the payment of interest, including interest paid by the state, that creates the total public deficit. The public deficit thus does not lead to excess demand but is a consequence of the external (and, as we see below, also of the internal) indebtedness of the state.

The adjustment process so described was perverse—self-defeating—in several ways. First, it was achieved by a reduction of imports, an increase in transfer of real resources, and a reduction of investments. Second, it was accompanied by the nationalization of the external debt, which aggravated the imbalance of public accounts. Third, the increase in the interest bill to be paid by the state implies the reduction of public savings and thus—because current expenditures and public investments have to be minimally maintained—an increase in the public deficit. Fourth, real devaluations of the exchange rate, in addition to accelerating inflation, increased the public deficit even more. Fifth, as foreign banks decided not to increase their exposure in highly indebted countries, the financing of the public deficit caused by interest to be paid on a large external debt had to be done by increasing internal indebtedness or printing money.

In theory, the public deficit, E, can be financed by increasing public external indebtedness, $dDXG$; increasing public internal indebtedness, $dDIG$; and printing money, dB—that is, by increasing the monetary base (high-powered money):

$$E = dDXG + dDIG + dB$$

During the 1970s and early 1980s the public deficit in Brazil was financed more or less evenly by these three sources. But when the debt crisis appeared, the source of external finance for the state was reduced and ultimately closed. The state had to pay the interest on the external public debt but could no longer finance it externally. Thus, the only answer was to increase internal debt, print money, or both.[4] The increase in internal debt could be achieved only by increasing the interest rate and reducing maturities; the increase in the interest rate aggravated the public deficit. The alternative of printing money validated the going rate of inflation.[5] The perverse character of the suppression of external indebtedness as a source for financing the public deficit is fairly obvious. Whereas a great effort was being made to reduce the public deficit, the suspension of external finance for that deficit, which was not eliminated by the 1981–1983 adjustment, led to an increase in internal indebtedness, an increase in the internal interest rates— which aggravated the public deficit because interests were paid mostly by the state—and a reduction in the maturities of the public debt.[6]

A nother effect of the increasingly high interest burden, in addition to increasing the public deficit, is reducing public-sector savings. Public savings, SG, are equal to state revenues, T, minus current public expenditures (total public expenditures), G (here already including interest in order to simplify), minus public investment, IG.

$$SG = T - (G - IG)$$

Thus, the public deficit, E, is equal to public savings minus public investments.

$$E = G - T = IG - SG$$

During the 1970s public savings in Brazil were strongly positive. In 1987, given the level of interest paid by the state (see Table 5.3) and the reduction of the gross tax burden and the increase in personnel expenditures (see Table 5.2), they became negative for the first time.[7]

Table 5.3   Public Sector's Interest Payments (percentage of GDP)

	External Debt	Domestic Debt	Total
1983	3.70	3.01	6.71
1984	3.89	3.30	7.19
1985	4.47	3.44	7.91
1986	2.89	2.23	5.12
1987	2.62	2.17	4.79
1988	2.85	2.88	5.73
1989	3.20	2.72	5.92
1990	3.28	0.02	3.30

Source: Central Bank, *Brazil Economic Program,* several issues.

Public savings are supposed to finance public investments. When public savings are around zero—as is usually the case in a highly indebted country where a fiscal crisis has developed—the public deficit is equal to the public investment that has to be made and that cannot be reduced. In this case one can speak of a structural public deficit. The real cause of the deficit is the interest burden originating in the external and internal debt, but as long as public savings are around zero, the unpleasant relationship between public deficit and public investment becomes evident.

Minimum public investments in Brazil are relatively high (around 5 percent of GDP) given the fact that the state—directly or through state-owned enterprises—is responsible for most of the investments in electricity, oil, communications, transportation, and steel production. Given that the state was reduced to zero savings mostly (not exclusively) as a result of the interest payments it has to make (around 6 percent of GDP) and that it must invest at least 5 percent of GDP, the public deficit at that level becomes structural; that is, very rigid downward.

This does not mean it is impossible to reduce and eventually eliminate the public deficit. But first, this fact emphasizes that a reduction in the public deficit without an increase in public savings makes no sense; this reduction without the recovery of public savings is possible, as the experience of the highly indebted countries in the 1980s demonstrates, but extraordinarily damaging for the country's growth prospects—it is enough to reduce public investments. In fact, the reduction of public investment is only feasible, in the long run, after a successful program of privatizations has been undertaken; in the short run, if the state is responsible for investing in crucial sectors of the economy, this strategy is self-defeating. Second, the situation described here says that the elimination of the public deficit is very difficult when the public sector is highly indebted as long as it accounts for an important share of investments in the economy.

T he previous discussion demonstrates in several ways how the debt crisis developed into a fiscal crisis. The increase in the external public debt in the 1970s was a consequence of a growth strategy (PND II) based on the public deficit. The internal adjustment, which occurred between 1981 and 1983, was accompanied by the nationalization of the external private debt. In Brazil, as in practically all highly indebted countries, the adjustment was also an opportunity for private businesses to pay their debts in local currency and pass on the responsibility for the external debt to the public sector.

The 1981–1983 adjustment process reduced (in an unsound manner) but did not eliminate the public deficit. Internally, its major consequence was to accelerate the reduction of public savings as it stimulated the nationalization of the external debt. The reduction of the public deficit was achieved by reducing investment rather than current expenditures (thereby increasing public savings). The limited reduction in current expenditures between 1981 and 1983—achieved by reducing wages and salaries rather than deregulating the economy and reducing the labor force in the public sector—was compensated by the increase in the interest bill that occurred, first, because of the increase of the external public debt and, second, as a result of the internal public debt.

Whereas the internal public debt increased as a result of the impossibility of obtaining additional external funds, the rate of interest on the internal debt—and the public deficit—increased or tended to increase.[8] The public deficit, which was reduced in an unhealthy way (through the curtailment of public investment and wage and salary reductions rather than personnel layoffs, deregulation, and privatization) during the adjustment process, started to increase again in 1985 as real wages and salaries in the public sector recovered their previous level.

I am not discussing solutions for the external debt crisis and the fiscal crisis that are being described. The fiscal crisis is clearly an outcome of the debt crisis. As the fiscal crisis is aggravated, the debt crisis remains the same, given the practical absence of new external loans.

S ervicing an excessively large debt—especially interest payments— leads to a reduction in a country's ability to save and invest, an increase in its public deficit, and inflation. In fact, the adjustment process imposed by creditors to make interest payments more feasible becomes self-defeating. The more a country tries to adjust when it has an excessively large debt, the greater the distortions the economy faces.

The fall in investments is directly related to the foreign debt or, more precisely, to the increase in the real transfer of resources (see Bacha 1988; Batista, Jr. 1987; Dornbusch 1989).[9] Not only in Brazil but in all highly indebted countries, as the real transfer of resources has increased the investment rate has decreased. Rather than investing (or consuming internally),

Brazil began to achieve high real transactions surpluses.[10] This phenomenon can be seen clearly in Table 5.4. The fifteen most heavily indebted countries, as identified in the October 1985 Baker Plan, also saw a real transfer of resources, whereas investment and the GDP growth rate fell, demonstrating a clear relationship between excessive debt and economic stagnation. This can be seen in Table 5.5, which shows the same tendency for these fifteen

Table 5.4   Brazilian External Accounts (US$ million)

	Real Transfers	Current Account	Debt	External Debt/ Exports
1979	(5,199.4)	(10,741.6)	49,904	327.4
1980	(5,774.9)	(12,807.0)	53,848	267.5
1981	(2,863.2)	(11,734.3)	61,411	263.6
1982	(2,816.1)	(16,310.5)	69,655	374.6
1983	4,170.6	(6,837.4)	81,319	371.3
1984	11,515.7	44.8	91,091	337.3
1985	11,017.2	(241.5)	95,857	373.9
1986	6,302.4	(4,476.9)	101,759	454.4
1987	8,889.0	(812.0)	107,514	409.9
1988	17,020.0	4,175.0	102,555	303.5
1989	14,426.0	1,564.0	99,285	288.8
1990	8,820.0	(2,347.0)	96,546	307.3

Source: Central Bank, *Brazil Economic Program,* several issues.

Table 5.5   Macro Variables of the Fifteen Primary Debtors

	GDP Growth (%)	Investment (GDP)	Inflation (%)	Public Deficit (% GDP)	Current Account/ Exports
1970–1979	5.9	24.0	31.7	(2.6)	(17.0)
1980	5.4	24.6	47.2	(0.8)	(18.0)
1981	10.1	24.0	53.7	(4.3)	(30.7)
1982	(0.5)	21.5	55.9	(5.9)	(35.8)
1983	(2.7)	17.4	91.6	(5.0)	(11.2)
1984	2.3	16.6	118.4	(3.6)	(1.0)
1985	3.8	17.1	121.8	(3.4)	(0.2)
1986	3.8	17.8	77.2	(4.8)	(11.9)
1987	2.5	17.1	116.2	(6.5)	(6.1)
1988	1.5	18.1	222.9	(5.1)	(6.4)
1989	(1.8)	–	485.9	(4.7)	(3.3)
1990	(0.8)	–	628.8	(0.7)	(2.5)

Source: IMF, *World Economic Outlook,* several issues.

countries that I showed for Brazil earlier: the fiscal crisis, represented by the public deficit, is not solved through adjustment efforts. As debt ratios continue to grow, the public deficit does not decrease, even though—as the IMF recognized—this group of countries registered an important external adjustment between 1981 and 1982 and between 1984 and 1985 as their accounts went from a deficit of 33 percent of their exports to almost an equilibrium (Cline 1988:40).

Less directly but not less importantly, the foreign debt is related to the fall in the investment rate as a result of the financial imbalance of the public sector. This imbalance can be measured by either the reduction in public savings or the operational public deficit (see Table 5.2). The lower investment rate is related to the fall in public savings because increased public investment raises the public deficit but does not diminish public savings. When public savings become negative the government has two alternatives in relation to investments: it either reduces its investments, or it borrows, thus increasing the public deficit. This happened in 1983 and 1984, when the deficit was reduced mainly by cutting public investment.

The drop in public savings and the increased public deficit on the one hand and the inverse movement of a reduced public deficit resulting from investment cuts on the other are directly related to the foreign debt. The second case is more evident. If a country has a balance-of-payments problem, it is forced to make adjustments that are invariably at the expense not only of consumption but also of investment. In Brazil's case, this has been very clear.

As long as an external debt that is far too high precludes additional external finance, the only form of financing a deficit is through perversely increasing internal indebtedness, printing money, or both. The perverse macroeconomics of adjustment when the public sector is highly indebted both externally and internally in turn leads the economy to inflation. The external debt acquired in Brazil in the 1970s was a basic cause of the fiscal crisis in the 1980s; in turn, both the external debt and the fiscal crisis were at the root of the acceleration of inflation rates during the 1980s.

As inflation accelerates, it tends to become more and more rigid downward because economic agents become increasingly inflation-conscious. The maintaining factor of inflation—the formal and informal indexation of the economy—assumes growing importance and gives rise to an autonomous or inertial type of inflation. In turn, high and accelerating levels of inflation lead to a larger public deficit, reduction of the investment rate, and reduction of the efficiency of accumulated capital. I will briefly examine these three aspects—the acceleration of inflation, its growing autonomy or inertialization, and its perverse consequences—after I describe the theory of inertial or autonomous inflation.[11]

According to the theory of autonomous or inertial inflation, we can define the rate of inflation, p', as a result of past inflation, $p'I_{t-1}$ (where I stands for the different indices economic agents use for past inflation), plus the action of exogenous supply shocks, G^z (where the superscript z stands for the several possibilities of supply shocks), and/or the action of exogenous demand shocks, u, where u stands for the unemployment rate in the Phillips curve,

$$p' = ap'I_{t-1} + b_u + cG^z$$

where a, b, and c are coefficients adding to one; in most cases b and c may be equal to zero.

In this model the maintenance of the level of inflation is defined by the indexation of prices according to past inflation, whereas its acceleration can be explained by: (1) an endogenous change of indices used by economic agents as they perceive that the going rate of inflation is too high, so that the index they are using to correct their prices is no longer a safe protection in the distributive conflict; (2) an exogenous (to the model) pressure of demand manifested by the reduction of the unemployment rate; and (3) an exogenous (to this specific model) supply shock caused by the exertion of some kind of power over prices (state, labor, or monopoly power of business firms).

This endogenous acceleration of autonomous or inertial inflation is important because it shows clearly that it is impossible to expect high and, simultaneously, stable rates of inflation, as we believed when we were formulating the theory of inertial inflation. High rates of inflation are always accelerating rates. In spite of its name, inertial inflation is permanently in a slow process of acceleration.[12] The endogenous mechanism of acceleration of autonomous inflation is based on the tendency of economic agents to change their indices as they perceive inflation to be higher and more threatening to their income share. I call this mechanism endogenous because it is based on the definition of inertial or autonomous inflation: present inflation determined by past inflation. In fact, however, it works only in combination with the exogenous (thus called because these factors are not based on past inflation) accelerating factors of inflation. At first, while autonomous inflation is perceived as relatively low, economic agents define past inflation as their cost increases; second, as the rate of inflation is perceived to be higher—and indeed is higher as a result of some exogenous shock—past inflation, defined as the index to be adopted by the economic agents, becomes the rate of inflation proper; third, when the rate of inflation is too high, economic agents tend to define as their index the price increases above the rate of inflation of some relevant sector. Each change of index represents an endogenous acceleration of autonomous inflation. In addition to this strictly endogenous mechanism of acceleration of inflation, all of the factors analyzed here that relate the acceleration of inflation to external and internal public debt and the public deficit are also endogenous factors of acceleration of inflation.[13]

During the 1970s the annual rate of inflation in Brazil averaged 40 percent. The acceleration of inflation to 100 percent, which occurred in 1979 and persisted until the end of 1982, coincided with the onset of the debt crisis (see Table 5.6). This crisis actually began in 1979 with the second oil shock, the increase in nominal and real interest rates, and the recession in the United States. The major supply shocks in this period were a maxi-devaluation of the cruzeiro in 1979, the increase in internal interest rates, a new wage policy, and the increase in some public prices to correct relative prices ("corrective inflation").

Table 5.6   Money and Inflation (percentages)

| | Inflation | | Monetary | | | Internal |
	(INPC)	(IGP-DI)	Base	M1	M4	Debt[a]
1979	70.7	77.2	84.4	73.6	65.1	26.4
1980	99.7	110.2	56.9	70.2	69.1	55.2
1981	93.5	95.2	67.2	87.6	140.5	137.8
1982	100.3	99.7	100.4	66.6	110.7	126.7
1983	178.0	211.0	79.8	97.4	150.5	95.7
1984	209.1	223.8	264.1	201.8	292.7	457.3
1985	239.0	235.1	257.3	304.3	303.9	387.0
1986	58.6	65.0	293.5	306.8	94.8	39.0
1987	396.0	415.8	181.5	127.4	352.6	531.2
1988	994.3	1,037.6	622.3	570.3	928.1	1,118.9
1989	1,863.6	1,782.9	1,754.1	1,384.2	1,743.1	2,068.6
1990	1,585.2	1,476.6	2,304.2	2,335.7	683.2	934.6
Accumulation[b]	10.963	14.089	8.087	4.986	7.355	13.477

Sources: Bank Central's Bulletin, vol. 20, April 1984; Central Bank, Brazil Economic Program, vol. 20, March 1989, and vol. 31, December 1991.
Notes: a. Internal debt includes federal bonds and bills outside the Central Bank.
b. Times rather than percent (in millions).

In 1983 inflation accelerated again to 200 percent and stayed at that level until the end of 1985. The major accelerating factor was again a maxi-devaluation of the cruzeiro, directly related to the debt crisis. Agricultural prices also contributed to the general price increase.

The deep recessions of 1981 and 1983 were unable to control inflation. In 1981 inflation maintained its previous level of around 100 percent; in 1983, this rate doubled to about 200 percent (see Table 5.6). The first recession led a group of economists in São Paulo (at the Getúlio Vargas

Foundation) and Rio de Janeiro (at Catholic University) to formulate the theory of inertial inflation; the second recession led them to propose a general price freeze, which they called the "heroic solution to control inflation" (Bresser Pereira and Nakano 1984), later called the "heterodox shock" (Lopes 1984). The Cruzado Plan of February 1986 sprang from this theoretical proposal. Its subsequent failure stemmed from its populist administration rather than its original conception.

This plan, along with the Bresser Plan (June 1987) and the Summer Plan (January 1989), was unable to eliminate inflation. As an emergency plan, adopted to cope with the acute crises of the Cruzado Plan, the Bresser Plan did not have eliminating inflation as its objective, but the other two plans were clearly aimed at reducing inflation to a rate similar to the one prevailing in the OECD countries. The literature on the causes of the Cruzado Plan's failure is growing continually. At one point it became popular to say that the Cruzado Plan had failed because it was unable to combine heterodox with orthodox measures.[14] Starting from this assumption, the Summer Plan tried to adopt an orthodox monetary policy by setting the real rate of interest at a very high level, but it failed as well. The Cruzado and Summer plans ended with an acute economic and financial crisis, which can be explained, first, by their populist implementation and, second, by their orthodox conception.

If we are to look for the basic reasons that a price freeze combined with monetary policy is unable to control the autonomous inflation prevailing in Brazil, the answer is fairly simple: until a definitive solution is found for the debt crisis and the related fiscal crisis, inflation will not be controlled. A solution to the debt crisis means reducing the debt to around 50 percent of its present level; a solution to the fiscal crisis means—in addition to reducing the public debt—eliminating the budget deficit. However, as long as inflation is not controlled, it remains a cause as well as a consequence of the fiscal crisis and, more broadly, of the economic crisis.

The Olivera-Tanzi effect, by which state revenues are reduced as inflation accelerates, is a basic cause of the public deficit. High rates of inflation, together with the public deficit and the dimension of the internal public debt, make economic agents distrustful of the indexation of the internal debt. As compensation for continuing to finance the state, they tend to demand higher interest rates, which implies a higher public deficit. Under the Summer Plan—when the loss of confidence among economic agents, leading to a loss of credit for the state, became evident—this vicious circle was aggravated by the government decision to promote the elimination of the indexation mechanism of the internal debt while at the same time setting the interest rate at an artificially high level.

In this type of economy, where high rates of inflation prevail and the source of external finance has dried up, financing the nominal public deficit (nominal public-sector borrowing requirements), Ep, where p is the price index, plus the increase in external reserves, dV, is achieved by increasing the size of the monetary base, dB, and the internal debt, $dDIG$:

$$Ep + dV = dB + dDIG$$

The question now is how this financing process will be shared between increasing the monetary base and increasing internal indebtedness. According to the monetarist view, the increase of internal indebtedness would be the independent variable. The limit to internal indebtedness would be the crowding-out process manifested by the increase of the interest on Treasury bills. The residue would be financed by seigniorage—the increase of the monetary base. Since this residue tends to be high, given the intrinsically populist character of governments in Latin American countries, inflation will be high and accelerating.

The neostructuralist theory of inertial inflation takes the inverse position. There is not necessarily a limit to internal indebtedness if the economy—as is normally the case in Brazil, except during the Cruzado Plan—is working in conditions of unemployment and idle capacity, and private business enterprises are liquid and unwilling to invest more than is strictly necessary to maintain their market shares. In fact, internal indebtedness is the residual variable, whereas the nominal growth of the monetary base is endogenously determined by the demand for money.

In this model the real demand for money, Bd/p, is a decreasing function of the rate of inflation: the higher the rate of inflation, the smaller the real demand for money (and the higher the income velocity of money). In consequence, as nominal GDP, Yp, increases, the nominal demand for money increases less than proportionately. The real demand for money is a decreasing function of the rate of inflation, and the nominal demand for money is a decreasing function of nominal income because, as inflation accelerates, economic agents reduce their liquidity preference, and demonitization takes place. These relations can be expressed by Cagan's money demand equations (1956):

$$Bd/p = aYp/p \ e - bp'$$
$$Bd/Yp = a \ e - bp'$$

where a is a coefficient that corresponds to the share of money in GDP when the rate of inflation is zero, b is the coefficient that expresses the negative elasticity of money demand to the rate of inflation, and e is the base of the Neperian logarithm (2.7182).[15]

The increase in the nominal demand for money defines the required increase in the monetary base. Given the rate of autonomous inflation, the nominal monetary base necessarily increases as the real monetary base decreases (see Table 5.7). If the nominal money supply does not increase as required by the increase in inflation, which is reflected in the increase in nominal GDP, a liquidity crisis will develop. Thus, given the required increase in the monetary base, the difference between it and the nominal public deficit plus the change in external reserves will determine the residual increase of internal indebtedness.

Table 5.7   Money and the Domestic Debt (Cr$ million)

	Monetary Base		Internal Debt[a]	
	Balance[b]	% GDP	Balance[b]	% GDP
1979	0.3	4.7	0.4	6.4
1980	0.5	4.1	0.5	3.9
1981	0.8	3.2	1.3	7.3
1982	1.9	3.1	3.4	7.8
1983	3.5	1.9	6.6	5.2
1984	12.7	2.0	19.1	8.4
1985	45.5	2.0	128.9	11.3
1986	179.0	4.4	354.9	8.9
1987	504.0	2.3	2,293.0	10.6
1988	3,637.0	1.5	25,575.0	10.4
1989	67,436.0	1.4	615,004.0	12.9
1990	1,621,271.0	2.2	1,886,793.0	2.6

Sources: Central Bank, *Annual Report,* several years; Central Bank, *Brazil Economic Program,* vol. 20, March 1989, and vol. 31, December 1991.
Notes: a. Internal debt includes federal bonds and bills outside the Central Bank.
b. Balance on June 30 of the respective years.

According to this point of view, the attempt to control inertial inflation with monetary policy is self-defeating, not only because the money supply is endogenous and is already decreasing in real terms as inflation accelerates (see Table 5.7) but also because an active monetary policy would have the perverse effect of aggravating the fiscal imbalance. We know that an active monetary policy means, basically, an increase in the interest rate. In Brazil, as in all countries that have autonomous inflation, it is the state, not the private sector, that is highly indebted. It is the state that pays interests. When interests increase, both the public deficit and the internal debt increase.

If the real interest rate is higher than the GDP growth rate (which is very likely because the economy is stagnant) and if interests have to be financed by increasing the internal debt, that debt will increase in such a way that economic agents will be pessimistic about its future payment. In the first two months of the Summer Plan, when the Brazilian government decided to raise the real interest rate to extremely high levels, the consequent loss of confidence in the government and the state's loss of credit reached an all-time high, capital flight and the public deficit increased, and the possibility of hyperinflation became evident.

Seigniorage, the issuing of money, is the independent variable for financing the public deficit, but it is a decreasing source of revenue for the state as long as the real monetary base and the inflationary tax (the devaluation of cash balances) decrease as inflation accelerates. The real resources the public sector obtains by issuing money (inflationary tax, $p'\,M/p$) correspond to the difference between real seigniorage (the increase of the monetary base in real terms, dM/p) and the reduction of the outstanding monetary base, $d(M/p)$.[16]

$$p'\,M/p = dM/p - d(M/p)$$

The monetary base, which was around 5 percent of GDP at the end of the 1970s, was little more than 1 percent of GDP in 1988 (see Table 5.7). Thus, the reduction of the monetary base $(d(M/p))$ becomes increasingly larger. Inversely, the internal debt tends to increase in relation to GDP (see Table 5.7). The reduction of the real monetary base is certainly a source of the ineffectiveness of the monetary policy, but it is also a possible source of hyperinflation. As inflation accelerates, the issuing of money—the seigniorage process—must continually increase in relation to the prevailing monetary base to finance the same public deficit; that is, to collect the same inflationary tax. And the share of the deficit financed by internal indebtedness must become larger and larger. If, at a given moment, economic agents lose confidence and stop financing the state, hyperinflation will be the necessary outcome.

Inflation plays a decisive role in the overall economic crisis I am examining—a crisis marked by economic stagnation. But before I examine the perverse logic of stagnation, I need to explain the paralysis of the state with respect to structural reforms. The fiscal crisis and its more terrible outcome—the acceleration of inflation—have as a consequence the paralysis of the state with respect to long-term economic policy. And nothing is more important for the less developed countries than an overall strategy of economic development.

A deep economic crisis, such as the crisis in Brazil in the 1980s, is a clear signal that the old strategy of economic development was exhausted. The fiscal crisis is an indication that the model of the state in Brazil no longer functioned.

This crisis is also a sign that, in addition to the model of the state, the model of society in Brazil had also lost its power. Brazilian society is characterized by a very high degree of income concentration. When the country was growing rapidly, income concentration was not a major problem. But as soon as this development stopped, income concentration became a major source of continual and aggravating social conflict—a conflict that lies at the root of the public deficit and the acceleration of the inflationary process.

The three basic strategies the Brazilian state adopted to promote industrialization were: (1) trade protection; (2) subsidies for private enterprises; and (3) direct investments in public services and basic input industries (electricity, oil, steel, communications, railroads). The change today is necessarily toward: (1) eliminating subsidies to fight the public deficit; (2) trade liberalization to stimulate international competitiveness; and (3) privatization, which will help to solve the financial crisis of the state.[17] Given the fact that Brazil is a large country, trade liberalization will necessarily be limited in comparison with smaller countries, but it will be an essential feature of any future industrial policy. State-owned enterprises played a decisive role in the first phase of industrialization, but currently, when efficiency has become crucial and the state urgently needs financial resources to balance its accounts, privatization is a natural solution.

An increasing consensus is developing regarding these reforms, but they have only started and are far from being completed, mainly because of the paralysis of the state in moments of crisis such as this. A fiscal crisis means the state has no funds to finance new economic policies; the policymakers have neither the time nor the tranquillity to formulate and implement new strategies. If to a fiscal crisis is added a social crisis stemming from excessive income concentration, the consequence is a legitimacy crisis that permanently threatens the political system and aggravates the paralysis of the state.

We now have all elements necessary to define the perverse macroeconomic logic of stagnation in a highly indebted country, where a fiscal crisis has developed and inflation has reached unthinkable levels and is nearing hyperinflation. An external debt too high to be paid— and inconsistent with growth and price stability—leads to a transfer of real resources (a surplus in the trade balance, including services) and the elimination of external savings (a deficit in the current account), which has a direct effect on reducing the global (private and public) rate of investment. This same debt leads, as we have seen, to a reduction of public savings and, consequently, to a fall in public investment.

The increase in the public external debt, which occurs as the private external debt is transferred to the state, and the increase in the payment of interest by the state cause a fiscal crisis. This crisis is aggravated the moment the public deficit can no longer be financed by external loans and must be financed by increasing the internal debt and printing money. The increase in the internal debt leads to an increase in the internal interest rate and thus to a further increase in the public debt. Printing money validates the going rate of inflation.

Prevailing high rates of inflation tend to become inertialized or autonomous. This means they are rigid downward, have an endogenous accelerating mechanism, and are subject to exogenous supply and demand shocks. As a consequence, inflation tends to become higher and higher.

High rates of inflation plus an increasing internal debt and a decreasing maturity for this debt lead economic agents to fear the financial breakdown of the state and cause an increase in capital flight, which used to be minimal in Brazil but has become substantial in recent years.[18] All of these factors obviously have a depressing effect on the rate of investment (which is already depressed by the transfer of real resources, the disappearance of external savings, and the reduction of public savings).

Finally, new investments and the existing stock of capital lose efficiency, as can be seen by an increase in the capital-output ratio. This increase is very large if we calculate the investment ratio at current prices; it is smaller if we measure investment at constant prices.[19] In current prices the rise in the capital-output ratio is greater because prices of capital goods—both imported and internally produced—increase in relative terms. In constant prices, where the variation of relative prices is neutralized, however, the capital-output ratio also rises. This should not be the case because investments in the 1980s tended to be less capital-intensive than those in the 1970s, when the PND II was launched. The best explanation for this decline in the efficiency of capital in the 1980s is probably the rate of inflation. It is usually believed that the Brazilian economy is used to inflation, that indexation neutralizes most of its evils. This was not true when inflation was 40 to 50 percent a year; it makes even less sense when inflation is no longer calculated on a yearly but on a monthly basis—that is, when inflation is 10, 20, or 30 percent a month rather than 10, 20, or 30 percent a year. This type of inflation disorganizes the economy, makes economic calculations increasingly more difficult, stimulates speculation, and leads economic agents to spend most of their time trying to gain, or at least not to lose, from the inflationary process. New investments are not necessarily less efficient, but the measurement of the marginal capital-output ratio shows an increase because part of the existing stock of capital becomes idle and loses efficiency as the economy is disorganized by inflation and an increasing number of people in business enterprises worry much more about inflation than about production. In fact, what is increasing is the total capital-output ratio, but this ratio cannot be measured.

It is fairly clear that to overcome this economic crisis, in addition to severely cutting the burden of the external debt and controlling the fiscal crisis, it is necessary to find a new pattern of capital accumulation or, in other words, a new scheme for financing investments in Brazil. I discussed this matter in Chapter 4, so a summing up is adequate here.

We can define the pattern of financing investments in terms of the sources of savings as:

$$I = SP + SG + SX$$

where I is total investment and SP, SG, and SX are, respectively, private, public, and external savings. The pattern of financing investments has undergone deep transformations in Brazil. Prior to the 1970s external savings were negligible, and savings were roughly divided between the private and public sectors:

$$I\text{–}1950s \text{ and } 1960s = 0.5SP + 0.4SG + 0.1SX$$

During the 1970s, with the increase in private savings and the huge current account deficits being financed by external indebtedness, a tripod model emerged. The state remained an important actor in the process of accumulation, but public savings began to decrease. Again, in very rough terms we have:

$$I\text{-}1970s = 0.5SP + 0.3SG + 0.2SX$$

In the 1980s public and external savings practically disappeared or became residual. Public savings were still positive because the savings of publicly owned enterprises were still positive. The source of savings for financing investments, however, became almost exclusively private:

$$I\text{-}1980s = 0.8SP + 0.1SG + 0.1SX$$

This pattern for financing investments today is clearly unsound. The external and the public sectors may not have such a small role in the process. And in relation to the public sector, as we have seen, in normal circumstances the public sector would still be responsible for around one-third of total investments (5 to 6 percent of GDP).

The required reduction of the external debt, the internal fiscal adjustment, and the structural reforms must have as one of their objectives to change this pattern of financing investments. This is the challenge of the 1990s. The 1980s was a lost decade for Brazil. But given that we now much better understand the logic of the debt, the deficit, inflation, and stagnation in Brazil and that we have been able to identify the ill effects produced by populism and the neoliberal orthodoxy, it is reasonable to hope that this vicious circle will be broken.

✠ 6 ✠

The Debt Crisis

In 1982 the debt crisis was a world crisis, threatening the major commercial banks in the First World. Today, in the mid-1990s, it is usually thought of as a bad memory, as something that existed in the past, although the highly indebted countries, particularly in Latin America, still feel its effects. The 1980s were marked by high interest rates and rationed international liquidity; in the early 1990s low interest rates prevailed in the North, whereas the supply of loanable funds to the highly indebted countries—including those that did not negotiate their debts—exploded, perversely attracted by the high local interest rates the debt left as a heritage. Until 1989 elites and governments in the creditor countries viewed the debt crisis as an unsolved problem; today it is basically assumed to have been adequately addressed by the Brady Plan, although the highly indebted countries' economic performance remains essentially unsatisfactory.[1]

Albert Hirschman (1974:152) once said that the "understanding of a problem and motivation to attack it are two necessary inputs into policy-making and problem-solving, but the timing of the two ingredients could be significantly out of phase." This is exactly the case with the developing countries' debt crisis. The diagnosis of the crisis and its possible remedies have been well defined and are known, but the solution that was found—the Brady Plan—was unsatisfactory to the debtor countries. The debt reduction involved was limited and did not present an effective remedy for the fiscal crisis of the state created by the debt crisis.

In the First World the motivation to face the crisis disappeared as soon as the threat of a world financial crisis was overcome. The Brady Plan is supposed to have solved the problem. In contrast, in the highly indebted countries the motivation to face the crisis exists or should exist, but the local elites realize that they have no power to obtain larger concessions from the creditors, given the unity of the elites in the creditor countries.

The foreign debt of the heavily indebted countries was the fundamental, although certainly not the sole, cause of the fiscal crisis that plagued Latin America in the 1980s. It still imposes a serious burden on the region, given the interest Latin America is supposed to pay to the creditor countries. Because of the strong adjustment, the entire region was engaged; and, later, because of the reduction of international interest rates, the region's indebtedness was reduced and debt ratios improved. Yet the fiscal crisis originating in foreign debt was not fully overcome in most Latin American countries, which were able to stabilize their economies but face low growth rates.

The idea of a global solution to the debt crisis, based on the creation of an International Debt Facility that would securitize the debt, is dead. The Brady Plan, proposed in February 1989, ended the debate on how to solve the debt crisis. It acknowledged that the debt crisis was not merely a liquidity problem—as the IMF, the Federal Reserve, and the banks had said when the crisis erupted in 1982—but also a solvency issue. Thus it adopted a debt reduction scheme through securitization of the old debt and the relative "delinkage" of the IMF and the World Bank in relation to the commercial banks. Yet the debt reduction made possible by the Brady Plan was meager. The Brady solution was timid.

The first country to negotiate its debt according to the Brady Plan was Mexico (August 1989). The reduction of its total debt was less than 15 percent.[2] But since that time, as the Mexican economy started to perform apparently satisfactorily, the confidence of local capitalists and international financial markets has increased, and capital flows to Mexico have boomed. The rate of growth has remained fairly unsatisfactory, and price stabilization has been based on an increasingly overvalued peso. However, because Mexico adopted or seemed to adopt all of the policy recommendations that originated in Washington and New York, confidence in the Mexican economy increased steadily. Only in 1994, when Mexico faced a current account deficit of around 6 percent of GDP, did the international financial system realize that the Mexican confidence-building strategy was ill founded. In fact, for the past few years Mexico has been engaged in a perverse trade-off between macroeconomic fundamentals and confidence building. In 1989 it had engaged in an equally perverse trade-off between the national interest—which was not adequately considered in the debt agreement—and, again, confidence building.

It is evident now that the correlation between the "solution" to the Mexican debt crisis represented by the 1989 Brady agreement and the flow of funds to Mexico was spurious. Mexico had not overcome its debt crisis. There is a relationship between the debt agreement and the performance of the Mexican economy because the country did gain the confidence of foreign investors, but this correlation is much weaker than is generally supposed. The moderately effective results the Mexican economy has shown are the consequence of a strict fiscal adjustment, a competent heterodox stabilization program that froze prices in December 1987, and bold structural reforms—particularly trade liberalization—rather than the result of the Brady agreement. The large capital flows that could be more directly related to this agreement—to the confidence the Brady Plan would have brought to the Mexican economy—in fact coincided with a strong increase in international liquidity and the reduction of interest rates in the United States. As a consequence, a country like Brazil, which did not sign a Brady agreement until 1994, has also received sizable capital inflows since 1991.

The creditors' and debtors' approaches to the crisis immediately following the definition of the Brady Plan in 1989 were conflicting. Among the creditors, I should distinguish: (1) the official and dominant conception defined by the U.S. government and implemented by multilateral agencies in basic agreement with the major U.S. banks; and (2) a decreasing number of dissenters outside the executive branch of the creditor governments, which favored a significant and concerted reduction of the debt. Among the debtor countries I should distinguish the views of: (1) nationalists and populists; (2) government officials and business elites subordinated to foreign interests; and (3) a group of citizens that favored adopting a combination of pressures by the debtor governments—including quasi-unilateral measures—oriented to capture the discount in the secondary market in a concerted manner.

The views of the official creditor community, including governments and international financial institutions, have evolved over time. In the early years of the crisis, when major banks were at risk of insolvency, the dominant creditor approach was focused exclusively on saving the banks by demanding that the debtor countries pay—at least partially—their debts, no matter how desperate these countries' situation. Over time, as the countries adjusted their short-term balance-of-payments problems but remained in deep economic disarray, whereas the banks recovered, the focus has gradually shifted away from the banks and toward measures to relieve some of the pressures on the debtor countries. The interests of the banks and the national interests of the creditor countries, which at the beginning of the debt crisis were practically identical, have clearly diverged as the threat of a world financial crisis born of the debt crisis has disappeared, whereas U.S. exports to the highly indebted countries have continued to suffer. Following the Brady Plan and the Mexican and Venezuelan agreements, concern over the debt crisis waned because the problem was considered to have been solved, at least for the time being.[3] The creditors' strategy, in spite of the profound changes it had undergone, was still a "muddling-through approach"—a strategy of continual improvisation that avoided a definitive and rapid solution to the problem.

The phases of official management of the crisis are well known. In 1982 the debt was understood as a mere liquidity problem to be solved by a combination of new lending and sharp austerity in the debtor countries. In 1985 the Baker Plan was introduced, calling for more lending—which never materialized—and for growth with adjustment and structural reforms. The idea of a "menu of options" became popular. In 1987 and 1988 it became clear that the debt was a solvency problem, and the idea of debt reduction became mandatory. Securitization—that is, the substitution of the old debt for new securities with a guarantee provided by the multilateral agencies—and the relative delinkage of the multilateral agencies from the banks in the negotiation process became dominant.[4] During these two years a consensus was formed that a new initiative should be taken in relation to the debt crisis—an initiative that included debt reduction through securitization. The Brady Plan, presented by the new U.S. secretary of the treasury, Nicholas Brady, arose from this consensus. The focus was on "voluntary debt reduction" through securitization. The IMF and the World Bank were to have additional resources to provide guarantees and other "enhancements" of the new securities to spur debt reduction. This was a major change in U.S. policy toward the debt and was also inspired by the views of Japan, France, and Italy. These views were never fully defined, but since 1988 it has become clear that these countries support a major change in the debt policy and movement toward a global solution to the debt.[5] Essentially, the Brady Plan was created because an increasing number of people in the political and economic elites of the creditor countries did not accept the liquidity approach. As the Baker Plan failed, they realized the self-defeating nature of internal adjustment policies when such policies were not coupled with debt reduction, and they supported a global solution for capturing the discount on the secondary market, tied to limited debt relief.

Within the debtor countries radicals and populists supported a moratorium on the debt that would allow in the short run an increase in wages and internal consumption. The Peruvian disaster is the best example of this attitude toward the debt. At the other extreme, the governments in the highly indebted countries—and their subordinate business elites—were eager to please the creditors and always bowed to their demands while adopting, in their speeches and official communiqués, a national-interest rhetoric condemning the debt and asking for debt reduction. Finally, the third group, which appeared in Latin America in 1987, proposed the adoption of firm measures, including unilateral suspension of payments—to force a concerted or negotiated securitization of the debt—combined with strong internal fiscal adjustment measures. It is fairly clear that this group had an important ally in the dissenters from the official view in the creditor countries, but it is also obvious that, in addition to this support, it was essential to use the only bargaining power a debtor country possessed: the possibility of suspending payments of interest. This group lost influence as Mexico negotiated its debt according to the Brady Plan and the dissenters in the First World practically disappeared.

B y 1990 some basic propositions about the debt crisis were well established. They can be summarized as follows:

1. The excessive international indebtedness in the 1970s and the resulting debt crisis were a consequence, on the one hand, of the belief that devel-

oping countries should and could receive capital flows for an indefinite period, ignoring the fact that loans follow a necessary cycle of payments and reimbursements, and, on the other hand, of the "Ponzi scheme" adopted by the banks and the multilateral agencies, according to which original lenders are paid with money supplied by later lenders, permanently rolling over the old debt (Payer 1991).

2. The debt crisis was a crisis of the highly indebted countries, not of the creditors. The danger of a world financial crisis had vanished, given the improvement in the capital ratios of the banks.[6]

3. The debt was a major problem not only because of the huge transfers of real resources to the creditors it implies but also because of its fiscal consequences. The foreign debt was essentially a government debt in Latin America. Around 90 percent of the long-term debt is state debt. Thus, the debt is an essential ingredient of the fiscal crisis of the state.

4. The debt crisis was the major, but not the only, cause for the relative economic stagnation of most of the highly indebted countries. Populist policies, based on resistance to eliminating the budget deficit and on the attempt to promote economic development and distribute income in the short run, were a second reason for this crisis.

5. The relative failure of adjustment policies in the highly indebted countries may have an explanation in populist practices, but its main cause was the self-defeating character of adjustment when the external debt was too high. Because the private sector in the highly indebted countries was able to transfer the foreign debt almost entirely to the public sector, the payment of interest on this debt aggravated the fiscal crisis, rendering the efforts to reduce the public deficit partially ineffective or self-defeating.[7]

6. In the first years of the crisis real devaluations of the local currency, which were necessary to achieve high trade surpluses, strongly accelerated the prevalent high inflation rates, which—particularly in the case of Brazil and Argentina—were subsequently inertialized through formal and informal indexation systems.[8] Since 1990 an opposite movement has taken place. The huge capital flows to Latin America led to the overvaluation of local currencies. As a consequence, inflation rates were reduced, but trade deficits appeared, and the local manufacturing industries were endangered. The threat to these industries was augmented by the fact that most Latin American countries are engaged in long overdue trade liberalization programs. Trade liberalization is essential to Latin America, but, combined with currency appreciation, it may be fatal to manufacture, as was the case with Martines de Hoz's Argentina.

7. Inertial inflation is resistant to conventional monetary and fiscal policy. A combination of conventional (orthodox) fiscal and monetary policy and heterodox policies is required. In the 1980s the successful heterodox Israeli (1985) and Mexican (1987) experiments in controlling inflation showed that a combination of income policies and orthodox policies is indicated when inflation is high and chronic or inertial.[9] This view was chal-

lenged by several heterodox attempts to control inflation in Brazil and
Argentina, all of which failed. Yet when stabilization was eventually
achieved in these two countries—in 1991 and 1995, respectively—it was the
outcome of a combination of orthodox and heterodox policies.

8. Stabilization has been achieved in Latin America, and the economic
stagnation of the 1980s gave way in the 1990s to modest rates of growth.
Income per capita is finally growing again. Yet income concentration
increased, wages remain very low, and the new democracies that were established in these countries in the early 1980s are far from consolidated. The
coup in Peru in 1991 and an attempted coup in Venezuela in 1992 demonstrate this fact.[10]

9. Given the failure of the conventional (muddling-through) strategy, a
combination of adjustment and financing, to deal with the debt crisis, in the
late 1980s the consensus was that the debt burden should be reduced and real
resources transferred to the creditor countries. The Brady Plan was the
response to this realization. Yet because the flow of funds to Latin America
again became positive as a result of the low interest rates in the creditor
countries and the high interest rates in the region, the motivation for a real
or definitive solution to the debt crisis vanished.

10. The Brady Plan was a major advance because it meant the creditor
countries recognized that the debt must be reduced; that securitization is the
best way to achieve this end; that the IMF and the World Bank should support the policy of debt reduction, including the supply of collaterals; and that
these two institutions should be partially delinked from the banks.[11]

11. The strategy of the creditor countries eventually changed in the
right direction, but the limited scope of the Brady Plan indicates the hesitation and dilemmas faced by the governments of the creditor countries
regarding the debt. They knew a solution should be found to the debt crisis,
but they did not want to confront their own banks. The Mexican agreement
demonstrated this fact. Debt reduction was unsatisfactory; the fiscal crisis of
the state was not fully overcome; macroeconomic balance was only partially achieved; growth rates remained very modest despite large cash inflows;
and eventually, in December 1994 the country faced a very serious crisis.

The Brady Plan was limited as a solution to the debt crisis. To
understand why this was the case, it is necessary to distinguish clearly
the two basic strategies regarding the debt crisis that dominated the debate
on the subject in the late 1980s. The idea of debt reduction, which had been
taken as a threat to the banks a few years earlier, was eventually accepted.
Securitization was the basic strategy used to achieve this result. Yet the
problem was how great this reduction should be. On one side were those
who favored a concerted and global reduction of the debt based on the creation of an International Debt Facility that would manage the entire process

on a case-by-case basis. On the other side, since February 1989, was the Brady Plan—firmly supported by the major creditor countries—which favored "voluntary," market-controlled debt reduction.[12] I call the first the concerted approach and the second the voluntary or, more precisely, the free-rider approach to debt reduction.

The concerted approach can be summarized as follows. First, the securitization of the long-term debt of the highly indebted countries—that is, the conversion of the debt into long-term bonds, capturing the discount in the secondary market—should be the basic financial device used to solve the debt crisis. These new bonds would make sense for the banks only if they were guaranteed by the creditor countries. The organizations to offer this guarantee should be the IMF and the World Bank, given that both multilateral institutions were directly involved in managing the debt crisis and that their main stockholders were the creditor countries.

To reconcile their policies, the Bank and the IMF should create an International Debt Facility (IDF), which, in addition to giving guarantees to the new bonds, would administer the debt crisis. The board of the IDF, after evaluating a country's economic capacity to pay its debt—taking as the basis, but not exclusively, the discount in the secondary market—and after debating the issue with debtors and creditors, would make a concerted (but not necessarily unanimous) proposal regarding the discount the country would be entitled to receive. It would then make a once-and-for-all offer to the banks; the free-rider strategy would not be permitted.

To receive this discount, the debtor country would have to meet the conditionalities agreed on with the IDF. The discount would be permanently dependent upon the ability of the debtor to adjust and maintain its adjusted economy.

The cost of this alternative would be low to the creditor countries, although there would be a cost for offering guarantees. Thus a fund should be established by the creditor governments in the IDF.

If the creditor governments had adopted this approach, it would have been possible to envisage an effective solution to the debt crisis. The creditors, however, stayed with the Brady Plan—that is, the market or free-rider approach—rejecting the creation of an IDF and not supplying the IMF and the Bank with the special funds needed to back the guarantees. Thus the achieved debt reduction was unable to effectively contribute to the solution of the fiscal crisis. The burden of fiscal adjustment remained fully local.

The banks, which are specialists in semantics, liked to call their approach to debt reduction the "voluntary or market approach,"[13] as if the concerted or global approach were not also voluntary and based on the market. The first and more important difference between the two approaches is that one allows for the free-rider strategy and the other does not. A second difference is that the free-rider approach favors debt-equity conversions as a good strategy to reduce the debt, whereas the global approach excludes such deals.

The idea of market-controlled debt reduction had been around for some years before 1989, but the actual accomplishment of debt reduction had been rare. The main channel for debt reduction had been debt-equity swaps, which, ironically, are typically harmful to the debtor country. In fact, despite the enormous pressure from commercial banks for such programs, they have been suspended in almost every country that introduced them.

Debt reduction schemes should be measured against the standard of restored creditworthiness of the debtor country. Specifically, debt reduction should be extensive enough to allow the debtor country to service the external debt on the revised contractual basis without the need to refinance interest payments, and to allow the private sector in the debtor country to attract suppliers' credits, trade credits, and project finance on a decentralized basis.

Under "voluntary" arrangements, a small number of banks can frustrate the comprehensive settlement of a country's debt. In a voluntary debt reduction mechanism each creditor is free to choose whether to participate. Nonparticipation means the creditor continues to hold the original claim and can attempt to collect as much as possible on that claim. Thus there is a basic arbitrage condition attached to voluntary schemes: participation in the scheme must, on the margin, be no worse than holding out and sticking with the original claim. In a voluntary scheme the creditor must compare the value of the existing claim after debt reduction with the value of the alternative claim made available through participation in the debt reduction scheme.

But an obvious paradox arises, best illustrated by the case of certainty. A full restoration of creditworthiness would imply that all claims on the debtor, including "old" debt that does not participate in the debt reduction process, will rise in value to face value. The secondary market price of the old debt will be 100 cents on the dollar after the debt reduction if full creditworthiness is indeed restored. Thus under certainty there would be no motivation for an individual creditor who has a small share of the overall debt to participate in a voluntary scheme if the creditor receives something less than 100 percent of face value.

The result, which was formally demonstrated by Helpman (1989), is that voluntary debt reduction may be impossible as a market mechanism even when the creditors as a whole would benefit from the reduction relative to the status quo. Thus the insistence that debt reduction be voluntary actually hurts the creditors as a whole.

"Voluntary approach" is an appealing expression, but it is misleading. What was really the alternative to the concerted approach to reducing the debt was the free-rider approach—the last version of the muddling-through approach adopted by the creditors since the beginning of the debt crisis.

Stanley Fischer (1989:320–321), who analyzed the possible solutions to the debt crisis, favored the creation of a debt facility. But he warned that even this scheme "creates a free rider problem. If the International Debt Discount Corporation [IDDC[14]] buys up much of the developing country debt and makes some form of debt relief possible, then the credit of the debtors improves. Those creditors who stayed out of the IDDC have a capital gain. For that reason an IDDC would have to find some means of ensuring almost complete participation by the creditors."

We see then that the Brady Plan was insufficient to face the debt crisis. Its limited character stemmed from two other factors in addition to its insistence on the voluntary approach: it did not provide funds for the IMF and the World Bank to offer guarantees, and it said nothing about a joint action of the two institutions to create a debt facility. Given these limitations, the discount the highly indebted countries received under the Brady Plan was small, if any. More important in solving the debt crisis were, domestically, the exchange rate devaluations and fiscal adjustment and, internationally, the reduction of interest rates in the early 1990s.

I f a concerted securitization of the debt is a better solution to the debt crisis, why has it not materialized? Why has the Brady Plan set a limit for the creditor countries? It is not difficult to identify the obstacles to the concerted approach—obstacles that originate in both the creditor and the debtor countries.

On the creditors' side, the barriers to a concerted reduction of the debt were: (1) the inherent collective action barrier to comprehensive debt reduction; (2) the problem of precedents; (3) the problem of public-sector bailouts; (4) the distorted incentives of the large banks; (5) the structure of the bargaining cycle (see Sachs 1989b); and, more recently, (6) the relatively strong performance of the countries that signed a Brady-type agreement.

The inherent collective action barrier is related to the insistence on the voluntary schemes I have already discussed. The problem of the precedent applies especially to small countries; a solution to the debt is not reached, given, as the banks would say, "the risk of a precedent." Concerted debt reduction is also difficult because of the continuing signal from the official community that public money will rescue the faltering negotiation process; to the extent that the banks limit new lending or debt reduction, they know the official community will make up at least part of the difference in official lending to the debtor countries. Additionally, the large U.S. banks strongly resist debt write-downs because of the less developed countries' greater exposure relative to capital, because they have superior access to debt equity swaps than do small banks, and because they will be better off if another, smaller creditor voluntarily makes a concession to the debtor. Finally, in the negotiating cycle the bargaining power of the debtor countries is weakened because an agreement with the banks has been made the sine qua non of good relations with the creditor governments. In the case of the Brazilian moratorium in February 1987, this phenomenon was quite clear. Solidarity among creditor governments, multilateral agencies, and banks was fairly evident.

T he debtor countries were obviously interested in reducing their debt when the problem was on the agenda of the creditor countries. This interest was first officially manifested at the Acapulco meeting of eight Latin American presidents in November 1987. But the elites in the debtor countries and their respective governments were unable to exert sufficient pressure on the creditors to adopt the unilateral decision of suspending the payment of interest and reducing the debt for three reasons: (1) they feared retaliation; (2) they identified ideologically with the creditors; and (3) the elites suffered less as a result of the debt, which, particularly in the case of debt-equity swaps, may be a source of speculative profits.

Bankers always threaten retaliation, and despite the fact that these retaliations never materialize, they continue to frighten debtor elites. In all instances of moratoria retaliations have been minor. In the case of Brazil the declaration of the new finance minister in February 1988 that the moratorium caused more harm than benefits to the country because of retaliations is meaningless. He was merely trying to justify suspending the moratorium and signing a conventional agreement with the banks, which had solved none of Brazil's problems. In fact, retaliations against Brazil were minimal. The commercial banks moderately reduced their short-term credits, and the World Bank—for the first time that year—presented a negative cash flow with Brazil. This may have caused a loss of reserves of, at most, $1.3 billion against a gain of $4.3 billion—the interests that should have been paid in 1987 to the commercial banks on long-term loans.

In fact, the banks have no interest in suspending their short-term loans to the highly indebted countries. They receive large spreads from these loans, and the discount for them in the secondary market is very small. If they decide as a retaliation to suspend these credits, the debtor country will not pay, and the loan will be immediately transformed into a long-term credit with a much larger discount in the secondary market. The loss for banks will be abrupt and large. They are well aware of this fact and thus do not retaliate. Banks are interested in making profits—now and in the long run. Threats may help to achieve this goal; retaliations will not.

A second obstacle for the local elites seeking to exert stronger pressure on creditors, which in certain cases should include the declaration of a moratorium, is their ideological identification with the creditor countries. They want to be part of the First World. They want respect, and they identify the First World with the banks and the U.S. government. They are only now beginning to realize that elites in the creditor countries are divided, that the First World should not be reduced to only the bankers, and that an increasing number of very influential citizens in the First World are pressing for a concerted debt reduction.

Finally, the poor rather than the elites are the ones who suffer as a result of the debt crisis. For some, the debt offers a chance for speculation and profit. Debt-equity swaps in particular make possible huge gains for local bankers, brokers, investors, and lawyers. In fact, these swaps are not merely inefficient—as is the case with the "voluntary" debt-bond swaps—in solving the debt crisis; they are a false solution that harms the economies of the highly indebted countries. Few effective investments result from these conversions. For the beleaguered public sectors of the highly indebted countries, they represent the exchange of an external debt for an internal debt—generally at a higher real interest rate—or for printing money. In the case of Brazil, where the internal debt consists of quasi money (overnight maturity), we have the worst of both worlds: with debt-equity conversions, the state pays higher interest rates while printing quasi money.

The failure of the conventional (muddling-through) approach to the debt crisis, the limitations of the Brady Plan, and the lack of motivation to adopt a global securitization solution to the crisis led an increasing number of countries into a state of arrears in the late 1980s. Negotiations basically lost focus because the "new money" device—the basis of the conventional approach—proved illogical even from the standpoint of the banks. The only alternative to new money was sizable negotiated debt reductions, reductions professional managers of the banks could not accept.

Arrears are undeclared moratoria. They are the obvious and, in fact, the only alternative when negotiations fail. This is the situation with the debt crisis of the 1930s, as Robert Devlin (1989a:234) reminds us: "At the outset of 1988 the situation of [Latin America] began to display some remarkable parallels with the debt crisis of the 1930s. . . . Only a few countries maintained a regular payments status with their creditors; the majority of debtors in fact were, in one form or another, in a state of arrears even on rescheduled debt service."

Arrears are not a solution to the debt crisis. They are a negative form of responding to it, as long as nothing is really solved. Economic theory holds that economic agents behave according to expectations—expectations that are rational and self-fulfilling for some economists and that underline the uncertainty of economic behavior for others. But expectations are always based on facts. If the economies of the highly indebted countries tend to be victims of a fiscal crisis and if a substantial part of the budget deficit originates in the interest paid by the state on the foreign debt, expectations regarding inflation will necessarily tend to be high. On the other hand, investors will tend to have negative expectations about the economy of a country that has an enormous unpaid debt.

The arrears problem was eventually solved when exchange rate devaluations produced trade surpluses in most Latin American highly indebted countries. In some countries Brady agreements also played a role in regularizing debt payments. The problem was solved definitively when the cash flows changed direction and the transfer of real resources to the creditor countries was stopped.

I n 1989 the probability that a debtor country would incur a state of arrears or adopt a quasi-unilateral solution was high; today there is no such probability. The debt crisis was not fully solved, but today its burden is smaller than it was in the 1980s. The relative success of the Brady Plan, the reduction of international interest rates, and the change of direction of international cash flows led the elites in the creditor countries to see the problem as having been solved.

Between 1986 and 1989 the elites in the creditor countries were divided. The realization of this fact was a decisive factor in convincing me, as finance minister of Brazil, to propose a concerted solution to the debt crisis in 1987. I would not have made these proposals if I had not known that a large sector of the elites in the creditor countries favored some kind of debt relief.

At that time, however, the sectors of the elites that were sympathetic to the debtors always assumed that the initiative should come from the creditor governments. It was difficult for them to admit that an initiative to reduce the debt could come from the debtors' side. Today, even this mildly favorable attitude has vanished because the Brady-type agreements are supposed to have successfully provided a long-lasting solution to the debt crisis.

Thus the creditor countries' motivation to solve the debt crisis has vanished. The debt is no longer a source of crisis for these countries, and the new international liquidity has created a worldwide belief that the crisis is also over for the debtor countries. This is only partially correct because the interest burden remains high and straps a heavy fiscal burden on the highly indebted countries. Governments in the debtor countries owe around 90 percent of the debt and have a limited fiscal capacity to pay. Thus in addition to causing real resources transfers, the debt crisis remains a major fiscal problem that is reducing growth rates in the debtor countries and will continue to do so for many years. Yet it is no longer a problem for the banks or the creditor countries and thus is no longer a part of the international agenda. The problem survives only through its effects in the 1990s: modest growth rates and lagging living standards in Latin America.

❈ 7 ❈

Hyperinflation

At the beginning of 1990 the Brazilian economy experienced hyperinflation for the first time in its history. The rate of inflation reached 56 percent in January, 73 percent in February, and 84 percent in March of that year. Yet this was a moderate hyperinflation, which the Collor Plan (see Chapter 13) was designed to try to curb. Hyperinflation in Brazil was the outcome of the fiscal crisis of the state. Here I provide a brief account of that fact.

The general conditions that gave rise to hyperinflation in Brazil were somewhat similar to those that had prevailed in countries that had previously experienced hyperinflation. Brazil was not defeated in a war and was not required to pay war reparations, but the combination of the foreign debt accumulation in the 1970s, the external shocks of 1979 (the second oil and the interest shocks), and the suspension of new external financing in 1982 had comparable consequences. Brazil, which in the 1970s had received around 2 percent of GDP in foreign savings, was now required to transfer real resources of 4 to 5 percent of its gross national product to the creditor countries.[1] The reduction in domestic investment was basically proportional to this transfer: the rate of investment, which had been around 22 percent of GDP in the 1970s, fell to around 17 percent in the 1980s.

There are also the fiscal consequences of the foreign debt. The debt, which in the mid-1970s was 50 percent private and 50 percent public, was almost fully nationalized during the 1981–1983 adjustment: by the end of the 1980s, 90 percent of the debt was the responsibility of the public sector. In the 1981–1983 stabilization program there was a strong effort to reduce the budget deficit, but this effort was defeated, first, by the high rates of interest paid by the state and, second, by the increase in the foreign and domestic public debt (see Chapter 5). With the suspension of foreign loans, deficit financing depended increasingly on domestic indebtedness and seigniorage. The consequence was a fiscal crisis: the budget deficit remained high (see Table 7.1); public domestic debt increased to around 50 percent of GDP; and domestic debt maturities became incredibly short (most of the domestic debt began to be financed on the overnight market). The state's creditworthiness collapsed. The fiscal crisis immobilized economic policy, transforming the government into a passive instrument validating inflation through fiscal deficits and inflationary financing.

Table 7.1   Public-Sector Accounts (percentage of GDP)

	Tax Collection	Personnel Expenditure	Public Deficit
1979	24.7	7.0	8.3
1980	24.7	6.3	6.7
1981	24.5	6.4	5.2
1982	25.0	7.0	6.2
1983	24.7	6.5	3.0
1984	21.4	5.5	3.1
1985	22.0	6.8	4.4
1986	25.0	7.2	3.6
1987	22.2	7.5	5.7
1988	19.8	7.2	4.8
1989	21.4	9.2	6.9
1990	25.9	9.2	-1.4

Sources: First two columns, IBGE, *Anuário Estatístico,* several issues; last column, Central Bank, *Brazil Economic Program,* several issues.
Note: The first two columns refer to the public sector in the strict sense; the last column includes state-owned corporations.

The strong yet incomplete adjustment program of 1981–1983 and the 1983 real devaluation of the local currency led, first, to a reduction of real wages and the aggravation of the distributive conflict (given the widespread conviction that income distribution was deeply uneven in Brazil) and, second, to a wage-price spiral. This wage-price spiral was engineered by an informal but effective agreement between the labor unions and the firms of the modern and oligopolistic industries (Nakano 1989).

The wage-price spiral had its origins in 1978–1979, when the first major strikes since 1964 took place, but it gained momentum only in 1985, after the transition to democracy had been completed. It did not lead to hyperinflation earlier for two reasons: first, the heterodox stabilization plans (in 1986, 1987, and 1989) pushed down inflation for a time; second, given the high degree of formal and informal indexation, inflation in Brazil has a strong inertial component.

Inertial inflation tends to be rigid downward because future inflation is strongly influenced by past inflation through indexation. But it also tends to hinder the acceleration of inflation as long as it avoids or postpones the dollarization of the economy. In the 1923 German hyperinflation, for instance, the dollarization of the economy led to an exchange rate–price spiral. Economic agents received the local currency in payment and immediately tried to buy dollars to protect their assets. Thus the real demand for dollars increased, and real devaluations of the local currency followed—continually leading to hyperinflation (Merkin 1982). In contrast, in Brazil economic agents could protect their financial assets by buying indexed bonds, mostly

Treasury bills financed daily on the overnight market. These bills (LFTs) represented a remunerated, interest-bearing quasi money and thus constituted a better alternative to buying dollars.

In fact, buying dollars was risky because the parallel exchange rate tended to be artificially high, and it fluctuated a great deal. At times, speculative attacks against the cruzado caused the premium of the parallel market exchange rate over the official rate to increase sharply. Inflation, however, did not follow immediately, given the low import coefficient of the Brazilian economy (less than 5 percent of GDP) and the dual exchange rate market. The official exchange rate was under strict government control, protecting the trade balance from the wild fluctuations of the parallel exchange rate. It was indexed following a crawling peg rule, with daily devaluation. The parallel exchange rate was market-determined. After each speculative attack the premium fell, imposing heavy losses on the last buyers.

I ndexation of the economy delayed hyperinflation but did not avoid it. Inflation tended to accelerate continually, but its acceleration happened by shifting from one level or plateau to another (higher) and was interrupted by price freezes, starting in 1986 with the Cruzado Plan. However, after the breakdown of the Cruzado Plan and particularly of the Summer Plan (January 1989), inflation accelerated very rapidly because these plans helped to disorganize the economy (see Table 7.2).[2] Confidence in the indexation system, which was already very low, collapsed with the Summer Plan because conventional indexation is based on past inflation, and past inflation was no longer a good proxy for present inflation. With the bankruptcy of the indexation system, the price system lost its basic anchor. Inflation began to accelerate in a spiral fashion (see Table 7.3).[3]

Table 7.2   Annual Inflation Rate

	Percentage	Year	Percentage
1970	19.3	1980	110.2
1971	19.5	1981	95.1
1972	15.8	1982	99.7
1973	15.5	1983	211.0
1974	34.6	1984	223.8
1975	29.4	1985	235.1
1976	46.2	1986	65.0
1977	38.8	1987	415.8
1978	40.8	1988	1,037.6
1979	77.2	1989	1,782.9
		1990	1,477.0

Source: IGP/FGV, General Price Index; *Conjuntura Econômica,* Getúlio Vargas Foundation, Rio de Janeiro, several issues.

Table 7.3   Monthly Inflation Rate (percentage)

	1986	1987	1988	1989	1990
January	17.8	12.0	19.1	36.6	71.9
February	22.4	14.1	17.6	11.8	71.7
March	−1.0	15.0	18.2	4.2	81.3
April	−0.6	20.1	20.3	5.2	11.3
May	0.3	27.7	19.5	12.8	9.1
June	0.5	25.9	20.8	26.8	9.0
July	0.6	9.3	21.5	37.9	13.0
August	1.3	4.5	22.9	36.5	12.9
September	1.1	8.0	25.8	38.9	11.7
October	1.4	11.2	27.6	39.7	14.2
November	2.5	14.5	28.0	44.3	17.4
December	7.6	15.9	28.9	49.4	16.5

Source: IGP/FGV.

As the financial market lost confidence in Treasury bills, the government increased its interest rate. The result was an increase in the budget deficit and a perverse additional loss of credit of Treasury bills. The successive plans changed the inflationary behavior of economic agents, introducing new destabilizing factors into the economy. Agents anticipated possible government actions, such as freezes or domestic debt repudiation, by increasing prices and promoting capital flight.

As inflation accelerated every month, expectations that acceleration would continue assumed a self-fulfilling character. The economy was heading toward hyperinflation, which materialized in early 1990.

The Summer Plan was designed to have a very orthodox monetary policy. Thus interest rates were raised to extremely high levels, reaching 16 percent a month in real terms during the first two months of the plan. Subsequently, as economic agents realized the unpleasant arithmetic involved (the high interest rate would be paid primarily by the state itself, thereby dramatically increasing the interest component of the deficit), the rate of interest was reduced but remained very high.

The fiscal crisis of the state finally became evident to everybody. The government faced increasing difficulty with financing its deficit, whose interest component was now overwhelming (see Table 5.3). The suspension of payments of interest related to the foreign debt in August 1989 helped very little because the expectations of economic agents were already clear: hyperinflation and some form of cancellation of the domestic debt were viewed as highly probable.

During 1989 economic agents worked under these two expectations, trying to anticipate the more likely government action. They strove to protect their financial assets by selling their Treasury bills ("running away from the overnight"), but they had limited alternatives because the price of other assets—including the dollar on the parallel market—greatly increased. The premium on the parallel market exchange rate over the official rate, which had been around 25 percent, exceeded 150 percent several times during 1989.[4]

The money supply, which is usually endogenous, in this case was fully passive, increasing automatically as the nominal demand for money increased. When inflation is high and chronic (inertial), the money supply is endogenous—thus validating price increases—because the alternative to trying to keep it frozen while prices are soaring is a serious liquidity crisis. The government is supposed to finance its deficit on the overnight market. Speculation with Treasury bills was rampant. Financial intermediaries would often buy Treasury bills without having a final buyer for them. In such a situation the normal procedure would be for financial intermediaries to finance themselves on the money market. But because they usually lacked the credit to do so, the Central Bank would repurchase the Treasury bills. This repurchase, practiced in the early 1980s, became the rule in 1986. Paradoxically, this was a sound policy because it reduced speculation and lowered the state's interest burden. But the consequence was that the money supply became fully passive. Whenever economic agents fled from Treasury bills, leaving the financial intermediaries without reserves, the Central Bank would automatically repurchase the bills without cost to the intermediary. Hyperinflation was the necessary outcome of theses events: the official inflation rate (Consumer Price Index) was 53 percent in December, 56 percent in January, 73 percent in February, and 84 percent in March.

❧ Part 3 ❧
The Political Dimension

✧ 8 ✧
Crisis and Renewal in the Left

In the late 1980s the left reached the climax of a crisis that had begun almost twenty years before. In the developed countries it manifested itself as the crisis of the welfare state. In those countries that had previously been communist it was the crisis of the state and of the statist mode of production. In Latin America it was also a crisis of populism and of the national-developmentalist strategy. It is essential to reconsider the issue of the left in Latin America as well as in the rest of the world. Yet it is also essential to reconsider our view of Latin America, as I have been doing throughout this book. Only through a new approach to the causes of the Latin American crisis will we be able to understand the new left that is emerging.

In this chapter I briefly analyze the general crisis of the left and then examine the case of Latin America in particular. I will show that the analysis and development strategies of the Latin American left were appropriate for the period from the 1930s to the 1960s, but that since the early 1960s reality has moved beyond both this analysis and this strategy. The crisis of the left, which took place throughout the world beginning in the 1970s, came to Latin America somewhat later—in the 1980s—as an outcome of the breakdown in its development strategy. Finally, beginning in the mid-1980s, a modern social-democratic or social-liberal left began to emerge in Latin America that came into conflict with the old left of the 1950s.

It was the right that was in crisis from the 1930s to the 1960s. Two world wars, the increasing strength of unions, and the Great Depression of the 1930s made it clear that economic liberalism combined with political conservatism was incapable of promoting development and guaranteeing domestic and international peace.

The old liberal conservatism was a social philosophy based on the principles of tradition and social order. It defended inequality in the name of inherent rights. It was elitist if not racist. It was based on the belief that the market was the best and the only way to regulate the economy. This liberal belief, which went on the defensive in the 1930s, reemerged in the 1970s with new strength; it had been modernized and was intellectually sophisticated. Thus a new conservatism—neoliberalism—manifested the thinking of the right in a renewed and aggressive form.

Among economists this new right corresponds to the Austrian, monetarist, new classical, and rational choice schools. It is the neoliberal right. It
is the right whose rhetoric is based on the principles of efficiency and competition. As is characteristic of all conservative thinking, it values order over
justice. It justifies inequality, although in the name of stimulating the economy and promoting efficiency rather than in the name of racial or class
"rights."

As the right recovered its forces, the left entered a period of deep crisis
beginning in the 1970s, following the surge of renewal of the 1950s and
1960s and the 1968 student revolution. This crisis had one fundamental
cause: the statist development strategy espoused by the left, which had been
successful from the 1930s to the 1960s, was no longer successful in the mid-
1970s.

From the 1930s to the 1960s the development strategy of the left was
dominant throughout the world.[1] The experiences of the Nazi and fascist
right are a tragic exception to this general trend, as is the Stalinist experience in the Soviet Union. There are three lefts that are relevant to our analysis of this historical period: that of the Soviet Union, where the communist
left was dominant; that of the developed capitalist countries, where the
social-democratic and the Keynesian left (progressive or "liberal" left,
according to North American terminology) supported the welfare state; and
finally that of the developing countries in their initial phase of industrialization, where an interventionist and protectionist left was geared toward the
national-developmentalist strategy.

Since the 1930s these three lefts, each characterized by a strong bureaucratic or technobureaucratic social component,[2] have replaced the right in
defining socioeconomic strategy for their respective societies. They were
initially fairly successful. The economic crisis that fostered their rise to
power was overcome during World War II. The outcome was increasing
development and social advances. However, in the late 1960s problems
began to grow, and by the 1970s the state-led development model supported by the left had lost its strength throughout the world.

I have been describing a political cycle, but we must also consider the
effects of the economic cycle, the long Kondratieff cycles, as well as a cycle
of state intervention in the economy. These cycles reached their peak in the
early 1970s and subsequently began their descent. In the capitalist countries
the growth of production per capita began to slow down. The growth rate of
income per capita decreased to half what it had been twenty years before,
and the unemployment rate increased. At the other extreme is Soviet-style
statism, whose stated goal was to foster socialism through eliminating private ownership of the means of production. Here the initial growth was
based on a vast mobilization of resources and forced savings, but this growth
could not be maintained. The crisis of statism was unleashed with the advent
of perestroika in 1986 and reached its high point in 1989 with the demo-

cratic revolution in the Eastern European countries and the collapse of communism. Finally, there is the interventionist protectionism of the Third World, particularly that of Latin America. The import substitution strategy had been successful in establishing the bases for industrialization, but it had gone as far as it could by the 1960s, although it continued to survive into the 1970s, propped up by foreign debt. By the first years of the 1980s stagnation in income per capita and high inflation rates demonstrated the conclusive failure of this model.

This is the crisis of the left. More precisely, it is a crisis of the strategy of the lefts, which suddenly appear to lack a development project. The strategies of the welfare state in the First World countries, of sheer statism in the former communist countries, and of protectionism in the Third World are no longer appropriate.

Whereas it is clear that the left is in crisis, it is necessary in our definition of the left to differentiate what is essential from what is secondary. Only then can we understand why the left will always exist and why, with each new crisis, it must be renewed to continue to play its historical role as a transformer—a key ingredient of what is usually called the left. What is essential in conceptualizing the left is the priority it gives to justice over order, its willingness to risk disorder—up to a certain point—in the name of justice. It holds the optimistic belief that society tends toward transformation and improvement. Another fundamental conviction is that the market alone is incapable of automatically regulating the economy and society, requiring some degree of state intervention. Finally, it is essential to keep the vision (even if it is a utopian one) of democratic socialism on the horizon. This is not to be confused with the elimination of private property, much less with statism—rather, it depicts a degree of democracy and social equality far greater than that existing in capitalism today.

To attain these goals and overcome this crisis, the left needs a new development strategy. It must develop a new historical project. However, at this point, rather than delving into a discussion of the general crisis and the definition of this new project within the developed countries, I concentrate my attention on Latin America and the Latin American left.

In Latin America the Great Depression of the 1930s signaled the crisis of conservative oligarchic domination and the rise to power of populist parties and governments. Populism is not exactly an ideology or a political practice of the left, but Latin America's parties of the left did participate in populist governments and often became confused with them, even though some of the more radical sectors of the left were frequently repressed by these governments. This identification—although relative—of the Latin American left with populism does have some validity, especially for those political sectors that were moderate and reformist, but also for the communist left.

In the populist pact this left was allied with industrial entrepreneurs, with modernizing sectors of the agrarian-commercial oligarchy, with the middle-class technobureaucrats and intellectuals (where the left had its strength), and with urban workers. Its role was intellectual: to provide leadership in setting the framework for the analysis of Latin American underdevelopment and establishing a development strategy.

The analysis made by the left between the 1930s and the 1950s was fairly simple and basically correct. Latin America was an underdeveloped agro-export region in transition from precapitalism or mercantile capitalism to industrial capitalism. The cause of its underdevelopment or, more precisely, the major obstacle to development lay in the primary export nature of the Latin American economies and in the unequal trade established between industrialized products from the center and agricultural and mineral products from the periphery. Industry in Latin America was still in its infant stage and was permanently threatened by competition from the industrialized countries. The agrarian-mercantile bourgeoisie, allied first with English and later with North American imperialism, was opposed to industrialization, which ran counter to its interests, using liberal arguments—particularly that of the law of comparative advantage of international commerce—to justify its opposition to industrialization, which was viewed as "artificial."

Based on this economic and political analysis, the development strategy of the left was uncomplicated and coherent. Industrialization was defined as its primary objective. In order to industrialize, it was necessary to take a basically nationalist position against "imperialism"—in reality, against foreign competition. An infant industry called for protectionism as a fundamental strategy to promote its growth. A domestic market, varying in size, already existed in each country. This market, if duly protected, could be supplied by national industries. Here we have the import substitution model of industrialization. In those cases where raising import barriers alone was insufficient to stimulate private investment (especially in capital-intensive infrastructure sectors such as energy, transportation, and basic inputs), the state would have to make direct investments.

This long-term strategy was complemented by a populist tendency, in the short term, to disregard or minimize budgetary limitations. Terms such as *adjustment* and *stabilization* were prohibited or viewed negatively. The public deficit was understood as a "Keynesian" approach to stimulating effective demand and fighting unemployment and idle capacity. Nominal wage increases (which, in fact, did not turn out to be real increases because of the accelerated rate of inflation) were also viewed as Keynesian approaches to stimulating effective demand. Foreign debt was seen as a more appropriate way to finance development than direct investment by multinational enterprises. However, because there were no ready sources of capital, Latin America had to be content with multinational investments. Although this was opposed by the more extreme sectors of the populist pact, it was accepted in principle by the dominant tendency. This type of nationalism was only protectionist: it protected local industry against competition from imports, but it did not oppose direct investments by multinational companies.

Despite being subject to recurrent crises—because of its populist nature, which caused balance-of-payments crises and subsequent orthodox stabilization programs—this view was dominant and largely successful in Latin America from the 1930s to the 1960s. There were, of course, some internal disputes. The left, within the bounds of the populist pact, tended to favor more state control and to be more nationalist than the industrial entrepreneurs. The latter were not always disposed, at least in theory, to accept the analyses and strategies proposed by the left, considering it to lean toward state control and nationalism. But in practice the entrepreneurs benefited from and supported the populist national-developmentalist strategy. Industrialization in Latin America showed enormous growth beginning in the 1930s. And until the 1960s, the success of this strategy was undeniable—one need only look at the data on the growth of product and on the increased industrial share of this product to realize it.

Yet it is significant and paradoxical that the left's development strategy did not promote income distribution. Nationalism, developmentalism, protectionism, the emphasis on the domestic market, forced savings by the state, and the application of these savings in either creating state enterprises or subsidizing private enterprises—these were the foundations of the political economy of the left, but they fundamentally favored private accumulation. This explains how, following the crisis of the 1960s, this populist strategy—which had never been exclusively an approach of the left—became the national-developmentalist strategy of the Latin American establishment, including the military.

The first clear symptoms of the crisis of the populist development strategy began to appear in the 1960s. The authoritarian technobureaucratic-capitalist regimes that were established at that time in Latin America, starting with the 1964 revolution in Brazil—a model for other countries— were the response to this crisis. In fact, the new regimes were an extension of the national-developmentalist strategy of industrialization but with the radical exclusion of the left and the workers, who, during the populist period, had a voice. It is significant, however, that the right, which now held power alone, had no alternative proposal. Its goal continued to be industrialization, its fundamental strategy remained import substitution, and its main tool was still the state-owned enterprises. In fact, this last characteristic became more pronounced because authoritarian regimes are the fruit of the alliance between the bourgeoisie and the state technobureaucracy whose power, by definition, originates in the state.

Only one thing was new about the authoritarian development strategy, aside from its supposedly antipopulist "modernizing" character. What was new was foreign debt. This debt, which had not been possible in prior decades, had now become viable. The formation of the financial Euromarket and the need to recycle petrodollars made the supply of lending capital abundant in the 1970s. All of the Latin American countries went into debt. Debt became the form par excellence for authoritarian regimes associated with international capital to guarantee the survival of the old development strategy.

During this period, particularly in the 1970s, the left undertook some sort of self-analysis and self-criticism, but it was very limited. The left realized that until the 1960s it had not paid enough attention to the issue of democracy, and it began to do so. It also realized that multinational corporations were not necessarily opposed to economic development. Finally, it came to realize the concentrating effects of the existing model of industrialization, but it attributed them to the authoritarian policies adopted by the military regimes instead of recognizing the intrinsically perverse character of the highly capital-intensive import substitution strategy.

The import substitution model and the protectionism upon which it was based were not subject to criticism. Domestic market-oriented industrialization *(industrialization hacia adentro)* continued to be the priority. International competitiveness was ignored. Technological development was hampered because it was a victim of an analogy with import substitution. Although it was not really viable, the goal in terms of science and technology was also autarky—competence in all sectors—rather than excellence in certain sectors that could be internationally competitive. In terms of short-term economic policy, ideas such as economic stabilization, fiscal adjustment, elimination of the public deficit, and austerity measures were shunned. These would be the inventions of the monetarists, the proposals of the International Monetary Fund, and the creations of the right. Marx, Keynes, and Schumpeter were spuriously invoked to justify these views.

Since the 1960s the Latin American left has been in crisis because its development strategy lost validity. Yet the left was not aware of its own crisis because all of its strength was mobilized in the struggle for redemocratization. Through the 1970s, not only the left but the right as well failed to perceive that the old approach to the causes of Latin American underdevelopment was no longer adequate and that a new strategy was necessary to stabilize the economy and promote development once again.

The old approach was no longer correct because it had been superseded by the facts. Latin America was no longer a continent in transition to capitalism but, in fact, was capitalist, even if its capitalism was archaic and exclusionary. Latin American industry was no longer an infant industry but a mature one, although not internationally competitive. The inability of many industries to compete internationally was not the result of their being new but rather a result of the insufficient dimension of the national market and the lack of incentives to incorporate technical progress, given an excessively protected domestic market.

The old development strategy was no longer functional. With the decline of the import substitution model, it was necessary to orient the Latin American economies toward exports and international competitiveness. In the first phase of industrialization the state had been the principal agent of forced savings and accumulation of capital; now the fiscal crisis of the state required that these functions be transferred to the private sector. The import substitution model and strong state intervention are effective in the first stage of industrialization, when forced savings and accumulation take precedence over cost reduction or efficiency. But in a second stage countries should adopt a market-oriented, export-led strategy geared toward the efficient use of resources.

Through foreign loans the authoritarian regimes were able to postpone economic reform and fiscal adjustment in the 1970s. The outcomes were serious macroeconomic imbalances and a large foreign debt. When the process of increasing indebtedness ended in the early 1980s the state in the Latin American countries fell victim to a fiscal crisis. The time for its growth had ended, and it needed to be trimmed down. It was time for fiscal adjustment, privatization, deregulation, and trade liberalization. The renewed state was now supposed to intervene in new areas, promoting social welfare and international competitiveness.[3]

In the 1980s the crisis of the Latin American economies engendered by the foreign debt finally exploded. This was the time for the left to acknowledge that the national-developmentalist strategy it had promoted from the 1930s to the 1950s was no longer relevant. The change took place, but rather slowly. An intellectual transition that was similar—although in the inverse direction—to the one required by the conservatives in the 1930s was now being asked of the left. Broad sectors of the left continued to think in 1950s terms, with nationalism and state control as their basic tenets. This archaic group mixed what was essential to the left—the effective commitment to income distribution and democracy—with a development strategy that, by definition, was transitory.

The Latin American right, which also needed to change because it had adhered to a state-led growth strategy, understood the new situation more quickly. When it was in power with the military, it had also adopted a national-developmentalist strategy, but liberalism is germane to conservative thinking. Nationalism was never fully accepted by the right, given its ideological ties with international capitalism.[4] Its thinking tends to be ahistorical, regarding each strategy as either permanently adequate or permanently inadequate. It does not understand that a development strategy based on protectionism and state intervention can initially be efficient and later become inefficient. When the failure of the national-developmentalist strategy was made clear, conservatives forgot their previous commitment to a state-led development strategy and became liberal if not radically neoliberal. Many felt triumphant.

The left remained in deep crisis. In addition to the crisis of the old development strategy, there was a crisis of the left on an international scale, marked by the collapse of communism and the evidence that the mere elimination of private property no longer constituted the route to socialism. As an outcome, an intellectual transition took place among many of the left's representatives. Social democracy, which in the past had been viewed with mistrust, was now becoming increasingly accepted. Economic populism, old-time nationalism, and statism were shunned. Those among the left developed an awareness of its crisis and of the need for modernization.

A new left has been emerging in the central countries since the 1970s. On the one hand, it has strongly criticized the statist or bureaucratic social formations that prevailed in the so-called socialist countries and the reduction of Marx's thought to a bureaucratic orthodoxy. On the other, this new left recognizes new realities: the environmental and feminist movements; the conception of democracy as a radical process of change; and the struggle for less-alienating labor conditions in which, through participation, workers' creativity is stimulated. Further, it addresses the social-democratic project of managing capitalism (to which there is no practical alternative today) more competently and fairly than have the conservative political parties. This new social-democratic, moderate left remains faithful to Keynesian ideas but does not mix Keynesian economic policy with economic populism.

All of these new ideas and tendencies from various quarters make up the new left—a modern left that has been developing in many ways. During the 1960s we heard about a "new left" in the developed countries. In the 1970s in the United States, inside the Democratic Party a new current of progressive politicians, whom some people identified as "Kennedy's children" and William Schneider (1990) mistakenly called "neoliberals," was born. These young politicians gave far greater emphasis to the market than to efficiency, and thus they were often mistakenly seen as conservatives. Schneider (1990:4) asked congressperson Andrew Maguire, who belongs to this group, if he considered himself a "liberal" in the U.S. meaning of the word (therefore a member of the progressive, moderate left). He replied affirmatively and added, "We have been trying to redefine the word. We have been trying to say that the words liberal and conservative are misleading rather than enlightening." These new progressive politicians aimed at blending the "liberal [progressive] tradition with the values of pragmatism, efficiency and good management, so that things would work out" (Schneider 1990:5).[5] Bill Clinton's victory in the 1992 U.S. presidential elections was an outcome of this concept of modernity. The concept has some points of contact with the neoliberal perspective but is also clearly different from it. In fact, although the United States has no social-democratic political party, Clinton's modernity is a social-democratic modernity. Clinton and his associates are as committed to the market as they are to social welfare. They count on the market and the state to coordinate the economy. They know that a true democracy demands the assertion not only of political rights but also of social rights.

Thus there is a new left in the world and also in Latin America. It is a modern left or an archaic left, as opposed to the Latin American left of the 1950s. In Brazil the Workers Party (PT), founded in 1980, appeared to be preordained to take on the role of the modern left to the extent that its cadres were among the most modern sectors of the Brazilian working class. Yet this party has, to a great extent, incorporated the ideology of the nationalist and protectionist left. We do not yet know whether the PT can become a modern party of the left. In the late 1980s, after the Brazilian Democratic Movement Party (PMDB) turned into a merely populist party, the Party of the Brazilian Social Democracy (PSDB) was founded. The PSDB purports to be the Brazilian expression of the new left, but the difficulties it faces are great— to the extent that the party's modern left is continually confronted by the old left, together with center-right sectors and sectors representative of political favoritism very similar to those found in the PMDB. During the 1989 presidential campaign its platform paper, "Challenges Facing Brazil and the PSDB," exemplified this party's attempt to define itself as the voice of the modern social-democratic left. The victory of its candidate, Fernando Henrique Cardoso, a leading intellectual, in the October 1994 presidential elections finally opened the opportunity for this new left—committed to fiscal discipline and market-oriented reform, as well as to social justice—to put its program into practice.

Nevertheless, the old left still exists. It exists not only in political parties but also in the minds of many who think of themselves as members of the left, as well as among those of the right who, in criticizing the left, identify it with the archaic left. This old left does not understand the changes that have taken place in Latin America, does not understand that the strategy of the left has changed or needs to change, and accuses those who have changed of being conservative, of belonging to the right. My experience in the Finance Ministry in 1987 clearly illustrated this.[6] In the 1994 presidential election, the fact that Cardoso received the support of the moderate right was strongly criticized by the old left, which supported the PT candidate, Luiz Inácid Lula da Silva-Lula. Intellectuals and politicians of the right, for their part, do not see that a substantial part of the left has changed, and they continue to rhetorically define the entire left in terms of the archaic left.

The new left, however, is a reality. It is a reality in the social demo cratic parties in Europe. The new democrats in the United States and President Clinton are the U.S. manifestation of this new and very moderate left. It has not yet come to power in Latin America, except as a part of political coalitions (in Chile in 1990 and Brazil in 1995). The new left rejects populism, nationalism, a protectionist strategy, and the chronic imbalances in public finance that defined the old left. It also rejects internationalism, the belief that the developed countries embody truth and rationality; it rejects neoliberalism, a rhetorical argument in favor of the minimal state; it rejects individualism and radical pessimism and is moderately optimistic with regard to the possibilities of social solidarity; it rejects the merciless emphasis on production espoused by the new right. The new left affirms the creative values of democracy; it considers a more equitable distribution of income as its fundamental objective; it will risk disorder for the sake of democracy and social justice. It is a social-liberal left because it asserts the superiority of the market in coordinating the economy but does not disregard the complementary activity of the state in the social domain and in promoting science and technology. The new left wants to promote new forms of labor participation. It is prepared to govern capitalist economies, considering itself more capable than the capitalists themselves at managing those economies. The new left understands that social democracy is not the answer to all of the world's problems or even to those of the left, but it is convinced that by promoting a social-democratic capitalism, democratic socialism will one day be possible.

❧ 9 ❧

Political Obstacles
to Economic Reform

P olitical and ideological obstacles have been crucial in Brazil's—as in
any other country's—ability to adopt sound, consistent economic
reforms. Brazil's democratization in the 1980s was based on solid economic and social reality. Contrary to the conventional interpretation, it represented the victory of civil society rather than a concession of the military
regime. But it failed to address some of the basic ideologies and political
practices that are typical of middle-income, industrialized, yet underdeveloped countries—such as, on one hand, economic populism, developmentalism, anachronistic nationalism, political clientelism, and unrealistic worker
demands and, on the other, conservatism, monetarist orthodoxy, neoliberalism, and the inability of a shortsighted business elite to recognize and
defend the national interest.

In Chapter 8 I analyzed the political crisis in Latin America, particularly the crisis of the left, because the basic cause behind that crisis was the fiscal crisis of the state. In this chapter I examine the political obstacles to economic reforms, but I interpret them in a broader sense, relating them to the
ideological debate between the left and the right. In the developed countries
political obstacles are identified with nationalist and populist policies,
which are usually identified with the left but are also germane to the opportunistic right. In addition to the nationalist and populist practices, it is also
important to detect another type of political or ideological obstacle: the
adoption of inefficient, if not ineffective, economic policies as a result of the
adoption of dogmatic monetarism and neoliberalism.[1]

In the early 1980s the economic crisis was a major player in the down-
fall of the authoritarian regime. Later, stubbornly resisting a solution, the
economic crisis became a threat to democratic regimes. Recession and high
inflation are destabilizing factors for any political regime, whether authoritarian or democratic. In the 1990s, when most Latin American political
regimes are democratic, it is democracy that is being jeopardized by the economic crisis, as we saw in Peru and Guatemala. Despite an economic crisis
provoked by extreme orthodox measures, Venezuela was able to preserve
democracy in the early 1990s, but the entire region suffered anxiety.

According to conventional wisdom, the causes of the economic crisis in

119

Brazil and, more broadly, in Latin America are political. The political obstacles I examine in this chapter clearly buttress this view. But there are also purely economic causes for the crisis. Economic reforms and stabilization policies are often inefficient and excessively costly, if not outright incompetent. And market failures—not only the classical ones, related to monopoly power and externalities, but also new ones, such as the inertial character of inflation that the market is unable to tackle—are not political problems but strictly economic ones.

In Brazil today capitalism and democracy have been consolidated. There is little doubt about the dominance of a modern, industrial, capitalist mode of production, as well as of the political and ideological hegemony of the business class. But from 1987 to 1994 new doubts arose—doubts that had not previously existed—about the country's prospects for economic growth. Capitalism rather than self-sustained growth seemed assured in Brazil.

At one time I believed that, when a country had completed its industrial and capitalist revolution, self-sustained growth would automatically follow as a consequence of the demands imposed by the accumulation of capital and the incorporation of technological progress. Following the Brazilian economic crisis, which kept income per capita stagnant for almost fifteen years, I am no longer so sure. One is forced to concede that Brazil's continued economic development depends on the adoption of a number of short- and long-run economic policies (adjustments and reforms), which involves making decisions and taking initiatives.

Democracy in Brazil is more solidly entrenched in the economic and social system than is usually acknowledged, however. First, modern industrial capitalism is able to appropriate an economic surplus through the market, thus dispensing with the direct force needed in precapitalist and mercantilist societies. Also, the bourgeoisie, or business class, does not feel threatened by the left. Further, the military and, more broadly, the authoritarians do not have alternative projects for Brazil (they are as perplexed as the bourgeoisie over how to solve the economic and political crises). Finally, the United States no longer resorts to "big stick" tactics (such as coups d'état, military interventions, and the like) as part of its strategy to consolidate capitalism in Latin America, and it is sincerely committed to consolidating democracy in the region.

But it is not possible to say that democracy has been consolidated. Guillermo O'Donnell (1988:85) emphasized that if a military coup is not likely, the "slow death" of democracy—that is, the continued loss of the effectiveness and credibility of political institutions as a result of the government's failure to meet or resolve socioeconomic problems—is another possibility.

The failure of governments to address these problems directly cannot be attributed solely to country-specific limitations or to the sheer size of economic obstacles. Real economic obstacles do exist. It is not by chance that Latin America has stagnated for ten years, ever since the foreign debt crisis manifested itself. However, the failure of Brazil's government to lead the country out of this crisis is clearly related to political practices and beliefs that are not conducive to the adoption of bold, coherent, and firm economic policies.

What are some of these political beliefs and practices? They are discussed below, where they are classified according to their political origin as obstacles originating from the opportunistic right, the moderate left, or the ideological right. One political practice is common to both the opportunistic right and the moderate left: economic populism, the distinguishing economic policy of opportunists and a basic political disease in Brazil.

Because *populism* has several meanings, the adjective *economic* is appended to distinguish it from other connotations. Populism usually carries a different meaning in Latin America than it has elsewhere, being tied to the practices of political leaders who are able to establish a direct relationship with the people without the intermediation of political parties. It is also related to the class coalitions or "populist pacts" that offered political support to import substitution industrialization. Such pacts were based on some kind of alliance among industrialists, workers, and the new, bureaucratic middle class.[2] In contrast, economic populism refers to a more general, although related, political practice: fiscal laxity, usually tied to naive distributivism.

The first economist to write on economic populism was probably Adolfo Canitrot (1975). Guillermo O'Donnell, although he is a political scientist, has also written admirably on the subject (1977). Carlos Díaz-Alejandro (1979) has addressed economic populism, specifically in connection with the "populist cycle."[3] Populist policies usually precede and are also the cause of economic crises, which then require painful orthodox stabilization programs.

There are two types of economic populism: (1) populism of the left, often characterized by naive redistribution of income and the "refusal-to-adjust" attitude; and (2) populism of the right, a phenomenon very close to developmentalism. In any case it is a kind of fiscal laxity, defined by a tendency to acquiesce to most of the demands of workers and businesspeople. This course is invariably embraced by opportunistic and clientelist politicians.

Populist economic policies lead to increases in the public deficit and to an imbalance in the current accounts (balance of payments). Some of the more common populist practices include wage increases for public-sector workers and officials; expenditure increases by the state; increased consumption and investment subsidies; overvaluation of the local currency, provoking increases in real wages and artificial prosperity; and credit subsidies offered by the official banks. These concessions offer something to every-one—public officials, businesspeople, and workers.

The outcome of these practices is the populist cycle. It begins with the government adopting a combination of the following policies: overvaluation of the exchange rate, which reduces inflation, increases wages and consumption, promotes imports, and restrains exports; direct increases in public-sector salaries; increased public expenditure, leading to a higher budget deficit; artificially low domestic interest rates; and artificially low prices and tariffs for state-owned enterprises. Thus the first phase of the cycle is characterized by a high rate of consumption and investment, an accelerated growth rate, and a decline in the rate of inflation as a result of the overvaluation of the exchange rate and the reduction of real public prices.

However, this stage proves to be a short-lived paradise because these practices generate distortions in the economy. Disequilibrium appears in the balance of payments as imports increase and exports decline. The budget deficit soars. Eventually, as the threat of a balance-of-payments crisis becomes evident, the currency is devalued. Domestic prices increase, setting in motion an often dramatic inflationary spiral. This stage of the cycle often leads to a severe crisis, sometimes accompanied by, at the minimum, a change of ministers if not a coup d'état, and it inevitably ends with a radical change in economic policy.

The expansionist policies of 1979–1980 (probably the worst mistake in the history of economic policy in Brazil) and of the Cruzado Plan (an excellent plan and an opportunity lost to incompetent management) are typical examples of recent populist episodes in Brazil. The 1979–1980 experience was conducted by conservative economists under the military regime; the Cruzado Plan was designed by competent economists soon after the democratic transition took place, but its implementation was populist.

I t is important to distinguish the opportunistic right from the ideological right. Of course, opportunists exist all across the political spectrum, from right to left. An opportunist is, by definition, a politician who lacks firm ideological convictions. Opportunists command the right rather than the left only because capitalism is dominant in Brazil. In a capitalist country political opportunists, whatever their ostensible political persuasion (even if they purport to be left or center-left), will tend to be conservative because their fundamental interests require that all possible and imaginable concessions be made to the rich and the powerful.

To be developmentalist is to have economic growth as the major objective, subordinating stabilization and income distribution. This was a dominant ideology and political practice in Latin America from the 1930s to the 1980s.

Clientelism is a political practice halfway between populism and sheer corruption. Populism, clientelism, and corruption imply the use of public funds: in the case of populism public funds are used impersonally to assure the goodwill of those groups and communities that benefit from public expenditure; in the case of corruption public funds are privately appropriated. Clientelism also involves the use of public funds, but indirectly. Politicians engaged in clientelist practices do not steal but use state resources to enhance their personal careers. The Brazilian term for this practice is *fisiológismo*.

The fisiológismo politician is, by definition, an opportunist, one who treats politics like a business in which political influence is the means of exchange. He is *fisiológico* because he puts his own personal and material interests above the ideas and moral principles he has pledged to serve and that are supposed to orient political action.

These opportunistic practices are deeply embedded in Brazil's political system and are both a symptom and a consequence of the country's low level of citizenship. Lack of information, a poor political education, and mistrust of popular candidates are characteristic of the average Brazilian voter. Thus, in the words of Wanderley Reis (1988:24), "given the characteristics of the Brazilian electorate, it is not realistic to expect that the stabilization of the democratic game takes place around parties that are defined in ideological terms; it is more likely that the process of formation of the political parties will continue to be based on traditional clientelism with an electoral appeal of populist tones."

D ifferent, but producing similar results, are the ideologies and political practices of the left. The golden years of the left were the 1930s to the 1950s. Since the 1960s the left has faced increasing problems as the communist or statist model of society experienced hard times in the former Soviet Union, and the state-led import substitution strategy became disfunctional in Latin America. This strategy was appropriate for the 1950s, but by the early 1960s it became apparent—as I pointed out at the time—that domestic and international conditions had changed sufficiently to require a new analysis of the economy and a new strategy for economic growth.[4]

In the 1970s and early 1980s the moderate left severely criticized the orthodox economic policies put forward by the authoritarian regime. Sometimes this criticism was justified, but often it represented merely old-fashioned populist and nationalist slogans. When the transition to democracy was completed in 1985 the new democratic government (the Sarney-PMDB administration) proved to be the outcome of a populist and nationalist political coalition of the opportunistic right and the old left. The old left clung to its typical ideologies and policies, one of them being old-fashioned nationalism.

In the 1940s and 1950s the left espoused the proposition that "imperialists," or foreign interests (including multinational enterprises), had allied themselves with the interests of domestic agro-mercantilist capital to prevent or oppose industrialization. However, in the mid-1950s those same multinationals proceeded to make large investments in manufacturing, thus altering the situation and acting in contradiction to this proposition (Bresser Pereira 1963; Cardoso and Faletto 1969).[5] If this analysis had once been true, it was no longer so. Nevertheless, some old-fashioned nationalists still think in terms of the 1950s. As we will see in Chapter 16, these anachronistic nationalists fail to understand that to be nationalist today requires having a clear notion, in each case, of what the national interest really is rather than adopting a nondiscriminating attitude toward multinational corporations or, more broadly, imperialists.[6]

In the mid-1960s the authoritarian regime opted for an export-led strategy of development. This strategy benefited the country, although in the short run it produced the perverse effect of making sustained rates of internal demand compatible with a concentration of income. From the beginning, the moderate left opposed this strategy and adopted a domestic market orientation, failing to acknowledge that not only had the import substitution growth model exhausted its virtues by the early 1960s, but the alternative growth model—based on highly capital-intensive import substitution projects—was even more disposed to concentrate income over the long run than the model based on the export of labor-intensive manufactured goods.

During the 1970s it was common for spokespersons for the left to criticize Korea and Taiwan as mere "export platforms" for the multinationals, whereas Roberto Campos, one of Brazil's leading right-wing intellectuals, viewed these same countries as liberal societies. Today we know that both were wrong. The extraordinary development of these countries was based on an export-led strategy in which the state played a decisive, and the multinationals a minor, role. Korea and Taiwan were neither export platforms nor liberal economies. Furthermore, their development strategy proved consistent with a much more even distribution of income than that existing in Brazil. One cause of this better income distribution was the agrarian reform undertaken by these countries following World War II; another factor was the export-led growth strategy, which was necessarily based on labor-intensive industries.

A resistance to adjustment—which I am calling the refusal-to-adjust attitude—emerged as a consequence of an entrenched commitment to developmentalism (in this case also a form of economic populism) that characterized Latin American economists of the left, myself included, during the 1950s.[7] We severely criticized the adjustment of the 1960s. The fact that stabilization programs were usually based on reducing wages rather than on fiscal adjustment was indeed good reason for our criticism. However, the left predicated its criticism almost entirely on a "no to recession" slogan, and, in so doing, slopped over into economic populism. The left's only economic argument was a spurious adoption of Keynesian ideas favoring budget deficits and a demand-led development strategy.

In 1979, when some form of economic adjustment became absolutely necessary, the developmental, populist economic policy adopted by the right-wing military regime was—not surprisingly—supported by economists of the structuralist moderate left. When adjustment finally came in 1981, the left wrongly adopted the view that adjustment was unnecessary when, in fact, there was no other alternative. At the time it was impossible, as well as undesirable, to maintain large deficits in both trade and current accounts. The only serious innovative criticism of the orthodox adjustment policies to emanate from the moderate left came from those economists who developed the theory of inertial inflation.

A redistributive wage policy is typical of economic populism everywhere. Income concentration is recognizably a major problem in Brazil, which has one of the most uneven and unjust income patterns in the world. However, this fact alone does not legitimate unrealistic wage distributivism. A politically progressive economic policy in Brazil will necessarily have to fight this uneven distribution, which is uneven not only among wages and profits but also among wages and salaries. And when the policy proposes wage increases, it has to be careful not to increase real wages more than productivity.

Whenever such a plan was tried in the past, profits were threatened and the inflation rate accelerated. This is unavoidable. Wage policy should be limited to three objectives: (1) to protect real wages from inflation; (2) to assure that increases in productivity are transferred to the workers; and (3) to reduce wage and salary differences through a gradual increase in the minimum wage. Presumably it would be possible to increase wages more than productivity without affecting profits if either the difference were paid for by the rentiers or there were an increase in state efficiency that would allow for a tax reduction, which would be equivalent to the real wage increase. A third alternative is the prevalence of capital-saving technical progress, expressed in the increase of the output-capital relation. However, these alternatives are difficult to accomplish.

Efficient means of redistributing income include export-led industrialization, industrial policy oriented to the production of wage goods, agrarian reform, progressive tax reform, and orientation of public expenditures to the poor. Yet these ideas are rarely acceptable to the populist left. An oft-cited slogan is "wage increases are not a cause of inflation." This was true for a long period during the authoritarian regime because real wages either lagged behind productivity or were reduced in absolute terms. Nevertheless, a different picture began to emerge by the end of the 1970s. In 1984, following the defeat of the authoritarian regime, unrealistic demands from workers increased sharply. The salaried middle class, which was employed in the public sector, became particularly active in this area. As the distributive conflict deepened, the budget deficit increased, prompting the rate of inflation to accelerate. Real wage gains tended to be short-lived. Increased inflation soon wiped out any real gains, and the only lasting result was a higher rate of inflation.

In conclusion, some ideas and political practices of the moderate left, which are very much related to economic populism—old-fashioned nationalism, domestic market orientation, the refusal-to-adjust attitude, and wage distributivism—are not consistent with rational, coherent economic policies. Further, the political practices of the opportunistic right—developmentalism and clientelism—are not related to economic populism. They are political obstacles to stabilization and growth.

The ideological right is thus also an originator of irrational economic policy. This category includes the monetarist economists and neoliberal ideologues who adopt a militant theoretical view opposing virtually every kind of state intervention in the economy and who support only purely orthodox economic policies to stabilize the Brazilian economy. An increasing fraction of Brazil's business elite falls into this category. Its leaders may not be opportunists, but they are ideologically conservative. In developing countries conservatism means ideological subordination to the dominant value and belief system existing in the central countries, over and above typical conservative characteristics such as placing order above social justice and resisting change.

The ideological right is truly convinced that its views on economic policy are intrinsically rational, based as they are on both the logic of capitalism and their own logic. They rely on their own rationality to confront the irrationality of both the populist left and the opportunistic politicians. They control the means of communication, so they are usually able to convey their ideas to the general public, thus reinforcing their ideological hegemony.

Unfortunately, not only are the ideas of the ideological right less rational than they purport to be, but they also raise a major obstacle to the adoption of a consistent economic policy in Brazil, especially when the time calls for bold, far-reaching economic decisions. What are these views and political practices of the ideological right?

Social conservatism is an obvious problem in a country where income levels are so sharply skewed, with so much going to so few. In Brazil the tax burden is relatively low, and the tax system very regressive. Thus progressive tax reform is an obvious tool for reducing the public deficit and distributing income more equitably. The ideological right systematically opposes tax reforms that increase the tax burden in any way or that make it more progressive. On the one hand, it refuses to recognize that the tax burden in Brazil is indeed low, whereas on the other hand it exhibits a sincere concern for the lack of incentives to savings and investment. In reality, tax renunciation and tax incentives to business enterprises are a major source of Brazil's budget deficits because they serve to reduce the effective tax burden. Most of these "tax breaks" or incentives lost their raisons d'être long ago. Still, the ideological right tends to ignore the problem, and it fights for lower taxes.

Although the ideological right professes its concern regarding income concentration in Brazil, it does nothing to help solve the problem. A social pact, which is essential to control wages and curb inflation, would involve concessions to the workers in terms of social reform. However, as a rule the ideological right opposes any effort at social reforms. This behavior serves its interests as a class and is also based on the firm conviction that social order takes priority over social justice: order must never be endangered in the name of justice.

Monetarism began as a conservative counteraction to Keynesianism. Monetarism originally developed in the Friedman version and subsequently evolved through the theory of rational expectations of the "new classics" (Sargent; Lucas). It is based on a fundamental contradiction: it is a macro-economic theory, necessarily oriented toward economic policy, that professes radical abstinence of state intervention. However, this abstinence is not actually practiced. The stabilization policies monetarism recommends tend to be both active and aggressive. When and if the economy stabilizes, however, the stability achieved is always so precarious that continued intervention by the state is required to maintain it.

At the present time, monetarism, in its rational expectations variety, is the economic religion of the developed capitalist countries. As a result of the ideological subjection of the elites in the peripheral countries to those at the center, an almost unrestricted monetarism has been adopted by the ideological right in a peripheral country like Brazil. Two examples will suffice. Although in Brazil inflation has structural origins and an inertial character, making the money supply endogenous or passive, the right believes inflation can be controlled simply by the application of monetary and fiscal policies.[8] In an underdeveloped economy, such as that of Brazil, economic imbalances run very deep, but, based on monetarism, the ideological right believes market forces alone will be able to solve all problems.

The successive failures of this approach to solve the economic crises in Argentina, Brazil, and Chile contributed to a certain discrediting of monetarism in the early 1980s. However, after the failure of the heterodox Austral and Cruzado plans, monetarism recovered some of its lost prestige. Suddenly, as a result of a very interesting maneuver by the ideological right, conventional stabilization policies (based on fiscal and monetary policies, over which a relative consensus exists among good economists) were equated with orthodox monetarism and were opposed to Keynesian and structuralist theories, which were now thought to be heterodox. Through this rhetorical strategy, the ideological right was able to identify heterodoxy with economic populism. Whereas the theory of inertial inflation was being incorporated by mainstream economics in the developed countries,[9] and an increasing number of economists came to admit the advantage of combining conventional or orthodox (fiscal and monetary) with heterodox policies (policies that neutralize inertia), the monetarist neoliberal right in Brazil still insisted on shunning heterodox strategies and advocated only conventional policies to control inflation. When a stabilization program—the Real Plan—finally controlled inflation in 1994, monetarists refused to acknowledge its essentially heterodox character, although its authors were neostructuralist economists, and the URV was an ingenious strategy to neutralize the staggered contracts, that is, inertia.

In fact, economic policies that are specifically monetarist in nature are often inadequate or plainly irrational. It is obvious that a dogmatic rejection of state intervention, including macroeconomic regulation and an income policy, prevents a monetarist policy from dealing with the real problems of the Brazilian economy. Monetarism also tends to overlook certain characteristics specific to that economy. Inertial inflation may be a universal phenomenon, but the degree of formal and informal indexation in Brazil makes it specific to the Brazilian situation, creating a particularly Brazilian problem requiring measures especially tailored to its nature.

Neoliberalism is the complement of monetarism. The Washington consensus was one of its manifestations in Latin America. The theme has been well discussed in this book. The ideological right knows (or should know) that the state played a pivotal role in Brazil's industrialization, although it persists in ignoring that fact. In the 1980s, after becoming heavily indebted to foreign interests, the Brazilian state suffered a severe fiscal crisis that stymied economic growth. For those who subscribe to unvarnished neoliberalism, this indicates that the state should totally abstain from playing any economic role and be reduced to the condition of a minimum state. Although this may indeed be a sensible alternative, the primary task is to solve the fiscal crisis: the goal is not to expel the state from the economy but to enable it to assume new roles in promoting welfare and technological progress.

A natural aspiration of Brazil's business community is to further integrate Brazil into the international economy. If this were achieved, Brazilian capitalism would be less vulnerable, both economically and ideologically. I will not argue about these objectives because they are fairly consistent. If a clear economic and ideological hegemony of the bourgeoisie exists (as I believe it does), and if Brazilian capitalism is well established, this desire for greater integration with the developed world is rather natural. The problem is how to accomplish this integration. Brazilian conservatives frequently believe this can be achieved by "being international." However, right-wing internationalism often takes the form of an uncritical subordination to the interests of the developed countries. This attitude—which I am calling subordinate internationalism—is a phenomenon of everyday life in Brazil. It is a consequence of the economic and cultural domination the developed world exerts over the periphery. In the case of the ideological right, this subordination takes on a militancy as inconsistent with the national interests as is the old nationalism of the left.

Another name for subordinate internationalism is the confidence-building strategy, which business elites in Latin America often advocate. The idea is to follow all recommendations or suggestions made by Washington (the administration) and New York (the financial system) in an attempt to build confidence. Mexico has consistently followed this strategy since August 1989, when it irresponsibly signed the term sheet of a debt agreement with commercial banks just six months after the Brady Plan was announced. Debt reduction was insignificant, but, as it was then argued, it "built confidence." From that time until the December 1994 crash, the Salinas administration was engaged in building confidence at the expense of the national interest and of macroeconomic fundamentals.

Today Latin American conservatives see the Chilean experience as an example of sound, successful economic policy. They are basically correct. Chile was the exception to the rule. After making major mistakes and being immersed in a severe crisis in 1982, Chile's authoritarian administration was able to overcome fiscal crisis and resume growth. Since democratization in 1990 the new democratic government has kept the macroeconomic fundamentals under control while giving stronger emphasis to social policies. Neither the authoritarian administration nor the democratic one privatized the copper mines, the source of a large proportion of the strongly positive public savings that prevail in Chile.

Chile's per capita income at the end of 1988, however, was still below that of 1980; 1987 wages were 6 percent below the 1980 level (Piedra 1988). Additionally, both poverty and concentration of income had increased. The mixed (positive and negative) results achieved by the Chilean economy were the product of orthodox policies and an authoritarian regime. John Sheahan (1986:161) noted that economic policies typical of the authoritarian regimes in Latin America include reduced price controls, lower protection, serious efforts to limit budget deficits, strict control of wages, and conditions highly favorable to foreign investors. Sheahan mixes regime rhetoric with the actions taken. In actual fact, Latin American authoritarian regimes do not necessarily adopt orthodox or neoliberal economic policies. Their rhetoric is invariably opposed to state intervention and protectionism. Although they may preach fiscal austerity, they hardly practice what they preach. The excessive external indebtedness and the corresponding public deficits of the 1970s were all incurred by authoritarian regimes in Brazil, Argentina, Chile, and Peru. Sheahan is on firmer ground, however, when he worries about the ability of Latin America's nonauthoritarian governments to survive the increase in populist policies, a trend that has only intensified since redemocratization: wage increases above the growth of per capita income; increases in public expenditures; and a trend toward excessive protectionism.

In summary, the combination of populist, developmental, and orthodox political practices and ideologies constitutes a major obstacle to the adoption of consistent, rational economic policies in Brazil and, more broadly, in Latin America. These practices led to fiscal crises, balance-of-payments problems, and inflation; the ideologies resulted in incompetent macroeconomic management, recurrent recession, and concentration of income.

❖ 10 ❖

The Collor Administration: Recurrent Political Crises

In the history of Brazil, the Fernando Collor de Mello administration (March 1990–December 1992) will remain a dramatic case of contradiction. On one hand, it changed the country's political agenda because it was able to implement bold and badly needed market-oriented economic reforms and fiscal adjustment. Although there had been attempts in this direction since 1987, it was during the Collor administration that the old national-developmentalist ideas were effectively confronted and defeated. Yet in spite of having given full support to his two economy ministers, Collor's administration was unable to control inflation, and, sadly, his government ended with actual impeachment after charges of corruption had been fully demonstrated.

The Collor administration was characterized by recurrent political crises. In its first year President Collor clearly leaned more toward confrontation than conciliation with the business community and, more broadly, with civil society. At times he was courageous, if not heroic, implementing market-oriented reforms and fighting hyperinflation with strict monetary and fiscal measures. Yet this heroism was eventually impaired by its self-sufficiency and quasi arrogance. During this period he revealed an enormous difficulty with, if not resistance to, listening to and engaging in dialogue with the society. As a result, his administration began to face a serious problem of legitimacy and loss of support from civil society.[1] With the dismissal of Zélia Cardoso de Mello—who matched Collor in bravery and arrogance—and the choice of the low-profile Marcílio Marques Moreira as minister of the economy in April 1991, Collor began a second phase of his administration, the initial objective of which was to recover the support of civil society, especially the business community. Yet in May–June 1992 the government was again immersed in a deep political crisis, this time as a result of being accused of corruption. This crisis eventually led to the president's being impeached in September 1992, with Vice President Itamar Franco replacing him in office. In this chapter I try to present a broad picture of the political ups and downs of the Collor administration.

The government began with a vote of confidence from civil society. The Collor Plan I received broad support in its first months. Its failure, which I

131

analyze in Chapter 13, plus the increasing corruption charges led the government to its first political crisis.

A significant change occurred in the Collor administration, beginning in April 1991 with the replacement of Zélia Cardoso by Marcílio Marques Moreira in the Finance Ministry and ending in early 1992 with a complete change in the cabinet and the appointment of some well-known and respected intellectuals to some cabinet positions. As a result, the administration, which had been immersed in a serious legitimacy crisis, partially recovered the support of civil society. This positive change was underlined by the fact that the inflation rate, which had been accelerating in 1991, stabilized at around 20 percent a month in the first semester of 1992. This was viewed as a government victory.

Yet in May 1992 a new and very serious political crisis erupted, triggered by the president's brother Pedro Collor's disclosures about corruption in the government. The weight of the accusations, which soon multiplied, fell on the president, who lost the support he had recently recovered. In September of that year Congress temporarily removed Collor from office, and in December he avoided formal impeachment by resigning a few hours before the Senate decided to remove him permanently from office.

I n Brazil it is possible to be elected without the support of the business community, but it is not possible to govern without that support. This is true in any capitalist country, but it is particularly so in Brazil because a dual democracy exists: in an election a vast majority of the dispossessed chooses the president; the next day, however, only a small elite—a minute segment of civil society in relation to the mass of 80 million electors—can influence the government.

In this tiny civil society, where—in various organized and interrelated ways—the business community, the press, scientists, celebrities, labor leaders, and associations of all types play a part, the business community is the largest, most powerful, and most influential group. A president can be elected in spite of this group, as Collor was, or against this group, as would have been the case if Lula—the PT candidate—had been elected president in 1989, but no president can govern without its support.

However, precisely because this society is dual and it is theoretically possible to elect a candidate without the real support of the business community, it is very tempting, once elected, to govern without it, to continue to rely on the mass of electors for support. President Collor basically succumbed to this temptation during the first year of his administration. It was this fact, more than the failure of his anti-inflation policy and the recession, that plunged his administration into a deep political crisis, actually a legitimacy crisis (that is, a loss of the support of civil society) similar to those that had plagued the last three years of the Figueiredo administration and the last two years of the Sarney administration. The difference is that these other legitimacy crises took place when the respective administrations lost the support of civil society in spite of their efforts to prevent this, whereas the Collor administration had given the opposite impression. Seemingly ignoring the fact that popularity comes from the electors but that legitimacy, in the political and juridical sense of the term, originates in civil society and especially in the business community, the Collor administration almost deliberately attempted to govern without civil society. By doing this, it engaged in a dangerous and exhausting conflict that eventually, when the charges of corruption that involved him directly were pressed, led to impeachment proceedings against Collor at the end of 1992.

Although the participants in civil society—especially the business community—always complain about their lack of power, they in fact have enormous power. When for some reason they are not invited to participate in a government, they respond with words and acts. Words wield enormous power and an ideological hegemony in the social arena because, as a group, society is in the best position to form public opinion. Acts, in turn, constitute the daily decisions on prices and investments.

Capitalist societies are democratic in part because democratic values are a part of their ideological foundations, as are liberal and individualistic values, and in part because the democratic regime is the only one compatible with the effective participation of civil society in politics. Although the business community, intellectuals, and civil society in general represent a minority in society, they constitute a large mass of people who demand political participation.

It is clear that any ruler who hopes to be a statesperson cannot simply bow to society. Such a ruler would not govern. The relationship of rulers with the powerful, both at home and abroad, is always conflictive. The polar alternatives are always submission or confrontation. A middle ground between these two extremes must be found—not one of mediocrity but a strategic one in which advance and retreat, the affirmation of one's convictions, and the ability to compromise amalgamate in many ways.

Self-sufficient, almost arrogant in its first phase between March 1990 and April 1991, the Collor administration listened little and talked even less with society. The choice of Marcílio Marques Moreira as minister of the economy represented an attempt at change. The new minister was a conciliator who had a respected team of economists and bureaucrats. He seemed a good match for the younger, more aggressive president. With Zélia's departure, the heroic phase of the Collor administration ended; with the entrance of Marcílio, the accommodative phase began. During the heroic phase the administration lost its political legitimacy through its confrontations with society and its foreign creditors. As a trade-off, it initiated bold structural reforms—trade liberalization and privatization—that are fundamental for overcoming the crisis of the state. In the accommodative phase, reforms were continued, but no effective stabilization plan was adopted.[2]

In the second half of 1991, to deal with the legitimacy crisis and the deep friction between President Collor and civil society, Brazil's political parties initiated a debate on a possible "national understanding"—that is, a political agreement. Its goal, as the president saw it, was to obtain support for his proposed amendments to the Constitution. In fact, the goal of this national understanding could only be to reestablish confidence in the administration. This was well understood by Senator Fernando Henrique Cardoso, when, in a speech in the Senate, he formally proposed the political agreement.[3] Brazil was undergoing a very serious political crisis, a classical crisis of loss of legitimacy by the administration. A national understanding would make sense only if it resulted in renewed confidence in the administration, thus making it able to govern once more.

The Collor administration concentrated on a set of constitutional amendments, which were known as the *emendão,* or big amendment. Reform of the Constitution was indeed necessary. The 1988 Constitution was the last manifestation of the national-developmentalist ideas that dominated the political coalition that led the transition to democracy in Brazil between the mid-1970s and 1984. Although the outcome was a democratic compromise between the supporters of a state-led strategy on the right and the left, and the liberals, mostly on the right, the text was marked by some degree of nationalism and statism. Additionally, it decentralized fiscal revenue to states and municipalities without transferring responsibilities. It made public administration extremely rigid, particularly the management of universities and hospitals, which lost autonomy and were treated as government departments. It assured social rights, particularly retirement rights, that were incompatible with a balanced budget.

The Collor administration recognized this fact. The 1988 Constitution had become an obstacle to overcoming the fiscal crisis of the state. However, the basic cause of the political crisis plaguing Brazil at that time was not to be found in the Constitution. Its background was in the political vacuum that had formed in the country since the 1987 collapse of the populist democratic pact that produced the transition to democracy.[4] Its most general cause was the economic crisis—centered on the high and persistent rate of inflation and on the crisis of the state—I examined in the first part of this book. Its immediate causes were, on one hand, the failure of the Collor administration's stabilization strategy and, on the other, the wave of corruption charges involving almost the entire federal administration.

A political agreement such as the one proposed could only be based on a revamping of the administration, making it free from corruption and able to deal with the fiscal crisis, to stabilize prices, and to resume development. In its new form, the president would preserve his powers while sharing them with the sectors of society that had taken part in the political agreement.

This seemed to be understood by President Collor, who in early 1992 effected a sweeping change in his cabinet. The quasi arrogance of the first year of his administration was replaced with a more humble and negotiating attitude. His belief that all decisions should be based on his own judgment and courage was replaced by a greater willingness to listen to others. The idea that he could govern supported only by the small team that had helped elect him was replaced by a much greater willingness to include capable politicians in his cabinet. Clearly corrupt or incompetent members of what was usually called his intimate circle were removed. The president started to appeal insistently to national agreement while reaffirming his belief in a "social-liberal" course for Brazil.[5]

It could be said that the president decided to change because he had no choice. The fact is, he showed that he was able to learn and change. It could also be said that the negotiations were limited to Congress. They had not yet been extended to the rest of society, especially to business and labor leaders, but it would not have been difficult to have taken this step.

Collor's call for a new understanding, expressed in a series of newspaper articles, was in general poorly received. The failure of his radical attempts to control inflation was vivid in the minds of the people. Intellectuals and the left were mistrustful.

Collor had adopted a bold program of economic reforms led by trade liberalization and privatization. In the opinion of most left-wing intellectuals, these reforms identified the Collor administration with the neoliberal right. This was a mistaken view. Neoliberalism is the ideology of the new right. It is a neoconservative view of society that is radically opposed to the state's intervening in the economy. Neoliberalism is the old economic liberalism updated by the neoclassical views of the Austrian school (Haiku), by the monetarist and the new neoclassical microeconomics (Friedman and Lucas, respectively), and by the politico-economic critique of the state carried out by the rational choice school (Buchanan and Olson). Neoliberalism is what Margaret Thatcher tried unsuccessfully to implement in Britain for eleven years. Neoliberalism is what the Reagan administration preached rather than practiced. Because neoliberalism is a utopian view of society in which the state is minimal, deprived of any economic and social role, the U.S. neoliberal experience was wrapped up in a curious mixture of conservative and populist policies that led the economy to fiscal crisis and seriously aggravated the country's social problems.[6]

Neoliberalism is deeply pessimistic and individualistic about the possibilities of social cooperation and collective action. Its objective is the minimal state. Industrial and technological policies make no sense, and even short-range macroeconomic policies are fallacious. The market is perfectly self-adjustable in accordance with the expectations of economic agents. Moreover, the real neoliberal condemns social policy itself because it inhibits work and individual initiative. As Albert Hirschman (1991) demonstrated, this new right is founded on the "perverse effect principle," already present in Edmund Burke's social philosophy. This principle holds that the attempt to improve the distribution of income and reach greater social equality is perverse to the extent that its real effects are the opposite of its objectives. It does not matter that the history of the European social democracies refutes this proposition. The perverse effect principle is a powerful ideological argument against more-effective social and economic state action. Additionally, it is the standard explanation for all of the failures of such actions.

According to this concept of neoliberalism, Collor was clearly not a neoliberal; nor are most of the Latin American politicians who have adopted market-oriented reforms since the late 1980s.[7] The industrial and technological policy his administration attempted to execute was not neoliberal by definition. Trying to assign a key role to the market in the coordination of the economy is not neoliberalism; it is pure common sense if the state has grown too much. When the state faces a pressing fiscal crisis, fiscal discipline and privatization of state-owned enterprises are obvious outcomes. Through privatization the state can obtain the resources it needs to reduce its debt instead of investing further in productive activities the private sector can perform more efficiently. Of course, foreign trade should have been liberalized long ago, when the strategy of import substitution became exhausted in the early 1960s. Collor was called a neoliberal because of a much too broad interpretation of the term, which the left in Latin America insists on using.

In Brazil several forms of liberalism are found within the business class, but neoliberalism as such has not been adopted by any relevant sector of society. To be conservative in Brazil does not mean to be against state intervention except for rhetorical purposes. The authoritarian capitalist-bureaucratic coalition that ruled the country between 1964 and 1984 was both conservative and interventionist. In the late 1980s neoliberal rhetoric entered the discourse of Brazilian conservative politicians and businesspeople, but a corresponding political practice did not emerge. Even among the intellectuals it is hard to find true representatives of this perspective.

Criticism of the gap between Collor's words and his deeds was constant during his administration. On February 2, 1992, the president tried to respond to his critics in an article in the *Folha de S. Paulo,* followed by several others. His speeches and interviews showed a modern, democratic, socially oriented thinking. They contained conservative elements but could not possibly be confused with a neoliberal view. Collor's ideological inspiration was José Guilherme Merquior, who was definitely not a neoliberal but was instead a distinguished intellectual very close to—although a little to the right of—social democracy.

Collor's articles and speeches were aimed at national development. The business community, operating freely in the market, would be the main agent of this development, and competition would be a fundamental factor in an efficient allocation of resources. The market, however, is not the nearly perfect mechanism for economic coordination the neoliberal economic models claim it to be. Thus, the flaws of the market, according to Collor, should be compensated for by state action, not only in the social and environmental area—the distributive realm—but also in the productive realm: technological development and industrial-agricultural policies.

While occupying the presidency, Collor did not hold back from fighting inflation. In this area his administration was very different from the previous one. The Collor administration was not populist. The president was willing to face any political difficulty. He accepted unpopularity without hesitation if the objective was to stabilize the economy. In the almost three years he governed Brazil he gave full support to his ministers of the economy, both Zélia and Marcílio. A fiscal adjustment was in fact carried out, although incompletely. Continual Treasury surpluses were an objective fact. The reduction of both the public deficit and the internal public debt was undeniable. If inflation was not controlled, it was not for lack of strength and determination on the part of the president but rather was the result of the inefficiency of the stabilization programs, which were unable to address the particular character of inertial inflation.

If Collor's words were positive, his deeds—such as the selection of corrupt ministers and advisers in the first phase of his administration or the undiscriminating attacks on business and media critics or the inability to listen—contradicted them. The change in his cabinet in 1992 opened new perspectives for his administration. A moderate increase in its popularity in the polls indicated this.[8] Yet the political scandal that erupted in May 1992, involving the president in serious accusations of corruption, led immediately to a loss of popularity. A poll conducted in June of that year indicated this decline: 65 percent of respondents viewed the Collor administration as bad or very bad; 65 percent believed Collor was involved in corruption; and 32 percent believed he should renounce the presidency (*Folha de S. Paulo,* June 25, 1992). In September, when the impeachment vote was taken in the House of Representatives, the vote was almost unanimous (only 61 of the 505 representatives voted in Collor's favor or were absent). At that time opinion polls showed that around 90 percent of the population viewed the Collor administration as bad or very bad.

According to Philippe Faucher's observation at a conference in São Paulo in April 1992, "the current Brazilian economic policy is at the same time the only possible and the worst alternative."[9] It was the only one possible because society had shown itself to be unable to visualize another. It was the worst because it was destroying Brazil's productive capacity—the average real interest rate in 1992 was 30 percent—without controlling inflation.

The economic crisis Brazil faces is defined by stagnation and high inflation rates; the political crisis is delineated by the lack of a political coalition that could define national goals and give political backing to the administration. The result of this kind of crisis is to immobilize the government and society itself.

In a situation such as this it is understandable that Marcílio's economic policy during the second phase of the Collor administration was "the only one possible." It was the only one possible because it was a nonpolicy, a "nothing plan," as André Lara Resende suggested. The conventional stabilization plan resulted from the failure of the previous price freezes and from the fear of new real attempts to stabilize the index-linked or inertial high inflation. It was a nonpolicy because it defined itself as *laisser-aller,* because it hoped that all problems would be solved automatically by the market, and because it recognized the government's impotence to define and implement any program.

Actually, as we will see in Chapter 11, when there is no broader political coalition, no national goal has been defined, and the only possible policy is that of laisser-aller, the general solution is to transfer the costs to the state—which is seen as something distinct from society. Each group, economic sector, and region of the country discovers that the general solution is a very special one: it is to exact the costs from the state, to make it pay a bill it is unable to pay and thus perpetuate inflation and put off the necessary structural reforms. This perverse situation will last until it becomes possible to define a new political and social pact that makes feasible a concerted action by the administration and society against inflation and for structural reforms.

G iven the failure to stabilize the economy, an alternative is to wait for chaos to arrive, for open rather than indexed hyperinflation. In Argentina it was the economic chaos associated with hyperinflation and the liberal shock that made the alteration of economic policy possible. The country's economy was exhausted; Argentines were exhausted. In late 1992 Brazil had not yet reached that level of fatigue. The Brazilian economy is much more powerful, diversified, and resistant than the Argentine economy. But it had hit what we could call "the rational bottom of the well."

The rational bottom of the well is the point at which it is no longer even minimally rational to continue to try to muddle through the crisis. The bottom is not economic and social chaos. It is not radical impoverishment. Brazil does not need to become a Bangladesh, just as the United States— which is also facing grave macroeconomic maladjustment problems—does not need to become a Brazil before it starts to reform and to adjust. Long before this, the peoples of Brazil and the United States will understand that adjustment can no longer be postponed and that the net costs of adjustment (costs of adjustment minus costs of adjusting and reforming) have turned negative. Even for people with a very short time preference, adjustment will be less costly than its postponement.[10]

Literally, the bottom of the well is the bottom of the crisis, but what is the bottom of the crisis? The point at which it is no longer possible to go deeper into crisis? There is no limit except a rational limit. There is a time when the transitional costs of adjusting the economy and implementing reforms become equal to or less than the cost of not adjusting, of trying to muddle through the crisis. Even if people have an absolute preference for present consumption, even if the citizens of a given country adopt a very high discount rate over future consumption, it is more rewarding to make the adjustment immediately, and it is irrational to postpone it. When this moment arrives, the rational bottom of the well has been reached.

Economic adjustment and reforms can be anticipated and decided upon when the rational bottom of the well has been reached, or they can be decided upon only after that point. Brazil probably reached this point around 1990, when reforms began to be undertaken seriously. Yet fiscal adjustment remained insufficient. Argentina reached the bottom of the well before 1990–1991, but only at that time were adjustment and reforms effectively undertaken. Chile and Mexico were the first countries to undertake adjustment and structural reforms, but Mexico was unable to complete them. Chile anticipated the transitional costs. As a trade-off, it emerged from the crisis sooner. Argentina lies at the other extreme. It decided to carry out adjustment and reforms only when the costs of adjusting became much smaller than the costs of not adjusting. The Argentines clearly took a long time to perceive this, which is why their adjustments were made so late. Since 1990 Brazil has probably been at the point where the two cost curves are crossing. After this point in time, it no longer made sense not to undertake reforms, even for the shortsighted. Yet in this situation minority groups that are still profiting from the crisis may oppose the reforms and the adjustment needed, and this strategy may work because the country has not yet been plunged into complete chaos.

In 1994, when stabilization was finally achieved, it was clear that the Brazilian economy could no longer grow—even minimally—without adjusting and stabilizing. The short-term costs involved in continuing to adopt populist policies were greater than the benefits. Some indicators were pointing in that direction. Since 1990 the country had been almost permanently in recession. Recoveries were short-lived. Populist episodes such as Antônio Delfim's first stabilization plan in 1979–1980 or the Cruzado Plan in 1986, which brought a piece of paradise for a few months, could no longer occur. The recovery from recession was short-lived and very weak. It was no longer possible to expand income based on an increase in consumption, as had happened on other occasions, because the economic agents—investors and consumers—knew that inflation remained uncontrolled and that the administration would have no other choice but to try a new stabilization plan.

Brazil had, therefore, hit the rational bottom of the well. The Collor administration's bold attempts to stabilize demonstrated this fact. They did not fail for lack of political support; they failed because the stabilization plans were incompetent or inefficient (see Chapters 13 and 14). Stabilization became possible only in 1994 during the Itamar Franco administration, when Fernando Henrique Cardoso was able to select a competent team of economists who had helped to develop the theory of inertial inflation (see Chapter 15).

❖ 11 ❖

The Citizenship Contradiction

In this book I have been analyzing Brazilian society from around 1979, when the crisis of the Brazilian and the Latin American economies erupted, to the present. This crisis, which I define as a crisis of the state, can also be called a modernization crisis. Beginning in the 1930s Brazil, as with all of Latin America, adopted a capitalist, national-developmentalist strategy of development. This strategy was a successful road to modernity for some decades, but by the 1960s it began to present increasing problems. The bureaucratic-capitalist military regimes that then took power and the foreign indebtedness of the 1970s were artificial forms of overextending a weary national-developmentalist strategy. The consequence is well known: the modernization process collapsed. Economic stagnation and the rapid deterioration of social conditions followed.

Since that time Brazil and Latin America have been striving to overcome this crisis. Most analysts agree, however, that this will be possible only if the region is able to define a new development-oriented political pact that would assure the political elites of legitimacy. In this chapter I discuss this problem, starting from one question I have never seen put to Latin American interpreters: why do Latin Americans, particularly Brazilians, stress the need for a political pact, whereas in the developed countries people seldom speak about such a pact? To answer this question, I relate the problem to the radical heterogeneity of the Latin American and particularly the Brazilian societies. Whereas a Hobbesian social contract is sufficient for relatively homogeneous societies, which include the developed ones, dual and underdeveloped societies additionally require a development-oriented class coalition.

As we will see in the last part of this book, Brazil was prodigal in failed attempts to stabilize. Market economic reforms took place but in a contradictory and uncertain way. Why was it so difficult to stabilize and reform? We have seen that political obstacles played a role. It is clear that the inefficiency of the stabilization plans and the sheer incompetence of policymakers also constituted a major cause (see Chapters 13 and 14). In this chapter I adopt a broader, more political perspective. I discuss the relative failure to modernize. Why was Brazil only partially able to adjust fiscally and to adopt structural and social reforms? What does "modernization" mean in Brazil today, and what are the political reasons it is incomplete? Can this be

explained by the radical heterogeneity of Brazilian society and the consequent citizenship contradiction?

F ernando Henrique Cardoso's election to the presidency in October
1994 will probably be seen as a major step in the modernization of
Brazil. Yet the country is far from having achieved modernity.
Modernization is an open and imprecise word. It often means the transition
to capitalism, but not all types of capitalism. Modernity is identified with the
form of capitalism that prevails in the developed countries, which are a
model for the developing countries notwithstanding the problems they face.
A society is modern when, in the economic realm, it allocates resources in a
reasonably efficient way through the market and is dynamic in technological terms; in the social realm, economic inequality is not excessive, although
it is sizable; and in the political realm, democracy is solidly established.

Modernity has an ideological content, but this content is not to be confused with the political right. To be modern is not to be conservative, much
less neoliberal. The distinction between being conservative, or putting order
above justice, and being left or progressive—willing to risk disorder in the
name of justice—remains as important as ever. And one can be modern
regardless of whether one is politically right or left. Yet in times of transformations, such as exist today, the distinction between archaic and modern
becomes crucial. Here we have a two-entrance matrix and four combina-
tions: one can be right or left, archaic or modern. Hélio Jaguaribe (1990:4)
correctly suggested that "the distance between the modern left and the modern right is far smaller than the gap between them and their archaic forms.
Helmut Schmidt and Oskar Lafontaine are far closer to Helmut Kohl than to
the old East German leaders."

Modernity means democracy, the primacy of efficiency, and an effective concern with social equity. Moderate and modern conservatives, who
like to call themselves liberal democrats, accept a sizable intervention of the
state in social affairs and limited state intervention in economic matters.
Modern social democrats, whom I am equating with the modern left,[1] may
be liberal[2] because they privilege market allocation of resources, stress individualism—conceived as consistent with social rights—and see a clear sep-
aration between civil society and the state as essential to democracy. Yet in
contrast to conservatives, social liberals are more committed to egalitarian-
ism and have as their personal utopia something like a market, self-man-
aged, democratic socialism. Capitalism, despite all its shortcomings, may be
the most efficient way to reach such a utopia, but it is not to be confused
with it.

Between the 1930s and the 1960s modernity was tied to some degree of
state intervention and the welfare state. As state-led development came to a
crisis and was increasingly distorted by economic populism and narrow-
minded nationalism, modernity—especially since the 1970s—became
increasingly identified with market-oriented reforms and fiscal discipline.

Yet the modernization of Brazil will occur only when a new class coalition is able to celebrate an informal political pact that has an interpretation for the crisis and a strategy for overcoming it. This interpretation will probably be what I am calling the crisis of the state approach, and the strategy will be a social-democratic and pragmatic one—a strategy that is market-oriented and, at the same time, uses the state pragmatically to promote income distribution and technological innovation.

In the developed countries a social contract is sufficient to legitimize the government. These societies are relatively homogeneous, so that the constitutional principles expressing the classical social contract that contractualist philosophers—from Hobbes to Locke, Rousseau, and Ant—analyzed are sufficient. The state will have the power delegated by society to maintain order, administer justice, protect property rights, and enforce contracts, whereas citizens will be protected against the abuses of the state (abuses of their individual rights) and against the abuses of the powerful (abuses of their social rights).

Yet in developing countries—particularly in Brazil, where social heterogeneity is so dominant—a social contract is not enough. The legitimacy of the government additionally requires a growth-oriented political pact that endorses a concrete perspective of progress for the deprived masses.

According to Aspásia Camargo (1990:51–52), "the Brazilian crisis is in large part the outcome of the high burden that still today we bear for our archaic past. . . . This high burden is defined by the 'social debt' that resulted from a slave-owning society's cultural tradition, based on a contempt for productive work and on the hierarchical rigidity of social relations." The "social debt" is another way—which is well established in Brazil—of expressing the extreme income concentration that prevails.

If there is a consensus in Brazil about the basic character of Brazilian society, it holds that Brazil is a dual, extremely heterogeneous society. Sérgio Abranches (1990:174) underlines the fact that "the Brazilian institutional dilemma is defined by the need of finding a system of institutions able to efficiently aggregate and process pressures from an essentially heterogeneous social structure." The state and the political parties are, in principle, these institutions. But given the extreme heterogeneity of Brazilian society, both the political parties and the state lack political legitimacy. One of the main themes being discussed in Brazil is how to design more-appropriate political institutions. The major proposed political reform—the adoption of the parliamentary system—was defeated in the April 1993 plebiscite. But the political reform agenda is large. It includes a mixed, German-style electoral system that is half proportional and half based on districts. It also encompasses correcting disproportion in the representation of the federal states in the House of Representatives; limiting the number of political parties; and a new federalism, limiting the role of the central government in local expenditures.

All these institutional changes are necessary, and they have strong ratio-nal arguments to back them. Their inner motivation, however, is to reduce the acute lack of legitimacy of the governing elite. They will increase the representativeness of Brazilian politicians. Yet not all of these changes will be enacted. And they are no panacea; they will not solve the legitimacy problem of the Brazilian government because the basis of that problem is not institutional but social. It is derived from the extremely heterogeneous character of Brazilian society.

It is well known that Brazil has one of the highest concentrations of income in the world. In a 1991 sample of fifty-six countries—which includ-ed Uganda, the Philippines, and Guatemala—Brazil came out on top in terms of income concentration.[3] Even countries like Peru, which used to have a more concentrated income, perform better today. The ratio of first-quintile income to fifth-quintile income, which is around 6 in the developed countries and 7 in Asian middle-income countries, is 24 in Brazil. The poor-est 50 percent of Brazil's workers earned 12 percent of total income, where-as the richest 10 percent of workers received 48 percent. In 1990, 50 percent of the workers had wages equal to two minimum wages; in that year the min-imum wage was approximately $60 per month. Monthly wages of public schoolteachers in the richest state of Brazil—São Paulo—were only $200.

Social conditions have been improving in Brazil, but slowly. Com-paring 1960 with 1990, according to IBGE, the illiteracy rate decreased from 39 to 20 percent; life expectancy increased from fifty-two to sixty-two years; the infant mortality rate (deaths at less than one year of age) decreased from 118 to 85 per thousand. These figures, however, are still extremely unsatisfactory. Developed countries have around a 2 percent illit-eracy rate, life expectancy is around seventy-five years, and the infant mor-tality rate is around 9 percent.

These negative indicators are a consequence of both the low level of income per capita and the concentration of income. Until 1980 growth and productivity rates were increasing. From 1960 to 1980 per capita income increased 120 percent; the average yearly rate was 6 percent. Yet from 1980 to 1992 this rate remained stagnant; in fact, it decreased 8 percent. In 1993 it began to grow again. The level of the concentration of income was only accentuated, stressing the perverse or distorted character of the previous modernization process. In 1960 the average income of the tenth decile was thirty-four times larger than that of the first decile; in 1990 it was sixty times larger. In this period, whereas the incomes of the ninth and tenth deciles increased at an average annual rate of 2.9 and 3.1 percent, respectively, those of the first and second deciles increased at 1.3 and 1.7 percent, respec-tively, and those of the third, fourth, and fifth deciles increased at only 1.1 percent.[4]

According to Maurício Romão (1991), the proportion of poor in the population, which was around 40 percent in 1960 and 1970, declined to 24.4

percent in 1980. That figure rose again during the economic crisis of the 1980s, when an increasing number of families crossed the poverty line, reaching the 1970 level (39.3 percent) in 1988. Poverty was extremely uneven in regional terms. According to Sônia Rocha (1991), in 1989 in the northeast metropolitan areas the poverty level was around 40 percent, reaching 47.2 percent in Recife; at the same time the rate was 20.9 percent in São Paulo and 13.5 percent in Curitiba. According to Juarez Brandão Lopes (1993), poverty was more concentrated among children and nonwhites. Poverty is characterized by low income, little if any public health equipment, housing in *favelas* and slums, illiteracy, a larger number of children per family (three to four times more than in nonpoor families), and the absence of books, telephones, and television sets.[5]

Yet this immense mass of the poor, 40 percent of the urban and 45 percent of the rural population, does vote. In this intrinsically dual society, its members are citizens. As Table 11.1 shows, the proportion of electors in the population has not decreased. This was a quiet political revolution, the consequences of which have not yet been fully analyzed. The poor received the right to vote, but it is very difficult for them to exercise that right and protect their interests. They are citizens according to the law, although subjectively most are not citizens because they are not aware of their political rights and have little capacity to assert those rights and participate in political life. In a population of 160 million people, there are almost 100 million electors, but only half are effective citizens. This right to citizenship was a consequence of democracy, and it sends a clear warning to the conservatives that the social ghetto is inconsistent with modernization. But coupled with the radical dualism of Brazilian society, the right to vote is a "citizenship contradiction"; it is a short-term source of illegitimacy for every type of government and is the origin of authoritarian beliefs that, although subdued, are still alive.

Table 11.1 Proportion of the Electorate in the Total Population

Year	Percentage
1940	6.45
1950	22.05
1960	22.18
1970	31.10
1980	49.26
1990	57.03

Sources: From 1940 to 1980, IBGE, *Estatísticas Históricas do Brasil,* 1990; for 1990, IBGE, *Anuário Estatístico do Brasil,* 1993.

Radical social dualism creates tremendous political problems. First, it makes exploitation—that is, the continuation of extreme income concentration—easier. Second, it validates the traditional conservatism and authoritarianism of Brazilian elites. Third, it favors populist policies, particularly in electoral campaigns. Fourth, it deprives the elites of political legitimacy, thus blocking a broad democratic and popular pact that would facilitate governability. As Francisco Weffort (1992:25) observed, this "dual system, rather than an exclusion system, is a domination system." But, I would add, it is a domination system that works in an increasingly precarious way because it has fallen prey to a basic contradiction: the dominated are, or have the right to be, citizens.

It became commonplace in Brazil to say that the cause of the Brazilian crisis is political and that the solutions are also political. There is some truth to any such conventional wisdom. It reflects the contradiction Brazilian politicians permanently face. They are supposed to support sound, rational policies that solve the fiscal crisis of the state and reform the state, but they are elected by a mass of electors who have great difficulty orienting their actions in this direction. In consequence, they often become the hostages of special groups of businesspeople, bureaucrats, and union leaders who lobby Congress. If electors were well informed, and political culture and political education in Brazil functioned on a level similar to that in the consolidated democracies, Congress, the executive, and the judiciary would function more efficiently and effectively. Less room would exist for populism and the defense of special interests. Democracy would not be "delegated" (O'Donnell 1991) or "regulatory" (Weffort 1989, 1992).

All of this is obvious, but to say that the main cause of the Brazilian crisis is political either means nothing because it is too general an affirmation or creates an insurmountable vicious circle in which democracy and economic development become inconsistent. Further, it reveals either a technocratic bias of expecting too much of the state or an authoritarian belief that only an enlightened prince can solve Brazil's problems.

In fact, if this political explanation were true, economic and political development would have been impossible in all democracies. Thus the periods in which Brazil developed while a democratic regime prevailed would not have existed. I will not discuss this theme here. When primitive capital accumulation has not yet been achieved and a capitalist system is not yet consolidated, democracy is an improbable political regime. But once this has occurred—when the rate of investment is already sizable (although insufficient), a large capitalist class is well established, and this bourgeoisie is able to capture the economic surplus through market mechanisms instead of having to resort to force (as do the precapitalist and mercantilist-dominant classes)—democracy becomes both viable and by far the best political regime. Brazil has already reached this level.[6]

When an economic crisis exists, we have to look for the new historical facts that gave rise to it. In this book I am saying that the basic cause of the Brazilian crisis is the crisis of the state. In fact, this hypothesis is part of what I propose to call the economic vicious circle of the Brazilian crisis. Additionally, there is a social vicious circle. Together they offer an explanation for the crisis and clues for the reforms that will solve it.

The economic vicious circle can be described beginning with the exhaustion of the import substitution strategy, the debt crisis, and the adoption of populist policies—which lead to a fiscal crisis of the state. The fiscal crisis generates high inflation, which imposes a high interest rate and lowers the investment rate, bringing the economy to a slowdown and finally to stagnation, which reduces tax revenues, further diminishes public savings, increases the public deficit and the public debt, and—closing the circle—aggravates the fiscal crisis of the state.

We can describe the social vicious circle beginning with the citizenship contradiction—that is, from a radically heterogeneous society plagued by a high degree of poverty and illiteracy but in which a structural transformation gives everyone the democratic right to vote. From this citizenship contradiction an intrinsic lack of legitimacy of the elites evolves, which determines the difficulty of celebrating a political pact and further deepens the government's legitimacy crisis. The ensuing governability crisis—which is also a consequence of the fiscal crisis—paralyzes the state, which is constrained to act on behalf of private, corporatist, and regionalist interests rather than promoting economic growth and income distribution. In this way, modernization is stalled; social dualism and the citizenship contradiction are maintained. The vicious circle is closed.

These vicious circles are not impenetrable. I have discussed here primarily the economic vicious circle, particularly in Chapter 5 where I analyzed the perverse macroeconomics of the fiscal crisis. I have discussed the social and political vicious circles less thoroughly. Yet as the economic vicious circle has a "weaker ring"—high inflation—that, once broken, breaks the entire vicious circle, the citizenship contradiction also has a weaker ring: in the short run, the definition of a political pact; in the medium run, education.

I am not suggesting that it is easy to control inflation and stabilize the economy. But it is clear that this is easier than solving the other problems that characterize the economic vicious circle. I do not believe it is easy to define a political pact among capitalists, bureaucrats, and workers in Brazil, but I think doing so is easier than directly solving the citizenship contradiction.

In the medium run, there is no doubt that extending education to everybody is the basic solution to this contradiction. Education is essential to economic development, distribution of income, and political culture. But education itself is constrained by social heterogeneity. As José Márcio Camargo

(1993) observed, Brazil's failure to educate its citizens is related less to failures of the educational system than to extreme poverty. The high failure and large evasion rates of grammar school students may have direct educational causes, but their main cause is the fact that children have to work at a very early age. In 1988, 30 percent of children between ages ten and fourteen in families with per capita incomes 25 percent below the minimum wage worked. More than 50 percent of these children worked more than forty hours per week, contributing significantly to the family income.[7]

I n summary, in the 1980s Brazil and Latin America confronted the worst economic crisis in their history. Its basic cause was not chronic insufficiency of demand but rather the crisis of the state—a state that had played a leading role in promoting economic growth. The crisis of the state was defined by both a fiscal crisis and a crisis of the mode of intervention: the import substitution strategy. With this crisis the state was paralyzed. Rather than being a tool of economic development, import substitution became an obstacle to development.

The ensuing economic stagnation, defined by negative growth of per capita income, implied that the modernization process had been halted. Only one aspect of modernity was advanced: democratization. Many Latin American countries, including Brazil, made the transition to democracy. Yet the other two elements of a modern society—economic growth and distribution of income—were absent. And the new democracies suffered an essential evil: the lack of legitimacy of their governments. This lack of legitimacy is derived from the radically heterogeneous character of Brazilian society. In a dual society such as this, in which 40 percent of the population falls below the poverty line, a Hobbesian social contract is not enough to meld the society and to assure governments of legitimacy; a development-oriented informal political pact is also necessary. Brazil had a populist, national-developmentalist pact between the 1930s and the 1960s. It was replaced by a development-oriented, authoritarian, and excluding capitalist-bureaucratic pact from 1964 to 1977. From 1977 to 1987 a democracy-oriented populist democratic pact prevailed. Since the failure of the Cruzado Plan a political vacuum has afflicted Brazil.

Yet as growth resumes, the consolidation of democracy and the resumption of sustained economic development will depend on the definition of a new, broad, and informal development-oriented political pact—a modernization pact. This pact, by combining the capitalists, the bureaucracy, and the working class, as well as the multinationals, will correspond to a crisis of the state, European social-democratic, and East Asian pragmatic interpretation of Latin America, much as in the 1950s the national-bourgeois pact corresponded to the national-developmentalist interpretation, and in the 1970s the bureaucratic-capitalist authoritarian regime—that is, the alliance among local capitalists, the state bureaucracy, and the multinationals—corresponded to the new dependency approach. New pacts and interpretations emerged out of crisis—the World War II crisis and the crisis of the 1960s. The crisis of the 1980s and 1990s is now being overcome. And as this happens, it will produce its own interpretation of that crisis, its own development strategy, and a corresponding political pact. The evidence of the emergence of a new political pact is analyzed in Chapter 17.

Part 4
Formulating a Successful Strategy of Reform

12

Economic Reforms in Abnormal Times

In the first three parts of this book I examined the crisis Brazil and, more generally, Latin America faced in the 1980s—a crisis that has not yet been fully overcome. In this chapter I begin to examine the reforms and the attempts to reform and stabilize. Many reforms have failed or remain incomplete. I suggest a theoretical framework, deviating from conventional wisdom on the subject, to explain this fact. To back my argument I use one example from Latin America and another from Eastern Europe, whose problems may, in many instances, be paradigmatic to those in Latin America.

Price stabilization policies and balance-of-payments adjustments were initiated in Latin America immediately after the debt crisis became apparent, whereas economic reforms that acknowledged the crisis of the state were introduced only in the late 1980s. When the outcomes proved unsatisfactory, the standard explanation was a lack or insufficiency of political support for the required fiscal adjustment and reforms of the state. In Chapter 13 I will concentrate on the political obstacles. Now I propose that an additional and more meaningful explanation for the failures to stabilize and reform lies in the incompetence or inefficiency of those reforms, deriving mostly from the inability of policymakers to recognize that Latin America faced abnormal times. One basic problem involved in stabilization policies and market-oriented reforms is that they are designed to deal with normal situations, whereas in the 1980s developing countries in Latin America and Eastern Europe faced exceptional times that required exceptional remedies.

Until recently, the standard criticism of the IMF's stabilization programs and the World Bank's structural reforms was that they did not adequately consider the specificities of developing countries. Washington economists assumed there was only one type of economic theory, valid everywhere, and from it they derived standard policy recommendations. This criticism still holds water, but it is necessary to admit that the economic development the world has enjoyed during the past fifty years has reduced the weight of such criticism. Economies in which capitalism was just being introduced fifty years ago are today well-established industrial capitalist societies, even if still underdeveloped ones.

A second criticism is related to the fact that the IMF in particular and, more recently, also the World Bank tend to use inadequate economic theories and to derive improper economic policies from those theories. Economic theories—neoclassical microeconomics and monetarist macroeconomics—are inadequate not only because they are based on false assumptions about the behavior and efficiency of markets but also because they often reflect neoliberal ideologies about the minimum state, something daily practice denies.

The third criticism has to do with imperialism or, more broadly and mildly, with conflicting interests. The IMF and other aid institutions in the First World often represented the interests and ideologies of the developed nations, which frequently conflicted with the national interests of the developing countries. This claim may still hold in some circumstances, as the debt crisis has shown, but the proposition that the national interests of the developed countries are essentially opposed to those of the developing ones is false. Mutual interests are more common than conflicting ones.

However, in an endeavor to advise the developing countries—and, lately, the formerly communist ones—the representatives of the developed world, particularly of institutions like the IMF and the World Bank, made serious mistakes. These mistakes may have originated in the "monoeconomic" assumption, which development economics strongly criticized; they may also have derived from the support for ideologically burdened policies that proved ineffective even in the developed countries; or they may have emanated from conflicting interests between the North and the South. A fourth and more important source of erroneous policy recommendations is the fact that Latin America and Eastern Europe are enduring abnormal times.

W e have already seen that the crisis these two regions faced cannot be explained merely by "fiscal indiscipline" and "excessive state intervention," as the Washington consensus posited. Indeed, economic populism is a problem, but it is a normal problem that in Latin America coexisted with growth for many years. Since the early 1980s, however, a much more serious problem has emerged: the fiscal crisis of the state and the collapse of the former development strategy. In many Latin American countries the state lost credit and proved unable to guarantee the national currency. The ensuing economic crisis was related to excess state intervention, but its real cause was faltering or ineffective state action. In Latin America the country that suffered the most was Peru, which is a paradigmatic case of the crisis of the state. An informal process of privatization reduced the state apparatus to less than half its former size as the government was no longer able to collect taxes or to manage state-owned enterprises.

The crisis of the state in Latin America and Eastern Europe was translated into economic stagnation, high rates of inflation, and, in several cases, hyperinflation. In such a crisis the economic systems in these regions faced abnormal times and extraordinary, extremely difficult challenges. The state had to be reformed. The fiscal crisis had to be overcome. Fiscal discipline had to be restored. Structural reforms aimed at reducing the state, privatizing, liberalizing trade, and deregulating became urgent. But these reforms must start from the assumption that in abnormal times remedies must be somewhat different from those suited to normal periods.

I n abnormal times normal remedies will likely be inefficient—that is, highly costly or simply ineffective. The rewards they offer, if any, are not proportional to the austerity they impose. In some cases they will be perverse, producing outcomes that are the opposite of the desired ones. Thus it is not surprising that reforms will often fail or be abandoned. When this happens, a standard explanation is offered: fiscal adjustment and structural reforms failed for political reasons. The economic programs are sound, but they are hindered by populist and nationalist politicians. This is only part of the truth: the political obstacles to economic reforms are obvious, but they are not the main problem.

The contention that economic problems are essentially political in origin has several sources. I emphasize only two interrelated ones here: the arrogant monopoly of rationality; and the naive confusion of economics with social engineering.

It is self-reassuring to believe and say we have the monopoly of rationality—the rationality imbedded in economic theory. It is rational to observe fiscal discipline, to limit expenditures to what is earned, to behave parsimoniously and save, to limit state intervention, and to preserve the efficient allocation of resources by the market. Thus when these tenets are not obeyed, it is easy to attribute the deviant behavior to evil political interests.

Certainly, politicians are partly to blame for the crisis. But some questions must be asked. First, what do these political interests represent? Are they not usually the representatives of cartels of large businesses, of unions, or of middle-class interest groups? And are these cartels or economic coalitions not economic agents to be considered by economic theory and policy? Second, even when government economic policy decisions specifically represent political interests, when they reflect electoral politics, does this mean they are simply wrong and unacceptable, as the arrogant monopoly of rationality assumes? Or can we say they also reflect the resistance, if not the indignation, of the Latin American people aroused by the inefficiency of these supposedly rational policies—that is, their opposition to the unduly high costs involved in proposed economic reforms?

This question leads to the social engineering assumption. All economic problems will indeed be political if economic policy can be equated with or reduced to a branch of engineering—actually, of bad engineering. By reducing social science to engineering, we are able to abstract people from it. By downgrading it to bad engineering, we are able to ignore the costs involved. What matters are the outcomes: to honor debts; to stabilize prices and achieve balance-of-payments equilibrium; and finally, whenever possible, to resume growth. Romania's former dictator Nicolae Ceauşescu, for instance, did not doubt the engineering content of economic policy. It was this belief combined with absolute dictatorial powers that enabled him to fully pay Romania's debt before the 1989 democratic revolution in Eastern Europe.

When the costs involved in a given economic policy are too high, the decision not to adopt it is rational rather than political. Reforms that are inefficient—whose costs are higher than their rewards—are simply wrong.

T hree examples will illustrate my point: first, the debt crisis; second, the stabilization of economies that have high rates of inflation; and third, the "big bang" approach to Eastern Europe. In these three cases the IMF, the World Bank, and, more generally, orthodox economists were unable to provide appropriate policies as long as they tried to offer standard solutions when confronted with exceptional situations.

Washington economists' failure to realize the severity of the debt crisis when it emerged in the early 1980s and to offer solutions to it is well known. As late as 1984 some well-respected economists continued to insist that the debt crisis was essentially a liquidity crisis when it was fairly obvious that it was a very serious balance-of-payments problem coupled with a fiscal crisis of the state. And in 1988 the same economists advocated a fully voluntary solution aimed at reducing the outstanding debt when it was clear, as the Brady Plan partially acknowledged one year later, that debt reduction had to be administratively negotiated. The inability of these economists to assess and offer appropriate solutions to the debt crisis was derived essentially from the conflicting interests of the creditor and the debtor countries, but it also stemmed from the bureaucratic conservatism of multilateral institutions ill prepared to deal with exceptional situations.

The incapacity of the Washington economists to confront the high inflation that arose from the fiscal crisis of the state is another example. If we adopt as a parameter the intensity of the inflation rate, there are three types of inflation: regular or small inflation; high, chronic, or inertial inflation; and hyperinflation. Standard economic theory, taught in First World universities and used uncritically by the multilateral institutions, only has remedies for regular inflation, which is invariably a combination of fiscal and monetary policy. Economists also know something about hyperinflation but have little to say about it except that the remedy is essentially the same as that recommended for regular inflation, with the sole difference being the intensity of treatment. As for inertial inflation—inflation rates that remain chronically at 5, 10, or even 20 percent a month for a long time—this phenomenon only began to be recognized by the best macroeconomists in the First World in the late 1980s, whereas in Latin America the theory was fully developed in the early 1980s. But Washington and particularly the IMF continue to officially ignore it.

Hyperinflation is always connected with extreme fiscal crisis. The state is literally bankrupt, public debt is very high, and public credit nonexistent. In these circumstances the only alternative to hyperinflation, besides adopting radical fiscal discipline, is to introduce monetary reform that includes the cancellation or long-term consolidation of a large part of the public debt and convertibility of the new money. Yet such shock treatment is not found in textbooks. It is not part of Washington's recommendations, particularly not the debt cancellation aspect.

The essential characteristic of inertial inflation is that it derives exclusively from the phased character of price decisions in an economy where inflation is already high. Standard inflation theory usually relates inflation to excess demand and an increase in the money supply. The neostructuralist theory of inertial inflation attributes such inflation to the informal indexation of the economy that economic agents tend to adopt, quite rationally, to protect them from ongoing inflation. The theory holds that this type of inflation is autonomous from demand and asserts that the money supply, in this context, is endogenous. It consistently holds that in addition to fiscal and monetary policy, it will be necessary to influence price decisions directly through some kind of income policy. When inflation, except for inertial, is high—characterizing the prevalence of abnormal times—a shock, which has come to be known as "heterodox shock," is unavoidable. This is well known today. High, inertial inflation in Israel (1985), Mexico (1987), and Argentina (1991) led to such a shock. In Argentina, where inertial inflation was combined with hyperinflation, it was necessary to cancel the public debt and freeze (legal convertibility) the exchange rate. In Brazil all of the shocks that had been tried in the past failed, essentially because they were not accompanied by fiscal adjustment nor backed by a minimum social agreement on wages.

Nevertheless, the IMF continued to ignore these simple facts. In Brazil, where inertial inflation was particularly strong, the IMF supported—informally in 1990 and formally in 1992—orthodox stabilization plans that only caused recession and did not control the inflation rate. According to the 1992 IMF target program, inflation should have been reduced from 25 percent in January to 2 percent by December. Yet, as the theory of inertial inflation predicted, inflation remained fairly stable at around the 20 percent level for the entire year (see Table 12.1). The failure to reduce inflation was blamed on the inability of the government to meet the monetary targets and on the insufficient fiscal adjustment achieved. Admittedly, the fiscal adjustment could (and should) have been stricter than it was. Much remains to be done in the fiscal area. But it is important to note that between 1990 and 1992 the Brazilian Treasury had a cash surplus. In 1992, although inflation remained around 20 percent a month—contradicting the IMF inflation target—the budget deficit (public-sector borrowing requirements in real terms) target agreed upon with the IMF was met. The public deficit was $11,384 billion; the IMF target was $11,400 billion.

Table 12.1   Brazil: IMF Targets and Reality, 1992

	Inflation (percentage)	
	Target	Actual
January	26	26.5
February	23	24.8
March	20	20.7
April	17	18.5
May	14	22.5
June	12	21.4
July	10	21.7
August	8	25.5
September	6	27.4
October	5	24.9
November	3	24.2
December	2	23.7

Sources: For the target, Brazil's letter of intention to the IMF, December 1991; for actual inflation, the general price index from FGV.

In essence, the 1992 economic stabilization program in Brazil, endorsed by the IMF, was extremely inefficient. Its costs were very high in terms of a deep recession, whereas its results have been next to nil.

My third example relates to economic reforms in Eastern Europe. Here again, the failure of the reform programs proposed for the former communist countries is derived essentially from the inability to understand and to find solutions when the economies of the countries that are supposedly being helped face abnormal times. But whereas in the case of the foreign debt and of inertial inflation and hyperinflation this failure arises from the fear of adopting more-radical measures, in the case of Eastern Europe the problem lies in the temptation—fairly easily understandable from an ideological standpoint—to restore capitalism with one stroke.

Eastern Europe, like Latin America, faced a debt crisis that became a fiscal crisis of the state. The statist strategy of industrialization was exhausted in Latin America as well as in Eastern Europe; one could imagine that similar economic reforms would work in both regions. The only difference is the fact that statism is much more entrenched in Eastern Europe than in Latin America. Thus the liberal reforms aimed at privatizing, liberalizing, and deregulating the economy must be more radical; they should consist of a big bang.

There are at least two basic mistakes here. First, although the crisis in both regions has been and partially remains a crisis of the state, in Eastern Europe this crisis is more profound. The differences in state intervention are more than merely ones of degree; there is also a difference in quality. In Latin America, except for Cuba, the economic system has always been capitalist; in Eastern Europe, it has been statist. In Eastern Europe the mode of production was not socialist nor capitalist but statist. The ownership of the means of production belonged collectively to the bureaucratic class that controlled the state. Unlike Latin America, where the distinction between the state and civil society was always clear, in Eastern Europe no such distinction existed. Production and the entire society were state-controlled.[1]

In abnormal times macroeconomic reforms aimed at stabilizing prices and the balance of payments, as well as political reforms directed toward restoring democracy, must usually be radical to be successful. Microeconomic reforms—reforms dealing with the property system and the resource allocation system—intended to change fully and abruptly the entire economic and social structure make no sense. Eastern Europe's transition from statism to capitalism was revolutionary. It changed the structures of both the economy and society. In this context structural reforms such as privatization must keep control of the revolution by being implemented as gradually as possible.

The objective, to establish a capitalist system in the region, cannot be achieved overnight. First it is necessary to clearly separate the state from the business enterprises. The goal is not only to create a private sector, a civil society, but also to build a state—a state apparatus that effectively protects property and contracts, and promotes social welfare and economic development. A civil society and a market system will be created through privatization, but privatization does not need to be universal. In the case of very large corporations, at least in a first stage, it is more expedient and less conflictive to transfer the control of state-owned enterprises to foundations that represent civil society.

Regarding the state, it is necessary to increase—rather than decrease—the strength of the much smaller state that will remain after the state-owned enterprises have been excluded from the old state. The new state emerging in Eastern Europe is proving to be much weaker than its counterparts in the developed countries because it remains plagued by a fiscal crisis and the lack of definition of its real role. This is not what these countries need. They need a state with a small but competent bureaucracy able to raise taxes in the amount necessary to push forward with the required economic and social reforms. They need a state whose government is representative of civil society. A strong state is essential not only to guarantee justice and order, to back the local currency, to assure balance-of-payments equilibrium, to supply education and health services, and to promote technological progress but also to institutionalize the markets in which business firms are supposed to operate. Because there was no capitalism in Eastern Europe, there was no state in the capitalist sense, much less markets of the type found in the West.

The state must be reformed and the markets built from scratch. This is a long process, during which a big bang would only increase the risk of failure.

To understand why economic reforms and stabilization policies have been so costly and have often failed in Latin America since the onset of the economic crisis in the early 1980s, it is necessary to consider that the lack of political support was a problem, but not the only nor necessarily the main one. Another explanation is that these reforms were incompetently or inefficiently defined because they ignored the abnormal times Latin America (and also Eastern Europe) faced.

The multilateral agencies in Washington played a decisive role in these reforms. They had a double role: to both finance and advise the developing countries on the road to stabilization and growth. This role was and continues to be plagued with shortcomings. It is the task of the developing countries to refuse inappropriate advice. Their economic elites, however, tend to be so subordinated to the dominant ideas in the developed countries that it is difficult for them to criticize those views.

In this chapter I have added to the well-known criticisms of the policy recommendations coming from Washington an additional one: they fail to deal with abnormal times. This criticism is particularly relevant because Latin America has faced a deep crisis of the state—a fiscal crisis and a crisis of the strategy of state intervention—that has led to high rates of inflation and economic stagnation.

To support my contention, I presented three examples of the attitude of multilateral agencies: (1) toward the debt crisis; (2) toward high inflation in Latin America; and (3) toward the transition from statism to capitalism in Eastern Europe. In Latin America, where the fiscal crisis of the state and high inflation required a shock treatment and a substantial debt reduction, Washington policymakers limited themselves to proposing fiscal discipline and a tight monetary policy. Contradictorily, in Eastern Europe, where the transition from statism to capitalism implied a structural revolution, Washington tried to solve the problem with standard macroeconomic policies combined with big bang privatization, ignoring the fact that it is necessary first to build a much smaller state, separated from the rest of the economic system, and second to strengthen this state so that markets can be created and developed.

✳ 13 ✻

A Dramatic Attack on Inflation

On March 15, 1990, a newly elected president, Fernando Collor de Mello, took office; the next day he announced an ambitious stabilization program, including profound monetary reform. This was a dramatic attack on inflation that entailed canceling a substantial portion of the public debt and an eighteen-month monetary moratorium involving around 70 percent of domestic financial assets. The new president did his best to control inflation. He did not adopt the populist attitudes that had characterized the Sarney administration. Within ninety days it was clear that the plan had failed to meet the expectations of its authors: inflation had returned, much as had occurred with the previous plans, and a recession had begun, in contrast with previous plans. As we saw in Chapter 7, at that time the Brazilian economy was facing hyperinflation for the first time. The rate of inflation in February 1990 was over 80 percent. It was clear to everybody in the country that the new administration would have to take emergency measures. Following the failure of the Summer Plan, the policymaking capability of the Sarney government was exhausted; the government was immobilized. Everyone agreed that the old administration could do nothing. All expectations were directed toward the new government.

In 1989 the economic debate had been intense. Eventually a consensus was formed about the severity of the crisis, its fiscal character, and the need for a profound fiscal adjustment.[1] Because the exchange rate—both during and after the Summer Plan—was overvalued by around 40 percent, a consensus was also established about the need for a devaluation of the cruzado. No agreement, however, was reached on two issues: whether a new price freeze and a moratorium on the domestic debt were necessary.

The debate about income policy divided economists into three groups: (1) orthodox monetarist economists who believed no income policy and no mechanism to neutralize inertial inflation were needed; (2) monetarists who verified the high economic and social costs of orthodox policies in situations of chronic inflation and thus incorporated some neostructuralist ideas about inertial inflation (Blejer and Liviatan 1987; Kiguel and Liviatan 1988); and (3) neostructuralist (and post-Keynesian) economists who believed that in addition to fiscal and monetary policy, profound economic reform should be combined with a stabilization program, in which a new price freeze or some other form of neutralizing inertia was a necessary first step. The orthodox monetarist view was not considered or seriously espoused in Brazil. Although they would not say so openly, most monetarist economists knew that when inflation has a high inertial component, the economic and social costs of a monetary and fiscal shock that is not combined with some kind of income policy are too high.

The idea of a gradual deindexation of the economy, with decreasing targets of inflation, had more followers. Experience has shown that when inflation is chronic and reaches high levels, gradualist programs are ineffective, and only shock therapy can work (Dornbusch and Fischer 1986; Yeager and associates 1981; and the economists who developed the theory of inertial inflation in Brazil). The unpopularity of freezes with the Brazilian elites, however, given the failure of previous freezes, underlay the attitude of rejecting a new freeze. Theoretically, inertial inflation can be fought gradually. What was forgotten by these economists is that gradualism is possible only when inertial inflation is in its first stages: it is very difficult and implies an enormous social cost when such inflation is higher than one digit monthly; it is impossible when inflation is nearing hyperinflation.

The infeasibility of gradualism when inflation is very high is related to the free-rider issue. Let us hypothesize two situations: one in which inflation is 4 percent a month; and another in which it is 80 percent a month. In both cases the decision is to reduce inflation gradually over a four-month period, dividing inflation by half each month and defining guidelines for this reduction. In the first case the free rider's premium for not following the guidelines is only 2 percent; in the second case it is 40 percent. In both cases the risk is the same. If, instead of developing guidelines, the government decided to impose the gradual path, the same difficulties would arise several times. In fact, these difficulties would be greater because it is easier to control a full freeze than a partial one. In the first case the rule is very simple: prices are supposed to remain the same. In the second the rule may also be clear, but it is very difficult for government officials and economic agents to control: prices are supposed to increase according to a predetermined and decreasing rate.

The debate about the need for a moratorium on the domestic debt focused on two issues: the size of the debt; and its maturity. The proponents of a moratorium said either that the debt was the basic cause of the budget deficit given the amount of interest to be paid or that there was a great probability that economic agents—who were victims of monetary illusion— would spend their financial assets (which were invested in Treasury bills and savings accounts) as soon as they ceased to see huge nominal increases in their indexed financial assets every month. In this case the reduced nominal rate of interest would lead economic agents to consume or to invest out of their financial wealth, thus provoking a great increase in aggregate demand immediately following the price freeze. The Cruzado Plan was presented as an empirical demonstration of this hypothesis.

The first argument on the size of the public debt was very fragile. The domestic debt, although increasing, was not too high. Total Treasury bills represented 6 percent of GDP in 1979 and nearly 13 percent of GDP in 1989. To reach 50 percent of GDP (the total public debt), we have to add around 12 percent of GDP for domestic debt on state-owned enterprises and for states and municipalities and 25 percent of the total public foreign debt.

The interest burden on the domestic debt was indeed high. It averaged around 3 percent of GDP prior to 1989.[2] During that year, with the Summer Plan and the loss of control of an economy that was heading toward hyperinflation, real interest rates paid by the government exploded. The interest paid on the domestic debt jumped to 9.5 percent of GDP (see Table 13.1).[3]

Table 13.1   Interest Payments by the Public Sector (percentage of GDP)

	External Debt	Domestic Debt	Total	Public Deficit
1983	3.70	3.01	6.71	4.4
1984	3.89	3.30	7.19	3.0
1985	4.47	3.44	7.91	4.3
1986	2.89	2.23	5.12	3.6
1987	2.62	2.17	4.79	5.5
1988	2.85	2.88	5.73	4.3
1989[a]	2.80	9.50	12.30	12.4

Sources: The total figure for 1989 is taken from Central Bank, *Brazil Economic Program,* vol. 24, March 1990, p. 66. The interest on the foreign debt is estimated, and that on the internal debt is a residue.

Note: a. The difference between the public deficit (PSBR in operational terms) and the public-sector interest burden is the primary or noninterest deficit. Only in 1987 and 1989 did Brazil present a primary deficit.

The true problem with the government debt was the very short maturity of the Treasury bills. They were almost fully financed on the overnight money market, showing that the state had lost its creditworthiness as well as its credibility. This fact was presented as a second argument in favor of a domestic moratorium. Economic agents could turn their liquid financial assets into consumption or investments in real assets the moment these financial assets stopped increasing in nominal value. But this was only a possibility rather than a necessity. After the 1987 freeze there was no flight from the money market toward real assets. The costs and risks of such flight are usually very high. If this flight occurs, as happened in 1989 because of fear of hyperinflation and a domestic moratorium, the costs and risks of buying overvalued real assets (the dollar, gold, real estate) are very high. In fact, in these circumstances the degree of economic freedom of economic agents regarding their portfolios is rather small.

Taking these facts into consideration, a group of economists, including myself, refused the idea of a domestic moratorium as a first step—not only because the measure was too risky (a no-return policy) but especially because it could endanger the creditworthiness of the state and confidence in financial institutions. If, after the decision to proceed with a fiscal adjustment and a new freeze, economic agents started to flee from financial assets, sparking an undesired and uncontrollable increase in aggregate demand in spite of the adoption of a rigid but conventional monetary policy (a high interest rate), a domestic moratorium could be added to the stabilization program.

The stabilization plan—the Collor Plan—adopted by the new government on its second day in office (March 16, 1990) included four sets of short-term measures: (1) monetary reform, which included freezing 70 percent of the financial assets of the private sector; (2) a fiscal adjustment; (3) an income policy based on a new price freeze; and (4) the introduction of a floating exchange rate. Medium-term policies included liberalization of foreign trade and privatization.

These short-term measures were important, but the actual emphasis of the stabilization program was on the domestic moratorium, which attempted to control inflation through radical monetary constraint. In this sense, it was a typical orthodox stabilization plan. The heterodox aspect of the plan— the price freeze—was secondary because, first, the conversion tables required to neutralize inertia were not used and, second, the price freeze was suspended almost immediately following monetary reform.

The monetary reform adopted had some similarity to the reforms made after World War II in Japan, Belgium, West Germany, and other European countries, although it included different specific features. Instead of establishing a conversion factor larger than 1 between the old money (the novo cruzado) and the new money (the cruzeiro),[4] around 70 percent of financial assets (M4) were blocked in novos cruzados (which could only be used to pay past debts), whereas 30 percent were immediately converted into cruzeiros.[5] Whereas in Germany reichsmarks ceased to function as a currency, the novos cruzados—in addition to being used to pay debts incurred prior to March 16—were supposed to be redeemed in twelve tranches, with full inflation correction and a 6 percent annual interest rate, after eighteen months.

This 30 percent conversion in cruzeiros was the weighted result of the conversion of 20 percent of all financial assets (money market, time deposits, and even checking account balances) except savings accounts, where the conversion was limited to 50,000 cruzeiros. The same rules were valid for individuals and business firms, whereas in Germany, for instance, firms received—in addition to the deutsche marks corresponding to the exchange factor—60 deutsche marks per employee (the same minimum amount each individual received).

Why was it decided to impose such a radical domestic moratorium? We saw that if the problem were the possibility of economic agents fleeing from financial assets into consumption, the moratorium could be decided in a second moment if this possibility actually materialized. We were convinced, however, that different fundamental reasons caused the new economic authorities to impose the moratorium. They were confronted with the infeasibility of a drastic fiscal adjustment in a very short time. In addition, they felt the monetary crunch would defeat inflation.

This is the true logic behind the domestic moratorium. The medium-term fiscal adjustment that would provide the needed fiscal surplus was around 7 percent of GDP per annum. This number can be explained in two ways: in fiscal terms; and in national accounts terms. In fiscal terms or PSBR terms, the operational public deficit of Brazil in 1987 and 1988 averaged 5 percent. In 1989 there was an increase to 12.4 percent.[6] But this figure overestimates the permanent deficit, given the exceptionally high interest paid by the state that year. In national accounts terms, we can reach a similar number, considering that public-sector savings were negative by an amount close to 3 percent of GDP and should have been positive by around 4 percent of GDP to be able to finance essential government investment programs. According to this second reasoning, it is clear that we are assuming that the fiscal adjustment required could not impose further reductions in public investment. The fiscal adjustment had to be made by increasing taxes and cutting current expenditures.

The objective should have been to generate a small budget surplus, given that during the transition to stability the government was forbidden to resort to additional domestic or foreign finance. After stabilization the budget surplus would provide the government with some degree of freedom to stimulate aggregate demand and resume growth with stability.

It is fairly clear today that, given the political and constitutional limitations it faced, the new government did not have the power to impose such a fiscal adjustment within the required time. The Constitution establishes the principle of annuity for taxes. In political terms, there was not enough support in Brazil—either in Congress or among the business elite—to increase taxes in the amount that was needed at the time.

Immediately following the shock, it was not easy to figure out the size of the fiscal adjustment embodied in the plan. There is no doubt, however, that this adjustment was sizable. It was not fully permanent. The final cancellation of the public debt involved in the plan amounted to $28 billion—around 7 percent of GDP. In 1990 the Brazilian economy presented a budget surplus, and in 1991 the deficit was virtually zero (see Table 13.2).

Table 13.2   **Budget Deficits Before and After the Collor Plan (percentage of GDP)**

	Primary	Operational
1987	1.0	5.7
1988	−0.9	4.8
1989	1.0	6.9
1990	−4.7	−1.4
1991	−2.8	0.2
1992	−1.3	1.9

Source: Central Bank, *Brazil Economic Program,* several issues.

This fiscal adjustment was significant. It involved tax increases, reduction of expenditures, and permanent debt reduction. It is true that a stock measure such as a public debt cancellation is no real substitute for a permanent fiscal adjustment; it is also not to be confused with a monetary policy that effectively controls the flow of the money supply. The radical reduction of the stock of money could have some flow (fiscal and monetary) consequences in terms of a reduction of interest paid.

The debt cancellation took place in several ways. Three days of a banking holiday, during which Treasury bills bore no adjustment for inflation, represented an almost 8 percent reduction in the total debt. The capital levy (IOF) represented a reduction of around 9 percent in the stock of government debt. And some reduction was also achieved by not providing a full correction for financial assets in March 1990 (the BTN was limited to a 41 percent increase).[7] This debt reduction in addition to the forced reduction of the interest rate on the frozen public debt led to some interest reduction for the public sector.

The inability of the fiscal adjustment in the Collor Plan to control inflation dramatically confirmed the theory of inertial inflation. According to this approach, the public deficit was not the direct cause of Brazil's hyperinflation. Given chronic or inertial inflation, the public deficit is often a convenient way of validating the money supply expansion that is required by the increase in the transactions demand for money (Bresser Pereira and Nakano 1987:73–79). But when the time for stabilization arrives, there is no easy way to eliminate the public deficit.

A stabilization program usually involves a certain degree of recession of the economy, even if the previous inflation cannot be directly attributed to excess demand. Fiscal adjustment and monetary control have a recessive character, the control of wages indicates a slowdown of economic activity, and the need to maintain a nominal anchor (usually the exchange rate) requires a previous currency devaluation that is contractory. If a freeze is included in the stabilization plan, weak aggregate demand will facilitate the subsequent price liberalization.

The Collor stabilization program assumed a moderate recession as an objective—or as a necessary consequence. The general and correct idea was that it is impossible to stabilize an economy so deeply unbalanced without some sacrifice. The instrument used to impose this sacrifice was basically the reduction of the money supply. This reduction was so radical and hit businesses so hard that it disorganized production and led the economy into a much deeper recession than expected or desired, without achieving the sought-for control over inflation.

During the first sixty days after the plan was instituted the attention of the public and economists focused on the liquidity issue. First, the sharp reduction of liquidity was said to be both the cause of stabilization and the reason for recession. Second, when the money supply began to increase, it was blamed for excess demand and the resurgence of inflation. My view is, first, that this recession was the result—from the supply side—of the disorganization of production caused by the freeze of financial assets, including working capital, rather than the consequence of the reduction of liquidity provoking a fall in demand. Second, the increase in the money supply that immediately followed was a clear demonstration of the endogenous character of that money supply. And third, the resurgence of inflation cannot be related to this increase. I discuss first the former two points; the last is discussed later.

According to neostructuralist and post-Keynesian economics, the money supply is endogenous.[8] It is basically determined by the demand for money; it accommodates the increase of GDP and validates the rate of inflation. Government budgetary constraint, in a closed economy or a highly indebted economy, requires that the fiscal deficit, D, be financed by the net creation of government liabilities: an increase in the money supply, dM, and the issuing of Treasury bills, dB.

$$D = dB + dM$$

Conventional economics assumes that, in this equation, either dM or D is the exogenous variable. When D is the determining factor, the increase in the money supply is a residuum, given the government's incapacity to finance the deficit adequately with Treasury bills. If this is not necessarily true when moderate inflation prevails, it is clearly invalid when inflation is very high and is chronic or inertial. In this case the money supply—and thus dM—is determined by the demand for money, and the increase in government indebtedness is the residuum. In Brazil before the stabilization plan, the Central Bank projected the rate of inflation and passively established the required increase in the nominal supply of money that would balance out the demand for money, or in other words that would avoid a liquidity crisis. This practice was adopted independent of the orientation of finance ministers and Central Bank governors.

In fact, in the case of Brazil—where in addition to suffering chronic inflation the economy was fully indexed—the endogenous money supply included a portion of the Treasury bills traded on the overnight market, for which the maturity is one night. And the government, to reduce its interest payments and induce financial intermediaries to buy these Treasury bills, guaranteed the automatic and daily repurchase of Treasury bills that did not find buyers among the public. In this way the interest rate was fully determined by the Central Bank, and the money supply remained fully endogenous.

As a consequence, the overnight deposits represented quasi money—a remunerated money at that. The potential money supply was close to $M4$ because all financial assets were extremely liquid, but the actual money supply was really composed of $M1$ plus a portion of the overnight deposits.

The conventional concept of money supply makes it equal to $M1$. In equilibrium we would have

$$Md = Yp/V = M1$$

where Md is the demand for money, Yp the nominal income, V the income velocity of money, and $M1$ the money supply. In a situation of high inflation, V would increase sharply and the conventional supply of money would be much smaller. The actual velocity of money, however, does not increase as much as it seems because the actual money supply cannot be equated with $M1$. The actual money supply, M', should be considered as being formed of $M1$ plus a portion, z, of the overnight deposits, B. The z-coefficient, which is smaller than 1, is determined by the rate of inflation and the corresponding nominal demand for money. The higher the rate of inflation, the higher z will be. This share, zB, of overnight deposits is the amount of money economic agents in fact use as money. It is also the variable that endogenously equates the actual money supply with the demand for money. In this case the real income velocity of money, V', is smaller than the conventional or restricted definition of money, $M1$.

$$M'd = Yp/V' = M1 + zB = M'$$

In this equation zB represents money the same way $M1$ does; it is a means of exchange, as is conventional money. Economic agents habitually use part of their overnight deposits, zB, to make transactions. To do so they daily transform zB into $M1$, thus increasing $M1$. Because the recipients of the additional $M1$ invest it immediately in overnight Treasury bills, the $M1$

increase is automatically neutralized and disappears from the records—although not from the economic process.

Table 13.3 presents an estimate of the actual money supply as a proportion of GDP for Brazil at three points in time: fifteen days before institution of the stabilization plan and fifteen and forty-five days after institution. The estimation of the actual money supply is rather imprecise, but is not arbitrary.

Table 13.3   Money Supply in 1990 (percentage of GDP)

	February 28	March 31	May 14
M4 (potential)	29.0	9.0	14.0
B, overnight deposits	16.0	2.0	8.0
Savings accounts	9.0	3.0	1.0
Other	2.0	1.0	1.0
M1	2.0	3.0	4.0
zB	12.0	2.0	6.0
Actual money supply	14.0	5.0	10.0

The value of the money supply just before the implementation of the plan is somewhat imprecise because the quasi money stock, B, from which the actual money supply could be drawn, was very large. I estimated that the actual money supply should be around 14 percent of GDP. To reach this value I used the following data. $M1$ was around 15 percent of GDP in the early 1970s, when inflation was moderate but not negligible (20 percent a year), and it was reduced to 2 percent of GDP by the end of 1989 (see Table 13.4).[9] In my concept of actual demand for money, the demonetization caused by the acceleration of inflation is neutralized by the increase in zB that is considered part of the actual money supply. But inflation and financial innovations allowed for some reduction in the demand for money from 15 percent of GDP in the early 1970s to 14 percent of GDP in the 1980s. Of this 14 percent, 2 percent was represented by $M1$ and 12 percent by zB. Because B was 16 percent of GDP, I am assuming a z of 0.75.

With the moratorium on the domestic debt, the supply of money was reduced drastically. $M4$, which we can understand as a potential money supply, was reduced from 29 to 9 percent of GDP, overnight deposits decreased from 13 to 3 percent of GDP, and my estimate is that the actual money supply decreased from 14 to 5 percent of GDP. In this first moment (March 31) I am assuming that z was equal to 1—that is, that 100 percent of the overnight deposits were part of the actual money supply.[10]

Such a reduction was not in the minds of the authors of the plan. They

Table 13.4   Financial Assets (percentage of GDP)[a]

	Monetary Base	M1	Treasury Bills	Savings Deposits	Time Deposits	M4
1970–1974[b]	4.65	15.04	5.08	1.68	3.28	25.08
1975–1979[b]	3.75	11.70	6.85	5.62	4.44	28.60
1980–1984[b]	2.50	6.30	5.80	8.01	4.57	24.69
1985	1.56	3.73	10.39	9.20	6.17	29.50
1986	3.22	8.20	9.33	8.09	6.05	31.67
1987	2.19	4.62	10.07	9.69	4.86	29.24
1988	1.39	2.76	12.22	10.75	4.11	29.85
1989	1.26	2.05	13.94	8.13	2.78	26.89

Source: Central Bank, *Brazil Economic Program,* several issues.
Notes: a. Annual average, adopting end-of-period positions.
b. Average for these years.

confused the amount of cruzeiros left in the economy (9 percent of GDP) with the money supply. Several newspaper interviews quoted them as saying that in the second semester of 1986, following several months of price stability achieved during the Cruzado Plan, *M1* was 9 percent. Thus 9 percent of the money supply would be enough. In fact, the supply of money— even if we include overnight deposits—was only 5 percent, whereas the demand for money was at least 14 percent. During the period of the Cruzado Plan it was possible to live with a smaller *M1* because an enormous amount of overnight deposits were at the disposal of economic agents.

The effect of this reduction in the money supply on business enterprises was dramatic. It disorganized production. The working capital of enterprises was blocked, causing an immediate termination of activities. The freeze was made without any economic criterion. Thus the disparities in the situation among enterprises were very large. The prospect was that the banks would circulate the cruzeiros, but given the high interest rates, this effort was very limited.

According to a survey conducted by the FIESP, sales by industrial firms in São Paulo in the second half of March 1990 were reduced by around 70 percent. This was caused not only by a lack of money (globally and in terms of sectors of the economy) and the disorganization of the economy but also by psychological factors. The impact on expectation was very negative. Unemployment began to rise almost immediately. Many enterprises sent their employees on collective vacations while waiting for a clarification of the situation. Workers began to accept wage reductions coupled with a shortened work day.

The next month the amount of cruzeiros was increased by various means, reaching 14 percent of GDP by mid-May (16 percent by mid-June).

Part of this increase was under the control of the government, but part was not. The government assumed it would be able to control the increase in liquidity, but the market—taking advantage of the existence of two currencies—was able to increase the amount of cruzeiros, correspondingly reducing the stock of cruzados.

When this began to happen, banks gave notice that they were having difficulty making loans, given a reduced demand for loans. Several analysts and economic authorities concluded that the liquidity problem had been solved, even that at that moment there was excess liquidity that would provoke excess demand and bring back inflation.

As Table 13.3 reveals, in mid-May the potential money supply ($M1$ plus overnight deposits) continued to be relatively small (12 percent of GDP), and the actual money supply was below the level that had prevailed prior to the plan (around 10 percent of GDP in May compared with 12 percent of GDP in February). Why, then, was the demand for loans weak? Why was liquidity no longer tight but relatively loose? The increase in the money supply explains part of this change, but the real explanation lies in the lowering of the demand for loans. Given the pessimistic prospect for sales and the high interest rates (around 100 percent a year in real terms), firms were not interested in taking loans.[11] They preferred to reduce production. The demand for loans and the demand for money were reduced in accordance with economic agents' pessimistic expectations.

Recession in this case was not demand-led but supply-originated. Its basic cause was not a reduction of aggregate demand but the disorganization of production. Retail sales were the only indicator that did not point toward recession at the very beginning. Sales increased immediately following the freeze, as had occurred following the three previous freezes. There are some general reasons why this happens. First, although this fact is often overemphasized, with the end of the money illusion, people do tend to spend a little more on consumption. Second, because of either optimism or mistrust of the success of the stabilization, people tend to anticipate consumption. Third, as Helpman (1988) has argued, a price freeze in an oligopolistic economy has an effect similar to that of reducing real prices; thus demand will increase along the demand curve.

The Collor Plan contained three additional explanations for the increase in consumption. First, the loss of credibility of financial assets led people to consume; second, the resumption of consumer credit, which had practically disappeared as a result of hyperinflation, led to an increase in sales of consumer durables; third, the plan implied a real wage increase of 23 percent in March 1990.

This real wage increase took place in March because the government decided that the 70.16 percent February inflation should correct wages the following month, according to the existing wage indexation law. Inflation in

March, however, when calculated taking the end-of-the-month price level against the price level at the end of the previous month (rather than the usual comparison of the average of the entire month against the average of the previous month) was 79.11 percent.[12]

This wage increase could be interpreted as a basic contradiction of the stabilization plan (Sylvio Bresser Pereira 1990). In general, inflation is fought by reducing demand and, if possible, increasing supply. Under the Collor Plan the opposite was done: supply was curtailed through the money supply squeeze; and wages were increased. The problem, however, was less serious because—unlike what happened under the Cruzado Plan and similar to what occurred under the Bresser Plan—real wages had been decreasing in the months before the plan because of the acceleration of inflation. Thus the 23 percent wage increase only compensated for the previous reduction.[13] It did not represent a distributive incompatibility. Firms did not have to increase prices compensatorily.

This increase in consumption was necessarily short-lived, given the rise in unemployment. In May retail sales showed a decline when compared with the corresponding month in the previous year. Given the reduction of production and investments, depressed demand was becoming a generalized fact.

N inety days after the Collor Plan was launched, recession had taken hold of the economy, and it was fairly clear that inflation had returned. In fact, the slowdown of the economy had begun earlier. GDP growth was already slightly negative in the last quarter of 1989 (–0.3 percent) and was clearly negative in the first quarter of 1990 (–2.4 percent). In April 1990, as a result of the disorganization provoked by the Collor Plan, the FIESP index of economic activity showed a 22.3 percent fall in relation to April 1989; for February and March the corresponding figures were an 8.0 increase and a 6.8 decrease, respectively (see Table 13.5). According to a Getúlio Vargas

Table 13.5   Indicators of Economic Activity, 1990 (percent change in relation to previous year)

	Level of Activity	Level of Employment	Average Real Wage	Installed Capacity Utilization
January	6.2	3.8	–18.8	79.5
February	8.0	3.4	–22.7	79.0
March	–6.8	2.5	–10.5	72.5
April	–22.3	0.6	–22.4	62.5

Source: FIESP, data for São Paulo industry.

Foundation business survey, the level of capacity utilization of Brazilian industry in April 1990 (62.5 percent) was the lowest since this index had begun to be calculated in the mid-1960s; three months earlier, in January 1990, this index had been over 79 percent. In May, as the economy started to reorganize after the shock, the level of production began to recover, as the first figures on electric power consumption indicated, but the May record increase in unemployment in São Paulo in relation to the previous month (2.4 percent, against a 2.2 percent rate of layoffs during the previous month) suggested that the recovery was limited. That same month, according to the ABDIB, the rate of idle capacity in the heavy capital goods industry reached a 48.6 percent peak against an average of 38 percent during the 1980s. The recessionary trend seemed to be stronger than the recovery impulse.

Inflation had returned (see Table 13.6). Through May, the average inflation compared with average price indices was still showing a decline.[14] Yet any doubts about the resurgence of inflation were dismissed when FIPE's price index for the following months was released. By the end of the year, inflation was approaching 20 percent a month.

Table 13.6 Monthly Inflation Rate, 1990

Month	Percentage	
January	74.53	
February	70.16	
March	79.11	(3.3)[a]
April	20.19	(6.3)[a]
May	8.53	
June	11.70	
July	11.31	
August	11.83	
September	13.13	
October	15.83	
November	18.56	
December	16.03	

Source: FIPE/USP.
Note: a. The figures in parentheses refer to the end-to-end-of-the-month period.

Why did inflation resurge? There are three explanations—one monetarist, one Keynesian, and one neostructuralist or inertialist. The monetarist and the Keynesian reasoning is founded on the increase in the money supply in the three months that followed the institution of the plan. The neostructuralist analysis is based on relative price imbalances and the corresponding distributive conflict.

The government adopted a naive monetarist policy when it assumed that drastically reducing the money supply would eliminate inflation. In doing so, it forgot that inflation is not a stock but a flow problem. To control inflation, it is necessary to eliminate the budget deficit and control the money supply, not the stock of money. When inflation has an inertial component, as was the case in Brazil, it is also necessary to freeze prices or, more broadly, to promote an income policy that supports (but does not replace) fiscal and monetary policy. For the authors of the Collor Plan the freeze was an accessory measure. The essential part of the plan was the reduction of the money supply, to be followed by the elimination of the fiscal deficit. Inflation, however, had returned before the deficit could be controlled.

The true monetarist explanation for the resurgence of inflation is simple: prices increased again because in the two months following the institution of the plan, high-powered money increased four times. The liquidity increase provoked expectations that inflation would resurge—and rational expectation is a self-fulfilling prophecy. Monetarists do not accept the fact that the money supply has an essentially endogenous, passive character, and they forget that, following hyperinflation, a sudden stabilization provokes a strong increase in the monetary base. For the new classic monetarist, the belief that an increase in the money supply causes inflation has a quasi-religious character. The monetarist rhetoric—which is "true" because it is a part of mainstream economics—says that an increase in the money supply causes inflation; rational expectations theory adds that economic agents will form their expectations according to the "true" theory and, again rationally, will behave according to their expectations, thereby increasing prices. Thus the prophecy becomes self-fulfilling.

The monetarist explanation is implicit in most analysis. Pastore (1990) adopted it explicitly. Excess demand is not required for the resurgence of inflation; an increase in high-powered money is sufficient. For this explanation to be correct, the acceleration of inflation immediately following implementation of the Collor Plan should have been the result of business enterprises deciding to increase their prices as they noticed that the monetary base was increasing. The textile industry, suppliers of personal services, farmers, and the home appliance industry—the first to increase prices after the plan—would have made this decision after assessing the increase in the monetary base.

The Keynesian explanation is more reasonable, but in the present case it accounts for only part of the acceleration of inflation. According to this view, adopted by Toledo (1990), among others, inflation returned because the money supply increase caused excess demand. The halt to inflation as a result of the liquidity shock would have been temporary. As liquidity was restored, demand would recover and inflation would return. In fact, as I have shown, the trend is a result of recession rather than of growth. Retail sales increased in the first month after the plan was implemented, but soon slowed down. Some firms may have profited from this demand spurt by increasing their prices, but they were few because global demand was dwindling rather than expanding.

The neostructuralist or inertialist explanation for the resurgence of inflation is based on the nature of inflation in Brazil rather than on errors related to the money supply. Inflation in Brazil is inertial, and was very high—in fact, hyperinflation already prevailed—when the stabilization plan was launched. The neostructuralist explanation emphasizes relative price imbalances on the day of the freeze and the corresponding distributive conflict. In Brazil economic agents are used to fighting inflation. They believe increasing their prices is the best way to protect themselves from generalized distributive conflict. On March 16, 1990, when prices were frozen, relative prices were necessarily unbalanced because price adjustments were not synchronized. Thus there was an intertemporal relative price imbalance. Such an imbalance, which can be measured by the dispersion of relative prices, tends to increase with the acceleration of inflation up to the time the economy is fully dollarized.

On the day the freeze was implemented, firms that had just increased their prices gained from the freeze because their markups increased, whereas those that were at the point of raising prices lost. When inflation is chronic, firms that have lost—or think they have lost—as a result of the freeze will increase their prices as soon as possible. Under the Collor Plan, firms felt additionally injured by the retention of their financial assets. This was a second reason prices increased as soon as they did.

Some factors favored the price increase: (1) the increase in consumption expenditures immediately after the freeze; (2) the increase in the money supply, which kept pace with recession; and (3) the hasty liberalization of prices by some oligopolistic industries. These were the opportunities business enterprises had been waiting for. But the price increase would have taken place anyway, given the inertial character of Brazilian inflation. The price freeze and the freeze of financial assets induced a one-month truce, but immediately following the truce, business enterprises began to increase prices. Nobody wants to lose as a result of inflation or a stabilization plan. A few days after the freeze, according to *Gazeta Mercantil*, the leading Brazilian business newspaper, firms "were looking for an index on which they could link their prices." Fearing unemployment, workers halted their demands for a time, but two months after the beginning of the plan they were already making huge demands and receiving wage increases of 20 to 30 percent.[15] Firms that agreed to these wage demands would probably raise prices to offset the cost increases.

It is important, however, to underline that, since 1987, indexation in Brazil has not meant increasing prices only according to past inflation. Economic agents were so worried about not losing as a result of inflation that they either changed the index they utilized to obtain a more favorable one, or they "indexed" their prices according to their own predictions about the future inflation rate. In other words, they tended to add a risk premium to last month's inflation rate in their price decisions. Because all firms behaved similarly, each individual firm was not concerned that its price increase would not be followed by the competition. Thus inertial inflation was also, paradoxically, an accelerating inflation.

❧ 14 ❧
Attempts to Stabilize

From 1979 to 1994 inflation was the most obvious symptom of the crisis faced by the Brazilian economy. It was a high and persistent inflation that resisted all stabilization attempts. Following the heterodox stabilization programs, inflation would go down, but it would soon recover its previous level or would jump to a higher one. There was generally no response to the orthodox programs. In this case inflation would remain at the same level or would increase. Following the first orthodox stabilization plan, in 1979, inflation jumped from 40 to 100 percent a year. After the second plan, in 1981, it remained at the same level. After the third plan, in 1983, it jumped from 100 to 200 percent a year. Following the Cruzado Plan—the first heterodox attempt—in 1986, inflation decreased from 10 percent a month to almost zero, but one year later it was over 20 percent a month. After the Bresser Plan (1987) inflation fell to almost zero, but two years later it was nearly 30 percent a month. After the Summer Plan (1989) inflation fell sharply but rose to 80 percent a month one year later. The Collor Plan I (1990) reduced inflation to almost zero, but one year later it was around 20 percent a month. The orthodox Beans and Rice (1988), Eris (1990), and Marcílio (1991–1992) plans failed to reduce the inflation level.

Why was Brazil unable to stabilize its economy between 1989 and 1994? Was it because the lack of political will in the society blocked fiscal adjustment? Was it because fiscal adjustment was practically infeasible without a corresponding reduction of the public debt? Was it because stabilization programs have been inefficient, the fruit of technical incompetence? Each of these three questions corresponds to a hypothesis or a theory on the causes of the failure to stabilize. These theories hold that the high and inertial inflation that afflicted Brazil for years was not overcome because: (1) the public debt was excessive and its maturity too short, indicating the state's loss of credit—that is, a major fiscal crisis; (2) the economic teams that were charged with the programs did not receive the necessary political support from society; and (3) the local economic teams and the IMF (when the program was IMF-monitored) lacked competence in dealing with inertial inflation and adopted inefficient and ineffective stabilization programs.

I call the first of these hypotheses the political hypothesis, the second the extreme crisis hypothesis, and the third the economic inefficiency or the economic incompetence hypothesis. These three theories, however, are

complementary rather than exclusive. When a country reaches hyperinflation, as was the case in Brazil in early 1990, this means the state is bankrupt,
its creditworthiness is very low, its public debt is plagued by short-term
maturity or arrears, and it is no longer able to back its national currency. In
other words, the extreme crisis hypothesis is part of the explanation, and
reduction or consolidation of the public debt is required. When a country
recurrently fails to stabilize, this indicates that the economic policies that are
being adopted are not suited to the problem they are supposed to solve, that
they are too costly or simply ineffective. This, in turn, indicates that the economic inefficiency explanation plays a part in the situation. Finally, when
fiscal adjustment is never fully reached, this means political support for stabilization is lacking and society shows lassitude regarding inflation. In other
words, the political hypothesis is also meaningful.

In recent years the first explanation has become popular. The number of
conferences, articles, and books dealing with the political aspects of economic reforms has greatly increased. This explanation is true, but it does not
contain all of the truth. The inefficiency or incompetence hypothesis,
although never clearly expressed, was usually the most common explanation
in the past, but since the political hypothesis became popular the prevalent
assumption has been that well-prepared economists—whose doctorates are
from the best universities in the developed countries—know what should be
done; what is lacking is political support.[1] I believe this approach is mistak-
en, as was demonstrated by the failure of the orthodox stabilization programs in Brazil. Finally, the extreme crisis explanation, which is obviously
unpopular among both foreign and internal creditors, is also relevant but
leaves a great deal unexplained.

From 1979—when the Brazilian crisis began and inflation accelerated
from an average of 40 percent a year in the 1970s to 100 percent a year in
1979–1981—to 1992, the country undertook twelve stabilization plans.
Some were emergency plans; others were well-prepared programs. Some
were "heterodox," using price freezes, but most adopted "orthodox" strategies.[2] Some adopted the shock strategy; others tried gradualism.[3] In some
cases, even though inflation had not been subdued, the economic picture
improved, whereas in others the crisis only worsened. In some cases the
final outcome was only a high cost to be paid; in others there was a cost but
a benefit as well. After the failure of the Marcílio Plan (1991–1992) and the
impeachment of President Collor, when Fernando Henrique Cardoso was the
finance minister and Itamar Franco the president, the Real Plan—based on
the theory of inertial inflation—finally stabilized the Brazilian economy.
This plan is analyzed in Chapter 15, along with the other successful economic reforms that have taken place in Brazil since the crisis began.

In this chapter I discuss the three hypotheses behind the failure to stabilize, using the twelve stabilization programs as background. I illustrate the
inefficiency explanation with the last program, the Marcílio Plan, which had

the official support of the IMF. I try to show that behind the inefficiency hypothesis is the incapacity to understand the inertial character of Brazilian indexed hyperinflation.

The inefficiency hypothesis to explain the failure to stabilize can be illustrated by the Marcílio Plan, developed by Minister Marcílio Marques Moreira between May 1991 and September 1992, at which time President Collor was impeached for corruption. The Marcílio Plan was a gradual and fully orthodox plan—IMF-sponsored—that ignored the inertial character of inflation, raised real interest rates to around 40 percent a year in 1992, maintained the economy in permanent recession, perversely increased the budget deficit, and from a surplus in 1990 and 1991 returned to a deficit in 1992, although some fiscal discipline was maintained. The resurgence of the deficit was a result of the high interest paid by the state on its internal public debt.[4]

In the first months of 1992 the Collor administration lost its second great opportunity to achieve stabilization.[5] The budget deficit was still under control as a consequence of the fiscal adjustment measures adopted primarily in 1990; relative prices, including public prices and the exchange rate, were balanced; and inflation was high but stable. Additionally, the government had recovered political support, particularly the support of the elites, as the result of a combination of favorable factors: inflation had stopped accelerating; President Collor had changed his ministry, choosing a group of competent and highly respected intellectuals and politicians;[6] financial markets were tranquil; the support of the international community and the multilateral institutions was strong, given the market-oriented reforms initiated in 1990; and international reserves were increasing. At that time a nominal anchor, Argentina-style, combined with a temporary price freeze and a social agreement would probably have strengthened the fiscal adjustment process and achieved stabilization. By instead maintaining a gradualist strategy, which in addition to being inefficient was ineffective against inertial inflation, a genuine opportunity to stabilize was lost.

Under the Marcílio Plan inflation accelerated until November 1991, when it reached 25 percent a month. From then until April 1992 the inflation rate fell moderately, to near 20 percent. Between May and August 1992 it stabilized at around 22 percent. In October, when Marcílio left the ministry, inflation was back to 25 percent a month. Yet in early 1992, when for the first time since 1987 inflation had stopped accelerating and had even decreased a little, this orthodox plan raised hopes among economists and policymakers who were unable to understand the inertial character of Brazilian inflation.

The main reason inflation has accelerated systematically after each stabilization plan is found in the need economic agents feel to restore the balance in relative prices the plan in some way disrupted. But it is also a problem of a lack of confidence. The resurgence of inflation and the awareness of the fiscal crisis of the state—that is, the awareness of the lack of public credit—cause economic agents to lose confidence in the currency, to anticipate that inflation would accelerate, and to protect themselves accordingly.

Yet in addition to the confidence problem just mentioned, there is a real problem behind inflation and its inertial character that is directly related to a distributive conflict about relative shares. The acceleration of inflation after each price freeze during the Collor administration (there was a price freeze in March 1990 and another in January 1991) cannot have a conventional explanation—excess demand—because the Brazilian economy remained in recession. Also, it cannot be explained by the increase in the money supply as a result of the budget deficit because the Brazilian economy presented an operational (real) budget surplus in 1990 and 1991 and a Treasury (cash) surplus between March 1990 (when the Collor administration took office) and November 1992.

Inflation can always be explained by strict or tautological monetarism, which by using the exchange identity, $MV = Yp$, relates inflation, p, directly to an increase in the money supply, M, given a constant velocity of money, V, and a constant GDP, Y, in the short run. In fact, the monetary base increases with inflation, but it is well established today in the neostructuralist and Keynesian schools that the money supply is endogenous or passive when inflation is high and inertial.[7] The exchange identity is definitional; it does not establish a causal relationship. If V and Y are assumed to be constant, then either M could cause an increase in p, as the monetarists contend, or p—which increases for inertial reasons—could cause an increase in M.

The neostructuralist theory of inertial inflation provides a more sensible explanation. The maintenance of high-level inflation is based on the dynamics of relative prices, which are successively balanced and unbalanced, and a distributive conflict ensues among economic agents.[8] The acceleration of inflation is the result of the attempt to change, in real terms, the relative price balance. Inertia is derived from the acceptance of the fact that relative prices are balanced in real terms but that in the short run they are unbalanced because of the phased character of price increases.

According to this view, the acceleration of inflation that took place in 1991, after the Collor Plan II, was the result of the need to recover the balance of relative prices, lost with the price freeze. Inflation accelerated because, first, the last price freeze, with its *tarifaço* (sizable correction of public prices), had aggravated the imbalance of relative prices, acting as the motor for the resumption of inertial inflation to its prefreeze levels. Further, the postfreeze inflationary residue above 5 percent left it clear that economic agents had no alternative after the plan except to again engage in the inertial game of indexing their prices, correcting them in a phased and alternate way so as to guarantee their income share. Third, in this distributive conflict, economic agents, moved by their previous experience with inflationary acceleration, added a delta or an incremental value to past inflation to protect themselves against the probable increase in inflation. By acting this way, these agents transformed their expectations into a self-confirming prophecy. Finally, these agents knew that, because the state was bankrupt, it was in no position to guarantee the stability of the currency and would end up sanctioning inflation as it increased the monetary base.

This last characteristic defines the scenario of indexed hyperinflation or repressed hyperinflation that prevailed in Brazil from the failure of the Cruzado Plan until the implementation of the Real Plan. André Lara Resende (1988) called it the "hyperinflationary process." Actually, since the failure of the Cruzado Plan the Brazilian economy has been in an intermediary state between a purely inertial or autonomous inflation and hyperinflation. Indexation mechanisms, related to past inflation, continued to operate, but extremely volatile expectations—generally pointing to an acceleration of inflation—were added as a result of the fiscal crisis and the consequent loss of confidence in the government. Economic agents anticipated the acceleration of inflation and behaved accordingly.

Yet with the Marcílio Plan, beginning in November 1991, inflation stopped accelerating and even slowed down modestly. Why? I see three reasons. First, although the Collor Plan failed, it left a positive legacy: in 1990 almost US$28 billion of the internal Treasury debt was canceled. As a result, the fiscal crisis was objectively reduced. Second, Minister Marcílio was finally able to impose his calm, trustworthy style on the economy. At the end of October 1991 there was a speculative attack against the cruzeiro. The premium on the parallel market, which had been around zero, rose to 50 percent in three days. At this point the Central Bank, which had always sold gold on the parallel market when this happened, made a risky but correct decision: it decided to leave the market alone. To the surprise of the Brazilian financial market, this strategy worked. The speculative attack failed. The premium on the parallel market quickly fell back to zero. After this, economic agents altered their expectations. They recognized that they no longer had the power they had held in 1989 to carry out speculative attacks on the cruzeiro.

A third reason inflation ceased to accelerate was the recession caused by extremely high interest rates. Inertial inflation is autonomous from demand. This means that a strong recession has little effect on lowering the level of inflation. It can, however, keep inflation from continuing to accelerate. This must have happened in November 1991.

The partial recovery of public confidence and the recession interrupted the acceleration of inflation. Yet it did not break inflationary inertia. It did not eliminate the indexed nature of the economy. Economic agents in Brazil are used to correcting their prices in accordance with past inflation. Thus it is incorrect to suppose that, given the volatility of expectations, the reversal of expectations would gradually do away with inflation.

Monetarists, particularly the followers of rational expectations, confuse expectations with decisions.[9] They imagine that all expectations are self-fulfilling because they are automatically transformed into economic decisions. Yet an important gap exists between expectations and decisions. In the neostructuralist theory of inflation, economic agents, concerned with protecting themselves in the generalized distributive conflict that characterizes high inflation, are very cautious about changing their decisions. They can change their expectations and admit that inflation may decrease, but because decisions are volatile and untrustworthy, they do not change them. Averse to risk, concerned with protecting themselves, and aware that the economy is a real process of income distribution, economic agents conservatively maintain their decisions to raise prices.[10] Because this kind of rational behavior will be adopted by the great majority of economic agents, a reversal of expectations will not materialize.

In the case of Brazil a reversal of expectations was able to reduce the hyperinflationary component of Brazilian inflation but was unable to break its inertia. Inflation stopped accelerating at the end of 1991, but it did not go down, although expectations—strongly influenced by the dominant ideological character of monetarist views—held that it would do so. Distributive conflict, the protection of income shares, the prevalence of decisions over expectations, the tendency of economic agents in the real sector to base their price decisions on past experience (only in the financial sector are expectations dominant in defining price decisions),[11] and the fact that inflation is essentially a real process with monetary consequences rather than merely a monetary phenomenon, checked the expected reduction of the inflation rate. What was left was only an inefficient and ineffective economic policy.

L ike the Marcílio Plan, most, if not all, stabilization plans in Brazil have been inefficient. All of the purely orthodox programs—the two IMF-sponsored stabilization programs (the Delfim Plan III in 1983 and the Marcílio Plan, 1991–1992), the Beans and Rice Plan (1988), and the Eris Plan (1990)—were inefficient because they did not take into consideration inertial inflation and tried to stabilize gradually. All of the predominantly populist plans, such as the Delfim Plan I (1979) and the Cruzado Plan (1986), were inefficient for obvious reasons. They were also the outcome of a lack of political support for the necessary fiscal adjustment. Some plans were simply flawed, such as the Delfim Plan II (1981), the Dornelles Plan (1985), and the Summer Plan (1989).

The stabilization program I was responsible for, which came to be known as the Bresser Plan (1987), was an emergency plan left unfinished when I resigned from the Finance Ministry seven and a half months after taking office because of lack of political support for the fiscal adjustment plan I had formally proposed to the president.[12] I then insistently asserted that a stabilization program based on a new price freeze, coupled with the use of the exchange rate as a nominal anchor, could control inflation efficiently, provided the required fiscal adjustment was undertaken and a minimum social agreement was achieved. Yet since five previous price freezes had not been successful, this proposal was naturally received skeptically. This disbelief ignored, first, that all of the heterodox plans since the Cruzado Plan had included a heavily orthodox component; second, four other plans that were fully orthodox and three that were mixed had also failed.

I now briefly summarize the twelve stabilization programs the Brazilian economy undertook between 1979 and 1992.[13] Did they fail because they were heterodox or because they were orthodox, because they were shock plans or because they were gradualist? Which of the three hypotheses presented earlier was predominant in each plan?

1. The Delfim Plan I (1979), a populist right-wing program that was both developmental and monetarist, was based on the presetting of the exchange rate—that is, on a predicted or planned declining path for the exchange rate. This strategy was popular at the time among members of the Chicago school. The exchange rate guideline was intended to change expectations and to lead economic agents to correct their prices accordingly. Instead, inflation went from 50 to 100 percent a year, and the foreign debt grew from $40 billion to $60 billion in two years.

2. The Delfim Plan II (1981) was a classical orthodox program accompanied by a strong recession. GDP fell 3 percent in 1981, and inflation remained at 100 percent until the end of 1982.

3. The Delfim Plan III (1983) was an orthodox program monitored by the IMF and again marked by recession. Given the inertial nature of inflation—ignored by this plan as by the two previous ones—and the maxidevaluation of the cruzeiro in February 1983, inflation doubled to 200 percent, or 10 percent a month. Yet stabilization of the balance of payments was achieved. Since this time Brazil has presented high trade surpluses.

4. The Dornelles Plan (April–July 1985) was a partially heterodox plan based on freezing public prices and some private oligopolistic sectors, corresponding to about 40 percent of GDP, combined with a strictly monetarist policy at the level of the Central Bank. Inflation fell from 12 to 7 percent a month for three months, then returned—as was to be expected—to the previous level when the frozen prices were finally liberated or corrected according to inflation.

5. The Cruzado Plan (March–December 1986) was a heterodox program based on a price freeze. It was well formulated and received enormous popular support, but it became lost in populism and excess demand. Inflation went from 14 percent to almost zero as a result of the price freeze. In December, when it became impossible to keep prices frozen, inflation exploded.

6. The Bresser Plan (June–December 1987) was a heterodox emer-

gency plan. It did not include either deindexation or monetary reform. The exchange rate was not frozen. It was based on a provisional, short-term price freeze and incomplete fiscal adjustment. Relative prices were deeply out of balance, including the exchange rate, at the time of the plan. As was to be expected, inflation again started to increase slowly. The program should have been completed with a gradual correction of public prices (which was done) and a fiscal reform at the end of the year, which would have prepared for a final price freeze at the beginning of 1988. Because of a lack of political support, the plan was not completed.

7. The Beans and Rice Plan (1988) tried an orthodox program based mainly on the adoption of fiscal and monetary policy. The name *Beans and Rice* refers to the typical Brazilian meal, *feijão com arroz,* and implies a conventional policy in opposition to the heterodox, unconventional one. It was inefficient as a stabilization plan, and political support for the fiscal adjustment did not materialize. The plan ended as a muddling-through strategy, given President Sarney's unwillingness to proceed with a fiscal adjustment program. Inflation, which was at 14 percent a month in December 1987, went up gradually, reaching 30 percent a month by the end of 1988.

8. The Summer Plan (January–June 1989) used a heterodox approach—it was based on a price freeze, deindexation, and monetary reform—and also a monetarist, orthodox plan; it was supported by an extraordinarily high real interest rate (16 percent a month in real terms in the first month). At the time it was decided upon, President Sarney's term was ending, with very low popularity. The decision to adopt an extremely high real interest rate speeded the failure of the plan because it indicated that the government was bankrupt. The plan began to collapse in June 1989 and led to a kind of hyperinflation (an inflation rate above 50 percent a month) in December.

9. The Collor Plan I (March–April 1990) was an orthodox and heterodox program, combining the retention of monetary assets and stern fiscal adjustment with a price freeze. It was in fact essentially an orthodox plan, which received full support from Washington, because its heterodox component—the price freeze—was relinquished almost immediately. Further, it ignored the theory of inertial inflation and did not include in the price freeze a *tablita* (conversion table) that neutralized the relative price imbalances derived from the staggered character of price adjustments when inflation is inertial. The plan succeeded in lowering inflation from 82 percent in March to 3 percent in April. After that, inflation was supposed to be controlled by a mixture of fiscal and monetary policies and an income policy. The formal abandonment of the income policy, which was intended to control residual inflation, on May 15 marked the end of an incomplete plan.

10. The Eris Plan (May–December 1990), the second phase of the Collor Plan I, should be considered a new plan. It was the most strictly mon-

etarist and orthodox strategy ever adopted in Brazil. Its objective was to eliminate the residual inflation left by the Collor Plan I. The fiscal adjustment effort, to which President Collor continued to give full support and that produced a budget surplus in 1990 and 1991, was complemented by the definition and pursuit of a monetary target: a 9 percent increase in high-powered money in the second semester of 1990. The plan was not officially adopted by the IMF but, given its orthodox character, received full support from Washington, as I testified when I visited that city in July 1990. A few days earlier I had presented a paper with Y. Nakano (Bresser Pereira and Nakano 1991) in which we predicted the failure of the plan, which indeed occurred. The Eris Plan illustrated once again the endogenous character of the money supply when inflation is high and inertial. Notwithstanding an enormous recession caused by the tight monetary policy, inflation gradually accelerated, rising from 6 percent in May to 20 percent in December, when the money supply finally went out of control.

11. The Collor Plan II (January–April 1991) was a heterodox plan combined with a big increase in public prices (a tarifaço). This was a totally inefficient program. Inflation increased again immediately following the plan, reaching almost 7 percent in April and 10 percent in June.

12. The Marcílio Plan (May 1991–October 1992) was an inefficient, fully orthodox, IMF-sponsored stabilization plan. It started with 10 percent a month inflation and ended with 20 percent a month inflation.

These plans failed not only because of inefficiency or the incapacity of the government to devise a comprehensive stabilization program based on past experience, free from previous mistakes, and able to predict the reactions or defenses of economic agents to the stabilization policies. The extreme crisis and political hypotheses also played a role in their failure.

The explanation based on an excessive public debt is powerful. There is no doubt that an excessively high foreign and domestic debt causes stabilization efforts to be self-defeating.[14] It is no mere coincidence that most of the highly indebted countries failed to stabilize and that a reasonable—although insufficient—solution (the Brady Plan) was not found. When countries face an acute fiscal crisis and hyperinflation, it is not by chance that they almost invariably resort to some sort of internal debt cancellation and some kind of international financial support.

Yet public debt reduction, whether foreign or domestic, is a stabilization strategy with clear limits. Foreign debt reduction does not depend only on the debtor countries. Arrears are always an alternative but are costly. There are some classical cases of unilateral cancellation of part of the foreign debt. This was the case with the United States in the nineteenth century and with Germany in the 1930s and again in 1953. It was the case with Britain after

World War II. To a certain extent, it was the case with Costa Rica before a Brady Plan legitimated it. But countries do not usually have the external power and the internal unity to execute such a move.

Brazil did not have the power to reduce its foreign debt unilaterally. This fact helps to explain Brazil's failure to stabilize. Yet, although substantial sectors of the economy hoped for a large foreign debt reduction, this possibility hindered the required internal adjustment. When the debt was eventually negotiated according to the Brady Plan (1993), the hope of transferring a larger share of the fiscal adjustment cost to foreign creditors disappeared. Foreign debt reduction was small and unsatisfactory, but it was all that was politically possible at the time.[15] The burden-sharing process was over. Given that the foreign debt is a public debt, since 1993 Brazilians have known, at least presumably, the adjustment costs they have to face.

A partial cancellation of the domestic debt is much more common. But it is also risky and provokes strong political reactions. It can only be decided upon when the crisis is acute. Even in this case, it demands courage. And if it does not succeed in stabilizing the economy, the debt can easily be rebuilt. This was the case in Brazil. The Collor Plan I canceled almost half of the domestic Treasury debt. This fact significantly improved the country's fiscal condition, but because the fiscal crisis was not overcome and stabilization was not achieved, the internal debt began to increase once again, particularly after November 1991 when interest rates were sharply increased. It is not by chance that in Brazil today the possibility of a long-term consolidation of the internal debt—a milder form of debt cancellation—is again being discussed.

Following the debt cancellation the Collor Plan I promoted (almost 7 percent of GDP), stabilization became easier. This is one of the reasons—combined with the political support the Collor administration enjoyed at certain times—that in early 1990 and early 1992 two concrete opportunities to stabilize the Brazilian economy arose. The fact that they were lost when political support was present and the fiscal crisis had abated is an indication that they lacked technical competence and were inefficient.

F inally, we have the political hypothesis to explain the delay in stabilizing Brazilian inflation. Behind the political theory are two complementary phenomena—economic populism and lassitude toward inflation—that exemplify the lack of political support economic teams face for the difficult fiscal adjustment measures any stabilization program requires.

Political support for economic reforms depends on society's perception of the need for reforms and of the net costs of transition. Reforms are not always felt necessary. When the inflation rate is still at a "reasonable" level, certain societies—such as Brazil's—are insensitive to inflation and ready to live with it. Other reforms, such as trade liberalization, may not be considered desirable for a long time because they confront hidden interests.

Once the need for reform has been perceived, it is necessary to consider the net transitional costs. These costs represent the difference between the costs involved in the reform (in terms of higher taxes, unemployment, and the restructuration of business enterprises) and the costs of postponing reforms, of muddling through the crisis.[16]

Net transitional costs tend to be high initially because the costs of not adjusting or reforming—of living with inflation, balance-of-payments problems, protectionism, and inefficient use of resources—are still small, and the costs of adjusting the economy—of stabilizing, getting prices right, and proceeding with market-oriented reforms—are high. Yet as reforms are delayed, the costs of muddling through the crisis increase and eventually become higher than the costs of adjusting the economy. At this point the nonadjustment costs curve crosses the transitional costs curve. In the limit, the increasing distortions will lead to an acute fiscal crisis and hyperinflation. When this happens, society should have no doubts that the costs of muddling through are much higher than the transitional costs, that the net transitional costs are highly negative, and that it is time to adjust.

Yet it may be a long time before the country arrives at hyperinflation. It is also possible that the net transitional costs are already negative, and society is impervious to reforms. This collective irrational behavior has several explanations. First, society may not have correctly perceived the situation. The previous growth strategy may have been so successful that it is difficult to admit that it has become distorted and disruptive. Second, total net transitional costs may be negative, but some groups within the economy may still be gaining from the crisis.[17] If we draw the two sets of curves for each significant group, class, and industry in society, we would probably find that, for some, the costs of muddling through the crisis quickly cross the transitional costs curve, whereas for others this intersection occurs much later, if ever, because these groups are profiting from inflation. If this is the case, they will resist adjustment; they will deny political support for stabilization as long as they can.

Reforms may also be delayed or may fail because of weaknesses in the institutions that facilitate the negotiations leading to the required decisions. If associations of workers and businesspeople are not representative, political parties are weak and disorganized, and the state is disrupted by a severe fiscal crisis and does not counter with departments that are able to mediate negotiations and enforce agreements, it will be much more difficult to reform successfully.

All of the twelve stabilization programs faced difficulties in this area. Yet it must be emphasized that the three stabilization plans of the authoritarian regime (Delfim plans I, II, and III) did not fail for lack of political power. The Cruzado Plan in the Sarney administration, and in the Collor administration the Collor Plan I, the Eris Plan, and the Marcílio Plan between January and April 1992, met with reasonable political support.[18]

The Cruzado Plan and the Delfim Plan I, however, failed for an essentially political reason: they were populist stabilization plans. The Cruzado Plan especially had enormous political support. But this support was perverse, derived from the populist aspects of the plan. The Cruzado Plan did not fail because of a lack of political support but because of an excess of it. The Collor Plan I, the Eris Plan, and the Marcílio Plan were not populist plans, and they did not fail because they lacked political support. The Brazilian and foreign elites strongly supported them. They failed because they were inefficient.

❖ 15 ❖

Successful Reforms

B razil did not pass through its worst economic crisis without making profound changes. Particularly in 1987, when the magnitude of the crisis began to be acknowledged, substantial fiscal adjustment and deep market-oriented economic reforms were undertaken. Major social, political, and ideological changes were also taking place in the country. The social changes were related to the enormous increase of the middle class and of university-educated people. The political changes were linked to the extraordinary increase of enfranchised citizens and to the consolidation of democracy. The ideological changes were expressed in the crisis of populism and national developmentalism.

Brazil in the mid-1990s is quite different from the Brazil of the late 1970s when this crisis started. Luís Nassif (1995) expressed this modernization or *aggiornamento* very clearly:

> The great Brazilian cultural "aggiornamento" was almost completed. Some principles are already hegemonic: decentralization favoring states and the municipalities, privatization with regulation and without depleting the public patrimony, trade liberalization, the precedence of productivity and competitiveness over protectionism, the view of the state as a regulating and surveying agent, not as an operator.

To the list of ideas embodying this cultural modernization I would add two additional ones: the concern with fiscal discipline; and the realization that wage and salary increases may be inflationary. Budget deficits, which in the recent past have usually been viewed as good because of the expanded aggregate demand, are now approached in an entirely different way. The concept of *trade-off*, which is foreign to the Brazilian culture (there is no corresponding word in Portuguese) has begun to be understood.

These cultural changes, which for many were the outcome of an intellectual transition from the old ideas, corresponded to concrete economic and state reforms: fiscal adjustment; trade liberalization; privatization; and the restructuration of business firms. Yet for two basic reasons, foreigners and even Brazilians had great difficulty acknowledging these changes, particularly the economic reforms. First, high inflation, which remained until the implementation of the Real Plan in July 1994, blinded everybody to the reforms that had been instituted. It was difficult, if not impossible, for peo-

189

ple who did not comprehend the logic of high and inertial inflation to understand how fiscal adjustment and economic reforms could be implemented while inflation remained in an incredible two-digits-monthly zone. Second, the Brazil-oriented character of the market-oriented reforms led neoliberal ideologues and business agents who were privately interested in more-radical reforms to say that these reforms were not occurring or that they were not bold enough.

In addition to being market-oriented, the economic reforms were Brazil-oriented because they actively considered the country's national interest as well as macroeconomic fundamentals. They were not confidence-building reforms, designed mainly to build confidence in Washington (the U.S. government and the international institutions) and New York (the financial system). The reforms could also have this goal, but they did not assume that Washington and New York were the depositories of economic rationality or that the national interest of Brazil was equated with that of the developed countries.

The mistake of using a confidence-building strategy was made especially by President Salinas (1988–1994) in Mexico. If one wants to understand the basic reason behind Mexico's financial collapse in December 1994, I suggest it was the militant confidence-building strategy Salinas adopted at the expense of Mexico's national interest and of macroeconomic fundamentals. This confidence-building strategy started in early 1989, when, just six months after the Brady Plan was announced, Mexico signed a debt agreement (the term sheet) in which debt reduction was insignificant. When analysts denounced this fact, observing that the agreement did not serve Mexico's national interest, the answer was immediate: indeed, the discount was small, but the agreement built confidence, and the interest rate paid by Mexico fell.[1] Following the apparent success of the confidence-building strategy, such a strategy became standard in the Salinas administration. Economic growth was not resumed, but Mexico became the model Washington and New York presented to Latin America. The way the privatization of the commercial banks was undertaken and the decision to maintain an overvalued currency—notwithstanding huge current account deficits—were manifestations of a confidence-building strategy that clearly conflicted with macroeconomic fundamentals. The strategy worked for some time, but it finally became clear that it was not Mexico-oriented, that it did not uphold the national interest and macroeconomic fundamentals.

In this chapter I present some of the reforms that were undertaken in Brazil, underlining their Brazil-oriented character—that is, their consistency with the national interest, with strong macroeconomic principles, and with reforming or rebuilding the state. I am not suggesting that these reforms were ideally designed. They have been carried out in difficult, if not abnormal, times, particularly since 1987. The obstacles they faced were huge. They have not been completed by the mid-1990s, but sizable advances have been made.

Particularly in the case of privatization, reforms were undertaken without ignoring the country's national interest. Trade liberalization was bold, but it was carefully planned and pragmatically implemented. Price stabilization was only possible when competent economists ignored the orthodox recommendations coming from Washington or from mainstream economics, which were based on either conventional monetary and fiscal policies that would gradually control inflation or a monetary shock, and which added to the obviously required fiscal adjustment a heterodox strategy aimed at neutralizing inflation's inertia.

Between 1987 and 1994 (see Table 15.1), growth rates were modest, becoming negative in 1988, 1990, and 1992. In this period fiscal surpluses were achieved, but inflation remained at extremely high levels. Only in July 1994 did prices stabilize. In this chapter I discuss the market- and Brazil-oriented reforms that took place during this period, as well as the Real Plan, which successfully stabilized prices after twelve failed previous attempts.

Table 15.1   Budget Deficit, GDP Growth, and Inflation

	Deficit (% GDP)	GDP Growth (%)	Inflation (%)
1987	5.7	3.6	367.1
1988	4.8	–0.1	891.7
1989	6.9	3.3	1,635.8
1990	–1.4	–4.4	1,639.1
1991	0.2	1.1	458.6
1992	1.9	–0.9	1,129.5
1993	0.7	5.0	2,491.0
1994[a]	0.0	5.7	929.3

Sources: Budget deficit, public-sector borrowing requirements in real terms: Central Bank, *Brazil Economic Program,* several issues; GDP growth: IBGE *Anuário Estatístico do Brasil,* several issues; inflation, consumer price index: FIPE/USP.
Note: a. Preliminary data for budget deficit and GDP growth.

There are two types of relevant economic reforms at present: reforms that stabilize the currency and the balance of payments, among which fiscal adjustment is the most relevant; and market-oriented or structural reforms, among which trade liberalization and privatization are paramount. In Brazil both kinds of reforms took place. Fiscal adjustment was started in 1981, just two years after the crisis broke out in 1979; adjustment resumed in 1983, was suspended during the 1985–1986 populist episode, resumed in 1987, dramatically deepened in 1990–1992, and again resumed in 1994 to make the Real Plan viable. Stabilization of the balance of payments was achieved as early as 1983, when the exchange rate was devalued; since that time huge trade surpluses have been presented every year. Only in late 1994, following the Real Plan, the appreciation of that plan, and the warming-up of demand, did this trade surplus become threatened. A considerable restructuration of business enterprises, with around a 30 percent productivity increase in three years, took place in 1990–1992 as a consequence of the recession provoked by President Collor's stabilization attempts and the trade liberalization process.

Trade liberalization was the most far-reaching economic reform Brazil undertook. It was long overdue and should have been initiated in the 1960s when the import substitution strategy proved exhausted, yet twenty years passed before it was seriously considered and implemented.

In 1987, at the Comissão de Política Aduaneira (CPA), its president, José Tavares de Araujo, Jr., a leading neostructuralist economist, initiated studies to liberalize trade. At about the same time, at the Banco Nacional de Desenvolvimento Econômico e Social, another group of state bureaucrats—working in the same direction—proposed that Brazil should change its long-term industrial policies, engaging in a "productive integration program" with the rest of the world. Tavares's project would eliminate all quota and administrative import controls, replacing them with a tariff system. To do that it was necessary, first, to fully revise the tariff system, which had been distorted by several years of misuse. Second, the plan would eliminate all tariff subsidies. Yet in this first stage the level of tariff protection should remain high. Only in a second stage should it be gradually reduced.

As finance minister, I gave full support to Tavares's project and started negotiations with the World Bank for a US$1 billion structural adjustment loan that would be based on trade liberalization. In December 1987, when I left the government, the revision of the tariff system was complete. A few months later it would be implemented. Yet the effective process of trade liberalization took place only after Collor's election. All administrative barriers to imports were eliminated, and a four-year program of tariff reduction was announced. Over the next four years the plan was implemented, transforming Brazil into an extraordinarily open economy. As Table 15.2 reveals, the average protection fell from 32.2 percent in 1990 to 14.0 percent in 1994. Nearly all import quotas and administrative controls were eliminated.

Table 15.2   Import Taxes

	1990	1991	1992	1993	1994
Highest tax	105.0	85.0	65.0	55.0	35.0
Average tax	32.2	25.3	20.8	16.5	14.0

Sources: Ministry of Industry and Commerce; Revista Exame, July 1994.

The trade reform followed the national-interest principle. There is an old nationalist interpretation according to which trade liberalization is the outcome of pressure by the developed countries, directly or through the World Bank. This view makes no sense. Conditionality and GATT pressures played no role. Only unilateral retaliations were relevant and only in one case: the radical market reserve for the computer industry. Yet even in this case domestic opposition to protection was the dominant factor leading to its being watered down. Another view suggests that the ideological hegemony of the developed countries played a major role (Nassuno 1995). This is certainly true. Brazilian culture, as a peripheral or developing society, is ideologically enormously influenced by the cultural and economic centers in the North. Thus such influence is part of what explains trade liberalization in Brazil. Yet the decision to open the economy was essentially a domestic one. When I supported Tavares's initial work, or when Collor and Zélia implemented a bold trade liberalization program, we were not trying to build confidence but were acknowledging that the import substitution strategy was long exhausted and that the best and first industrial policy was one that would constrain Brazilian firms—including the multinationals that were supposed to provide protection—to increase their productivity and compete.

It is usual in Latin America to identify trade liberalization with neoliberal reforms and to oppose this reform of industrial policy. Yet when President Collor decided to go ahead with trade liberalization in March 1990, liberalization was viewed as an essential part of an industrial policy. As Fritsch and Franco (1993:28) underlined, the document that introduced trade liberalization in Brazil presented it as the essential ingredient of an industrial policy that would create "stable and transparent rules for industrial competition." Selective incentives, typical of an industrial policy, would be utilized, but the main tool to promote a productivity increase would be trade liberalization. The reform remained a market-oriented reform, but it was also a Brazil-oriented one.

The trade liberalization program was a huge success. Firms had to restructure, dismiss excess personnel, give up some sectors, enter new ones, and become more export-oriented. Between 1990 and 1993 productivity increased around 30 percent. Around four hundred firms won the International Organization for Standardization–9000 certificate. Only a few firms had real problems. Nearly all revealed that they were able to face international competition. The program also proved to be pragmatic. In early 1995, when automobile imports became excessive, the government raised tariffs. The automotive industry is a strategic industry with enormous backward and forward linkages that deserves special treatment.

The privatization program, which had started timidly in the mid-1980s, gained new strength in 1990. Priority was given to competitive industries under state control. The steel industry was the first to be privatized. In 1977, when some small steel mills were being privatized, I asked the leaders of the local industry why they did not demand that large mills be privatized. They told me that this "was impossible." Yet in the early 1990s all of the big mills (Siderúrgica Nacional, Cosipa, Usiminas, Tubarão) were privatized. The privatization of the petrochemical industry is currently under way. Electrical plants will probably be next.

Brazil in 1995 is approaching the time of privatizing monopolies. In this case it is concurrently necessary to establish efficient regulatory systems. When the market is competitive, private enterprises are undoubtedly superior. In the case of natural monopolies, however, regulation becomes a key factor.

The privatization program in Brazil has been implemented cautiously and competently. The results are satisfactory. Between 1991 and 1994 thirty-two state-owned enterprises were privatized, for which the Treasury received $7.9 billion. The two basic motivations behind the program were to achieve more operational efficiency and to solve the fiscal crisis of the state. The first privatizations were subject to some criticism because *moedas podres*—old bonds the Brazilian government was not honoring—were accepted as means of payment in the public auctions. Given the fiscal crisis of the state, these old debts could be consolidated in the long run, and the government would receive cash. More recently, the government has been pressing bidders to offer a larger proportion of cash.

F iscal adjustment and privatization were other major reforms achieved by Brazil. The budget deficit, which was around 8 percent of GDP in the early 1980s, was brought down to around 4 percent between 1982 and 1984. It rose again in the populist New Republic (1985–1989) and fell dramatically during the Collor administration. After two surpluses, public-sector borrowing requirements in real terms were around 1 to 2 percent of GDP.

In spite of the stern fiscal adjustment, Collor's finance ministers failed to control inflation because their economic teams and, in 1992, the IMF, which approved a stabilization program for Brazil, were unable to recognize the inertial character of Brazilian inflation. In fact, they were victims of a monetarist or mainstream economic bias that made them unable to understand what inertia was and how to fight it. They thought that either a monetary anchor (Collor I and Eris plans, 1990) or a gradualist fiscal and monetary policy (Marcílio Plan, 1991–1992) was sufficient to control Brazil's high and persistent inflation.

A monthly inflation above two digits can be controlled only by a radical attack. If this inflation has a strong inertial component resulting from the informal indexation of the economy, some kind of coordination of expectations should be part of a stabilization program. It is impossible to stabilize an economy gradually through fiscal and monetary policies. This kind of conventional policy is suited to control moderate demand inflation. In this case reducing state expenditures, increasing taxes, and increasing the interest rate reduce aggregate demand, thus diminishing real wages and eventually reducing the rate of inflation. Brazilian inflation, however, was neither moderate nor a demand-push one. It was a high, persistent, cost-pushed or inertial inflation. To stabilize high inflation gradually is costly.[2] To stabilize high and inertial inflation gradually is simply not feasible.

In theory, a gradualist approach to control inertia is viable if the rate of inflation is still relatively low. In this case the stabilization plan would consist of the gradual presetting of prices according to guidelines suggested by government. In fact, however, such a strategy would work only if inertial inflation was moderate. When inflation is high, presetting is ineffective because economic agents are reluctant to take risks and to make decisions in terms of the prisoner's dilemma. For the presetting strategy to be successful, economic agents must believe inflation is falling and will continue to fall and must be ready to correct their prices accordingly. But if inflation does not behave according to predictions, the economic agents who believed in the prediction will suffer loss. If inertial inflation is low, say 2 percent a month, and a formal presetting has an error rate of 10 percent, the economic agents who followed this guideline—increasing their prices 1.8 percent instead of 2 percent in the first month—will have lost only 0.2 percent. However, if inflation is high, say 20 percent a month, their loss will be much greater—2 percentage points—if the guidelines were not followed by other agents. This is why, when inflation is high, economic agents will not obey government guidelines and will gradually reduce their prices in accordance with the expectation of a declining rate of inflation.

When Latin American economists developed the theory of inertial inflation in the early 1980s and concluded that stabilizing this type of inflation would require adopting heterodox policies, the idea was received with reservation in the First World. Some economists were aware that some inertia existed in inflation but, because they were used to moderate inflation rates, paid little attention to it. Most economists, following the conventional ideas on inflation, completely ignored the problem. Yet in the late 1980s a few First World economists started to recommend a combination of income policies and conventional policies.[3]

M.A. Kiguel and N. Liviatan, in an article with the suggestive title "When Do Heterodox Stabilization Programs Work? Lessons from Experience," presented two scenarios of high inflation in which the heterodox plan is not appropriate: when inflation suddenly becomes high; and when hyperinflation exists. In both cases inertia is irrelevant. They concluded, "The single situation in which the heterodox strategy may be useful, then, is in economies suffering from chronic high inflation" (Kiguel and Liviatan 1992:54). Brazil is the country that best fits this description.

The alternative would have been using a nominal anchor—the exchange rate or the money supply—without neutralizing inertia. All hyperinflations have ended when a fiscal adjustment was combined with the convertibility of the exchange rate at a fixed rate. Yet a necessary condition for this strategy is that the economy be strongly dollarized. At this point all price increases become synchronized, contracts are no longer staggered, and inertia is automatically neutralized, ceasing to be an obstacle to stabilization. This was, for instance, the case in Argentina in 1991. The economy was fully dollarized, so that the adoption of the exchange rate as a nominal anchor automatically stabilized prices. It was never the case in Brazil, whose economy was indexed rather than dollarized. Prices increased in a staggered way—each month, each fortnight—whereas when the economy is dollarized, prices increase every day, if not every hour.

A fter the Collor administration's four failed attempts to stabilize inflation, the successor Franco administration seemed paralyzed. In less than one year, four finance ministers succeeded each other without being able to formulate and implement a stabilization plan. Finally, in June 1993, when the inflation rate was over 20 percent a month, Fernando Henrique Cardoso assumed the Finance Ministry. New hopes were raised, given the political support he received and the excellent team of economists he put together.

The first positive outcome of the existence of a new and competent economic team was that the strong and irrational reaction against an economic shock vanished. It was clear that the new economic team would soon adopt a shock therapy, which would probably combine orthodox and heterodox economic policies, to stabilize the economy. It was clear that the major component of the high and persistent inflation in Brazil was inertia. The conventional explanation relating inflation to budget deficits, although valid in normal situations, had been recurrently proved wrong in Brazil. The budget deficit had been zero in 1990 and 1991, but inflation remained high. The other conventional wisdom, which attributes inflation to an increase in the money supply, had also been dramatically proved wrong. Even monetarist economists (Pastore 1994) acknowledged the passive or endogenous character of the money supply when inflation is high and inertial.

The proposal that high and inertial inflation should be controlled through a shock (a monetary reform), preceded or followed by a mechanism of neutralizing inertia, was formulated by Brazilian economists in the early 1980s when they developed the theory of inertial inflation.[4] Some of these economists, who had actively participated in the Cruzado Plan in 1986, were back in the government. The Real Plan, which stabilized prices on July 1, 1994, was drawn up by Pérsio Arida, André Lara Resende, Edmar Bacha, and Gustavo Franco. The first three of these economists contributed to the theory of inertial inflation in the early 1980s and were on the team that formulated the Cruzado Plan. When it became clear that this plan's administration was populist and would lead to disaster, they were the first to internally denounce the mistakes that had been made. They resigned from their posts before the complete collapse of the plan. In 1993, back in the government as part of Fernando Henrique's team, they had the opportunity to apply an alternative (to a price freeze) strategy to control inertial inflation—an alternative Arida and Lara Resende had developed back in 1983–1984.

It was clear to the neostructuralist economists who developed the theory that the stabilization of high and inertial inflation should be divided into four phases: (1) preparation, consisting essentially of fiscal adjustment; (2) coordination of expectations through the correction of relative prices to neutralize inertia; (3) a price shock, usually accompanied by a monetary reform and the adoption of a nominal anchor (the exchange rate), thereby dramatically reducing prices; and (4) consolidation through additional fiscal adjustment plus a tight monetary policy.

Phases 2 and 3 could be inverted depending upon the strategy adopted. Previous attempts in Brazil—beginning with the Cruzado Plan—had adopted first the price shock and second the correction of relative prices through conversion tables. Similar strategies were successfully adopted in Israel (1985) and Mexico (1987). In Brazil they failed. Thus in 1994 the decision was made to adopt the second, more complex alternative: first to neutralize inflation through the URV mechanism—a U.S.-dollar-pegged money index, to which all prices were converted in the three months previous to the monetary reform (July 1, 1994) when inflation was practically zero.

The original and extremely ingenious idea in the Real Plan was to have two currencies coexisting at the same time: the old currency, in which inflation would be high; and a new, indexed currency. This dual system would permit economic agents to convert their contracts in a voluntary, market-oriented way from the old currency, in which contracts embodied the expected rate of inflation, to the new currency, which—because it was linked to the dollar—would have no inflation. Then, when monetary reform eliminated the old currency, inflationary pressures, derived from relative price imbalances and from the fact that in inertial inflation prices are changed in a phased, nonsynchronized way, would be absent. Relative prices in the new currency would already be balanced, so that conversion tables (tablitas) aimed at eliminating expected inflation from contracts would not be necessary.

In the early 1990s, when the idea of a new shock was discredited, Lara Resende (1992) came back to his original idea and suggested a further step: that the new currency, convertible to the dollar, would be issued by a Currency Board that would hold the international reserves of the country. Fernando Henrique Cardoso's economic team viewed this alternative as too radical. Preference was given to Arida's simpler proposal. Rather than issuing a second currency, the government would create a daily "price-index currency" reflecting present inflation and attached to the exchange rate. It would not actually be a currency because payments would continue to be made in the old one, the cruzeiro. But as a price-index currency, contracts, including credit sales and wages, could be voluntarily converted to it to avoid the need for a tablita on the day of the monetary reform, when the old currency would be extinguished.

The Real Plan was divided into three phases. In the first phase, between December 1993 and February 1994, fiscal adjustment, based on public expenditure cuts and a tax increase, allowed a balanced budget for 1994. Congress, after some initial opposition, approved the fiscal adjustment, which the economic team defined as a prerequisite for launching the program's second phase.

The second part of the plan, from March to June 1994, consisted of neutralizing inertia by utilizing a currency index, the URV, which measured day-by-day, current inflation. This index was closely attached to the exchange rate variation. It was used to adjust all prices in the economy: wages, public and private prices, rents, long-term contracts, and financial applications. As contracts were converted to URVs, prices in URVs remained stable, whereas prices in cruzeiros changed every day—as happens under hyperinflation and full dollarization. As predicted, the market assured that the conversion of cruzeiros to URVs was made basically (not fully) according to the medium real value of the contracts rather than their nominal peak values.

The third phase of the plan was the shock—the monetary reform—that changed the URV into new currency, replacing the cruzeiro, which was extinguished. The rate of inflation was immediately reduced to near zero. The new currency, which economic agents expected to be pegged to the dollar at a one-to-one relationship, was actually evaluated at around 15 percent. Only then was it pegged to the dollar. Like the Cavallo Plan in Argentina, the major problem the Real Plan faces in 1995 is the real evaluation of the *real*. Eight months after stabilization, residual inflation neared 1 percent a month, but accumulated inflation was around 25 percent.

The Real Plan has not yet been consolidated, but clearly it has been an enormous success—an intellectual success for its authors, who were able to develop a heterodox strategy of controlling price inertia without a freeze; a political success for Fernando Henrique Cardoso, whose election to the presidency was basically the fruit of the plan. The Real Plan was a strictly Brazil-oriented economic reform. It was heterodox because it adopted the URV, but it was also orthodox because it never neglected fiscal adjustment and, since the shock, has been supported by an extremely tight monetary policy.

M arket-oriented economic and state reforms, fiscal adjustment, and stabilization did happen in Brazil. The conventional wisdom, dominant in the early 1990s in the developed countries, according to which "Brazil was the laggard of Latin America" was simply false. High inflation blinded everybody. And it was difficult for people who ignore the nature of inertial inflation to understand how such high inflation was possible while economic reforms, including fiscal adjustment, were being undertaken.

These economic and state reforms were Brazil-oriented as well as market-oriented. They were defined and implemented not to please international bureaucrats, government officials, and financial investors in the developed countries but to protect Brazil's national interest and to achieve macroeconomic equilibrium. It is too soon to celebrate victory. Fiscal adjustment will have to produce not only a balanced budget but also positive public savings. Structural economic reform will have to be deepened. Yet, there is no doubt that the crisis was not in vain, that economic reforms were indeed accomplished in Brazil.

✶ 16 ✶
The International Perspective

A country's economic alliances are directly related to its development strategy. In the case of Brazil and Latin America this is very clear. This region's dependence on England in the eighteenth century and later on the United States was related to the primary-export nature of its economy. When import substitution became dominant in the 1930s, relations with the central countries changed because local markets needed to be protected from international competition. This was done first at the national level; then, in the 1950s, Latin American integration was seen as a way to broaden import substitution markets. In this context regional integration was essential for the smaller countries, whereas for the larger ones, such as Brazil, it was a condition of development only if they wanted to prolong the import substitution program indefinitely.

The necessary consequence of the import substitution strategy was a certain degree of nationalism. The military regime in Brazil, which had employed antinationalistic rhetoric in 1964, eventually adopted a nationalistic foreign policy when it opted to maintain the import substitution strategy. However, when it became clear that this strategy had run its course—even for the larger Latin American countries—Brazil had to reconsider its approach to its international relationships.

In this chapter I argue that, because Brazil has dramatically opened its economy to foreign competition, it should take the next step: it should recognize that world trade and investment are increasingly being organized according to macro regional blocs, and, consequently, it should ask for admission to NAFTA and the EU. This should be done while economic integration with South America and particularly with Mercosul continues to have priority.

Developing a closer relationship with the United States and Europe is a defensive policy that bears no relation to the old, primary-export kind of dependency. It is not consistent with old-time nationalism, which feeds on a xenophobic attitude and begins with the assumption that one's country is unable to negotiate its interests with the developed countries.[1] The new nationalism is based on the concept of national interest, which will have to be protected on a case-by-case basis. All countries are nationalist in the sense that they defend their national interest, but the new nationalism is very different from Latin America's and Brazil's old nationalism, which began with the assumption that the Latin American countries were weak and defenseless, surrounded by imperialist powers. Because they lacked the capacity to negotiate their interests, they had no alternative but to debar foreign influence.

This attitude or policy may have been true in the past, when industrialization was only beginning and the national-developmentalist interpretation was dominant, but it is true no longer. In the context of the crisis of the state interpretation or a social-democratic, pragmatic strategy, the old nationalism gives way to the national-interest concept. Dependency still exists, but interdependency is also a fact; imperialist exploitation may still occur, but mutual interests coexist. Brazil is already able to negotiate its own interests in the international arena.

W hen one considers international trade, the multilateral option is the principle most consistent with the trade liberalization now under way. It also reflects the diversified character of Brazil's exports. Yet this option is viable only if the rest of the world is also effectively engaged in multilateralism and if managed trade and the formation of trade blocs are not basic characteristics of international trade. Europe led this movement. The United States, Canada, and Mexico followed with the NAFTA agreement. Thus the idea that Brazil is a "small global trader," which the current Brazilian Ministry of Foreign Affairs holds, may be a good description of what Brazil represents in international trade terms, but it does not imply a policy of continuing to be so.[2]

Trade blocs are discriminating institutions. They liberalize trade within the region, but they also establish preferences among its participants while discriminating against outsiders. They are often trade-diverting rather than trade-creating. Thus participation in trade blocs is not a case of pure economic rationality but a pragmatic issue of self-protection. If Brazil insists on staying out of NAFTA and the EU, it will be a victim of trade discrimination.

The argument against participating in a trade bloc is that, if it were to join such a bloc, Brazil would no longer be able to protect its industry against foreign competition. This is an old protectionist argument that was significant in import substitution strategy times but that no longer makes sense because Brazil has opened its economy. Additional opening will be necessary, but as a trade-off huge markets will also be open to Brazil.

Brazil's most obvious partner outside South America is the United States, but in 1994 the European Union showed increasing interest in celebrating a free trade agreement. Only Japan, which leads a production rather than a trade bloc in East and Southeast Asia, has shown no particular interest in Brazil.

The U.S. interest was shown in the June 1990 Bush Initiative (the American Enterprise), which ended with NAFTA approval in 1993. The

U.S. government opened three fronts for negotiation with this initiative: reduction of the public foreign debt, support for technological development, and the formation of a free trade zone with Latin America.

Brazil's reaction to this initiative was cautious, saying it "lacked real content" and that the country had decided to negotiate on a limited basis and to "wait for a better definition" of the Bush Initiative on the part of the U.S. government. This is dramatic proof that Itamaraty does not understand the new times and dismisses U.S. integration because of old nationalist and developmentalist ghosts. It is true that the U.S. offering was timid and that the free trade proposal was vague, but this does not justify Brazil's paralysis.

The proof that integration with Latin America was consistent with the U.S. national interest was demonstrated by the NAFTA agreement. Mexico gave content to the U.S. integration rhetoric. Inter-American rhetoric in the past has always been that of the United States. The rhetoric and practice of American integration could also be a Latin American rhetoric. At a December 1994 meeting, when all American countries met, a time schedule for American integration was established. Brazil was taken by surprise, but it signed the agreement. Prior to 1994, Brazil was clearly being led in this matter.

It is important to distinguish between rhetoric and practice. Brazilian rhetoric should be that of American integration, but its practice should be to defend this integration while protecting its national interests in each case. This national interest basically coincides with the concept of American integration, but is not necessarily identical to it.

The recent interest of Europe in Mercosul and particularly in Brazil was derived from Mercosul's economic success. It is also possible that the Europeans finally realized that they are losing interest in the Pacific's Latin America because it is so far away and in the Caribbean's Latin America because it is too close to the United States. But there is no reason not to be interested in the Atlantic's Latin America (which, by coincidence, corresponds to Mercosul) because Europe is as much an Atlantic power as is the United States.

With the collapse of the communist regimes and the failure of GATT's Uruguay Round, a new field has opened up for new models of international relations. Brazil is naturally concerned with this. Yet the consequent multipolarity could lead Brazil to deepen a multilateral policy, which could easily be transformed into a new wave of conflicts with the United States, similar to the one that prevailed during the Sarney administration. The realization that the United States has lost its world economic hegemony strengthens the multilateral option and favors mounting conflicts. In fact, U.S. hegemony has been waning since World War II because of the growth of Japan and Western Europe. Nevertheless, there is a big gap between concluding that the United States has lost its importance and concluding that Brazil should reinforce its independence in relation to all countries.

On the contrary, now more than ever it is important for Brazil to make a positive choice regarding the formation of regional trade blocs. The agreement may be with both NAFTA and the EU. It is not incompatible to sign two agreements. Precedence should probably be given to NAFTA because it is impossible, in practical terms, to negotiate simultaneously with both blocs. But the decision between one or the other bloc as Brazil's first partner will depend on the interest demonstrated by the would-be partner. Maintaining an independent course among these groups of nations is tempting but unwise. Competition among the world blocs will increase in the coming years, and each needs to know the countries on which it can depend.

C arlos Escudé (1991), who has been studying the confrontational nature of Argentina's international relations prior to President Carlos Menem, defined an alternative policy of "peripheral realism." He enumerated the following principles for such a policy: (1) reduce confrontations with the big powers to "material" subjects directly related to their well-being and power base; (2) submit foreign policy to a rigorous calculation of costs, risks, and benefits; (3) redefine the concept of national autonomy, replacing the concept of confrontational capacity with one of the relative costs of autonomous action; and (4) abandon the anthropomorphic concepts of "dignity" and national "pride," using public interests rather than state interests as the orientation for foreign relations.

The principles of peripheral realism clearly imply more criticism of Argentina's foreign relations than of those of Brazil. It is difficult, however, not to see that they can be applied to Brazil as well.

I must make a distinction between my ideas and those of Escudé. His analysis was based on the observation that Argentina is "a country that is dependent, vulnerable, impoverished and not strategic for the interests of the United States" (Escudé 1991:3). This is the source of the need to reduce confrontation with the great powers. I work from an opposite consideration. Although I recognize that Brazil is relatively impoverished and vulnerable, between the 1950s and the 1990s it changed into an industrialized country in the middle stage of development that has the capacity to promote its own interests and to negotiate with the big powers without fear and free from the need to be on the defensive.

My common ground with Escudé is pragmatism, the desire to avoid useless confrontations and theoretical discussions when what is important is results. The model for this kind of analysis, however, is not found in Latin America but in post–World War II Japan. Defeated in the war, Japan established a solid political alliance with the United States that did not prevent it from advancing its economic objectives. On the contrary, this alliance provided Japan with generous aid at first. It also never prevented Japan from keeping its national interest as the criterion for its decisions.

We see this process repeating itself in other countries in the Far East and Southeast Asia. In this region economists and technocrats are essentially pragmatic. They practice strong state intervention, but their rhetoric states that their economies are market-oriented because such rhetoric facilitates their international relations. They are not concerned with confidence building. They are not ready, as Mexico was, to build confidence in Washington and New York at the expense of their countries' national interests and of macroeconomic fundamentals. But they are ready to establish friendly political relations with the developed countries.

A country's foreign relations are heavily dependent on its international image. Its bargaining capacity increases or decreases depending on the credibility its government possesses in the international arena. To achieve a positive image, it is important to adopt the rhetoric Washington likes, as well as to adopt a competent diplomatic strategy, but what is really essential is to achieve results. Recently, Brazil's image has been negatively affected by bad rhetoric and unsatisfactory results.

In April 1991, on the eve of the change of command at the Ministry of the Economy, I testified before the Brazilian Senate's Commission of Economic Affairs in support of the provisional agreement Brazil had signed with the commercial banks, according to which the country would resume the payment of interest while negotiating a final agreement.[3] In my testimony I tried to answer one question: why did Brazil accede to this provisional agreement rather than demanding that an agreement on the principal be signed before paying interest in arrears?

The answer to this question is simple: given the support the commercial banks were receiving from their governments—especially from the United States—and the Collor administration's lack of international credibility, the alternative most in line with Brazilian national interests was to sign this agreement. It was necessary to recover a minimum level of international confidence, and a standby agreement with the IMF would contribute substantially to this end. The provisional accord with the commercial banks was a positive step in this direction. National interest is sometimes defended by confronting the interests of other countries. At other times it is necessary to be conciliatory and to make concessions; this situation is more common. Sometimes a strategic retreat is necessary, especially if one's adversaries, as in the case of the commercial banks, are capable of gathering extraordinary forces.

How were the banks able to obtain such strong support from their governments? Was it because the IMF refused to sign an accord with Brazil in 1990, although it had approved the Brazilian letter of intention? Was it because the G-7 decided at its February 1991 meeting to use the multilateral agencies to pressure Brazil to yield to the banks? Or was it because the Inter-American Development Bank refused a loan to Brazil because of the vote of the U.S. representative?

The main reason was, in fact, the Brazilian government's loss of credibility. This loss, which had been dramatic inside Brazil, was echoed on the international level. In the first half of 1990 the First World was very pleased with Brazil. But between July 1990 and April 1991 there was a complete change in attitude toward Brazil on the part of the directors of the multilateral agencies and, more broadly, the First World. In mid-1990 there were great hopes for the new Brazilian government, with its "modern attitude" and liberalizing, market-oriented reforms. In addition, the courage and strength of the fiscal adjustment involved in the Collor Plan I (March 1990) spoke well for the antipopulist character of the new administration. This support became complete when the Brazilian government adopted a rigorously orthodox monetarist strategy for fighting inflation in May 1990. This was a mistake the Brazilian authorities and Washington made together. The support of the Washington authorities for the monetarist policy was so clear that, in September 1990, the IMF approved the Brazilian strategy to fight inflation almost in toto. The agreement failed to be approved by the board of directors only because an agreement with the banks was lacking.

Predictably, this strategy failed because it was erroneous (see Chapters 5, 7, 12, 13, and 14). However, when it failed and inflation returned, the blame was placed exclusively on the Brazilian government. Rather than admit that the strategy was incorrect, that inertial inflation and informal indexation cannot be fought with monetary measures, the word in Washington was that the Brazilian government had failed because it was populist, because it lacked adequate monetary control, and because it did not force more corporations and banks into bankruptcy (in September 1991 there was a slight easing of the monetarist policy because of the failure of banks). The extremely high 1991 interest rates, a fundamental cause of that year's recession, were overlooked.

In the United States there is the saying that nothing succeeds like success. The reverse is also true—nothing fails like failure. Failure proliferates, and the guilty party is always the one that failed, not the one that supported erroneous strategies. After the Real Plan in July 1994, the Brazilian image in the First World radically changed, this time in a positive direction. But the Mexican financial crisis in December 1994 strongly reduced confidence in the Brazilian economy in the international markets. Again, as had happened in the debt crisis, the "winds of Latin America proved to be stronger."[4]

In its international relationships, Brazil's inability to carry on a dialogue with the First World, particularly the United States, clashed with the Collor government's "modern attitude" that had so charmed the First World. I have already mentioned Brazil's cautious reaction to the Bush Initiative.

Brazil's October 1990 proposal on the foreign debt, however, although correct, struck the First World as excessively daring. The commercial banks profited from the opportunity. They defined the proposal as arrogant and unacceptable. Based on the continuance of the moratorium, they were even able to convince the authorities in Washington and the G-7 governments of an obvious untruth: that Brazil did not intend to pay any of its foreign debt. The banks' strategy was helped by the fact that at that time the monetarist stabilization policy was floundering inside Brazil. The internal erosion of support for the government affected its external credibility. The government's loss of popular support had been accelerating and was disquieting because it was rooted in the deep recession and the reappearance of inflation.

One year later, when Marcílio Marques Moreira had replaced Zélia Cardoso as finance minister, Brazilian rhetoric regarding the debt changed entirely, and a final and reasonable agreement was reached with the banks. Yet Brazil's international image did not improve. The rhetoric had changed in the right direction—it even became submissive at certain times, remembering the Mexican confidence-building strategy—but Brazil was unable to stabilize. The developed countries are impressed by the right rhetoric, but they are more impressed by the right outcomes.

Greater integration between Brazil and the United States or Europe may be a positive factor in helping Brazil face its problems. Recently, we have witnessed arrogance and, subsequently, submission. Neither of these attitudes will achieve anything. U.S. or European integration is a priority for Brazil's international relations. This integration, however, makes sense only if two conditions are fulfilled. First, Brazil must prove capable of going ahead with fiscal adjustment and market-oriented reforms that are Brazil-oriented reforms rather than confidence-building reforms (Chapter 15). Second, externally, Brazil must be able to negotiate competently and to celebrate alliances with the developed countries—without fear and with a friendly but not submissive rhetoric. Brazil is large enough to negotiate with all countries, including the most powerful, and protect its national interests.

❊ 17 ❊

Toward a New Political Pact

I started this book with an analysis of the historical interpretations of Brazil and economic development strategies. I suggested that the most adequate interpretation for Brazil today should be called the crisis of the state approach and that the corresponding growth strategy should be social-democratic and pragmatic. Yet, as I suggested in Chapter 11, this interpretation and this strategy will gain historical relevance only if they are supported by a development-oriented political pact based on a new class coalition that can dominate the political center. A major question, which I discuss in this chapter, is whether such a political pact is already emerging.

Between the 1930s and the 1960s there was no contradiction between being modern and supporting a sizable degree of state intervention. Yet since the 1970s, as the state-led development strategy became increasingly distorted by economic populism and narrow-minded nationalism, and came to a crisis, the country's modernization has become increasingly identified with market-oriented reforms and fiscal discipline. Brazil, as with all of Latin America, resisted this intellectual and political transition. In the early 1980s the dominant views in the country, expressed in the political pact that led the transition to democracy, remained populist and nationalist. It was only after the Cruzado Plan failed that politicians, businesspeople, and labor leaders began to make the intellectual transition to the new ideas. And only in 1994, with the election of President Fernando Henrique Cardoso, did a modern political pact based on a broad political coalition of both the moderate left and the moderate right seem to emerge. In this concluding chapter I analyze this process, which is essential to the consolidation of democracy and the resumption of growth in Brazil.

If modernization is the transition from archaic to modern values and practices, it is this process that has been facing difficulties and setbacks in Brazil. In the 1960s the right, supported by the military, took power and was assumed to be modern, but it eventually proved to be merely a new breed of the old national developmentalism—a bureaucratic and authoritarian developmentalism—whereas the left remained tied to economic populism. Since the 1980s a transition to modernity has been taking place in Brazil in a dramatic and contradictory way. An effective democratization process, market-oriented reforms, sizable improvements in the labor organi-

209

zation of workers, substantial technological progress, and a generalized increase in productivity exist side by side with inefficient economic policies imported from abroad, the resurgence of populism, and the rise of neoliberalism.

The democratic transition that took place in Brazil in 1985 was a transition from an archaic and authoritarian right to a no less archaic populist coalition of businesspeople, middle-class bureaucrats, and workers. I called this political coalition, which was formed around 1977 and existed until 1987, the 1977 populist democratic pact. As should be expected, this political coalition, which assumed power with President Sarney in 1985, failed to resume the process of modernization and development.

João Paulo dos Reis Velloso (1990:24), who, through the prestigious Fórum Nacional he created, became a leading figure in seeking a new development-oriented political pact in Brazil, said that the first basic idea for the modernization of the Brazilian society

> is the option for a democracy that would be buttressed by a new political and social coalition, with a broader basis than the former one. Be the government from the center, the center-left or the left, it will have to incorporate some popular forces of the political coalition behind it, given the accumulated social demands that must be satisfied. Only in this way will we have large political majorities able to support stable governments.

Velloso was conveying a very general belief that modernization in Brazil requires a political pact that can in some way incorporate the masses.

Yet since the failure of the Cruzado Plan in 1987, Brazil has been experiencing a political vacuum. Industrialized countries do not usually require a clear political coalition for their governance. The existence of a broad social contract that defines the power civil society "delegates" to the state, or, more precisely, to the government that runs the state, is sufficient.[1] This institution, which is so powerful in the developed countries, is too weak in the developing societies. Political coalitions able to formulate a national project are required to guarantee political stability and a sense of direction for society. In Brazil such a political coalition has not existed since 1987. Only in 1994, with the election of Fernando Henrique Cardoso, did a new political coalition made up of both the center-left and the center-right become a real possibility.

Brazilian political history can be told by defining the major political coalitions or class alliances.[2] As we saw in Chapter 1, until 1930 an oligarchic political pact prevailed, based on the primary-export development model. From 1930 to 1964 the national-developmentalist or populist pact prevailed, in which the industrial bourgeoisie, the bureaucratic middle class, labor, and sectors of the old oligarchy united around import substitution industrialization. The 1964 authoritarian regime corresponded to the bureaucratic-capitalist pact, which brought together the bourgeoisie, the military, and the civil service and excluded most of the workers and the democratic sectors of the middle class.

In the mid-1970s the authoritarian party's defeat in the December 1974 Senate elections and, two years later, the April Package—President Geisel's coup within a coup, suspending the *distensão* that had begun when he took office in early 1974—were the two political facts that triggered the crisis of the authoritarian coalition.[3] A new political coalition—the 1977 populist democratic pact—began to form. This class coalition was formed when the bourgeoisie lost its fear of the communist threat, saw that the military was no better than civilians at running the economy, and decided—although through a long and uncertain process—to break its ties with the military regime and ally itself with the democratic middle class and the workers. Thus the transition to democracy in Brazil was not the outcome of an internal conflict within the military that divided the soft-liners and the hard-liners nor a gift of a military that had gradually converted to democracy, as the conventional and dominant literature on the subject in the United States suggests,[4] but rather was the consequence of the business class's decision to fracture its alliance with the military bureaucracy and to establish a new alliance with the democratic sectors of Brazilian civil society.

If one wants to be precise, the new political pact emerged in April 1977, following the April Package—a military coup within the already authoritarian regime, which caused an indignant reaction within civil society.[5] The pact fell apart in early 1987, when the failure of the Cruzado Plan proved it represented an unsatisfactory response to the crisis. This pact had been successful in its major and specific objective—to reestablish democracy in Brazil—but it failed in promoting the required economic reforms, stabilizing the currency, resuming growth, and fostering a more equitable income distribution. It failed not only because the crisis left by the authoritarian regime was extreme but also because this democratic political coalition was populist; it still believed import substitution, deficit expending, a widespread system of state subsidies, and naive wage policies could be effective in promoting growth and distributing income.

The New Republic was set up in Brazil in 1985 with high hopes and aspirations, but it fell prey to this populist attitude. It said no to recession and denied or ignored the facts that wage increases would provoke inflation, the public deficit was a serious problem, the state had grown too large, the protectionist development strategies were exhausted, and the state had become immersed in a deep fiscal crisis.

From the failure of the Cruzado Plan in 1987 until the 1994 presidential elections, Brazil gasped in a political vacuum. The great class coalition that characterized the populist democratic pact had died, and nothing had taken its place. The collapse of the 1977 populist democratic pact opened space for President Fernando Collor's reforms, but he was unable to lead a new political coalition.

C ollor was elected in 1989, during this vacuum, without the support of any major political power; his victory rested exclusively on his rapport with the masses. This fact was viewed by many as "normal" in an undeveloped Brazil. This is a mistake. The election of a president without political roots was only possible because the breakdown of the populist democratic pact had left a political vacuum. Collor's election was not the product of a class coalition, and it did not represent the victory of any party or even of a political tendency. It was simply the consequence of his ability to reach the people with a morally indignant stand at a time when the political parties and the social classes were disorganized.

Collor was elected under the banner of modernity, which he correctly defined as expressing the superiority of the market over the state in resource allocation and in the commitment to fighting poverty and inequality. In his direct, personal relationship with each elector there was a clearly populist element, but this fact did not lead him to adopt populist practices when in office. His stabilization policy failed, but this was not because he adopted populist practices, feared to take unpopular measures, or denied his support to the policies of his economic team. It was not because fiscal adjustment was not undertaken. The policy failed because the inertial character of Brazilian inflation was incorrectly appraised. Collor's impeachment in 1992 was not an outcome of resistance to the economic policies he adopted nor a result of their failure to stabilize. It was rather the consequence of proven corruption charges, which revealed a divided and unstable personality. On some occasions he was totally unable to distinguish the public sphere from his private interests; on others he demonstrated a bold and basically correct vision of how to modernize Brazil.

The Collor administration formally ended in September 1992, when he was replaced by Vice President Itamar Franco. Yet he suffered a first significant blow in 1990 with the failure of Zélia's stabilization attempts. Marcílio Marques Moreira's nonstabilization plan ("nonstabilization" because it was completely unable to control Brazil's high and inertial inflation), in addition to reflecting conventional monetarist views, revealed the anomaly of the Brazilian elites who, surviving in a political vacuum, had no national project and had accommodated high inflation.

The Itamar Franco administration faced the same problems. Initially the new president lacked the leadership qualities that were required to stabilize the economy and fill the political vacuum with a new development project. Only when Fernando Henrique Cardoso was invited to be finance minister in 1993 did the picture begin to change. In 1994 Cardoso was able to stabilize prices and a few months later was elected president. The political vacuum began to be filled. It is early, however, to say that the political crisis has been overcome. Cardoso's election demonstrates that a new and broader political coalition is being formed in Brazil. The recurrent failure to stabilize could be explained by the inefficiency of the stabilization programs. It could also be attributed to the fact that some sectors of society had not yet become totally aware of the gravity of the crisis or believed the costs of adjusting could still be avoided, postponed, or paid by others. This was true, but it was rapidly ceasing to be so. Only a few sectors of society profited from inflation, and social awareness of the crisis was much higher than it had been, for instance, in 1987.

Cardoso's election demonstrated that Brazilian society had changed, that modernization had taken place, and that populist and national-developmentalist rhetoric no longer made sense. Yet it remains clear that without a political coalition that encompasses a portion of the masses, the political elites will lack the political power to promote fiscal adjustment, permanently stabilize prices, and define a new strategy of development. They lack legitimacy.

Political elites in Brazil have lived in disarray and perplexity. The basic cause for this must be found in the political vacuum, in the fact that a modern democratic popular pact has not replaced, or is only recently replacing, the 1977 populist democratic coalition. This is why the crisis has been confronted so poorly. The political elites have no project for Brazil. They cannot assume the role of saviors, as they did in 1964. In spite of all of the difficulties, democratic culture has advanced in Brazil. As José Álvaro Moisés (1993:32) observed, "Empirical evidence confirms the existence in Brazil of a preliminary 'reservoir' of democratic legitimacy. Despite a growing and intense malaise among citizens about day-to-day workings of politics, adhesion to the normative principles of democracy persists among different segments of public opinion."

Society has been trying to reestablish a broad political pact. Agreements between the business community and labor are taking place on various levels. On the business side, FIESP and the PNBE, a group of young businesspeople, are more open to dialogue. On the labor side, trade unionism was renewed with Força Sindical, and the CUT became less radical, showing an openness to negotiations. On the bureaucratic and intellectual side, there are attempts to organize around parties near the center, such as the PSDB, or to lead the PT to positions closer to social democracy. Populism, statism, and nationalism, which the PSDB has criticized since its creation, are now being questioned by the above-mentioned sectors of society. Collor, coming from the right, tried to define a common ground between the liberal center-right and the social-democratic center-left with his proposal for "social liberalism." He failed. Cardoso, coming from the left, is proving that such a political project is viable, provided it is implemented with a clear notion of the national interest and with the conviction that the masses need a larger share of income and political power than they have today.

Yet the obstacles to the definition and consolidation of a new political pact remain formidable. First, national-developmentalist and populist sentiments in Brazil are still strong, although they are clearly in retreat. Sizable sectors of the working class and of the bureaucratic middle class are attached to an archaic view of development and either refuse to embark or have difficulty embarking on a modernization pact. As Lourdes Sola (1993:158) observed, "as important as the social and political impacts of economic reforms are, *intellectual adjustments* are required from the governmental, economic, and political elites, when the task of rebuilding the state on a new basis becomes necessary." Intellectual personalities such as Celso Furtado, who was the leading Brazilian intellectual—after Prebisch—in defining the national-developmentalist interpretation of Latin American development, have expressed this difficulty in a compelling way. In a recent book Furtado (1992:35) observed that the developed countries, through high indebtedness and high interest rates, are transferring income to themselves and promoting the disorganization of the national state in the developing countries. Additionally, and according with a basic tenet of the new dependency interpretation, "the predominance of the logic of the multinational enterprises in organizing economic activity will necessarily lead to the increase of inter-regional tensions, to the exacerbation of corporative rivalries, and to the formation of poverty enclaves that will make the country not viable as a national project."

Second, the state bureaucracy, whose role in any new political pact is crucial, lost influence and has been put on the defensive over the past fifteen years; it has been accused of authoritarianism by the democrats and of statism by the neoliberals. Luciano Martins (1993:12) observed, "The state, through the circles of its higher bureaucracy or through the intelligentsia in some way participant of the state, was the institution that, under authoritarian or democratic regime, always 'thought' the country's development. Today, this element, which was present in previous developmentalist strategies, is faltering."

Third, the gap between the elites and the people in Brazil is too large, as we saw in Chapter 11. The radical heterogeneity of Brazilian society turns the poor into half-citizens—into political subjects who are formally citizens but who have little notion of their rights and of how to protect them. Thus we have a citizenship contradiction: the masses, who have the right to vote, are easy victims of demagogical politicians coming from the right or the left.

In the long run, the only solutions to these problems are related to economic development, income distribution, and education. In the short run, however, the most obvious solution to the legitimacy crisis that is behind the citizenship contradiction is a political pact. This pact would embrace the political elites that represent the three basic social classes currently present in Brazil: the capitalist class; the working class; and, in the middle, the bureaucratic or technobureaucratic class. Sérgio Abranches (1993) described three possible political-strategic scenarios to face the present crisis: buffered stress; muddling through; and sustainable mobility. The response to hyperinflation would be the buffered stress strategy, through which the acute effects of the crisis would be controlled. If and when control mechanisms failed, a new rupture would follow. Muddling through is the usual response to a crisis. Stability always remains precarious. The effective solution will be the third scenario—sustainable mobility—which corresponds to the development-oriented political pact I am discussing in this chapter. In Abranches's (1993:21) words, "Consensus on rules and macro-objectives sets up the socio-political conditions required for the implementation of policies aiming at welfare and common goals, while business and individual strategies remain individual-oriented."

I am not speaking of a social agreement that would bring together business and union leaders, with the intermediation of government. A social agreement may help to stabilize the economy, but it is a more specific and short-term type of accord than a political pact. By a political pact I mean a much looser, more informal agreement—a class coalition in which the political representatives have a crucial role. In Brazil's recent history political pacts have included the populist pact between 1930 and 1960, the authoritarian capitalist-bureaucratic pact between 1964 and 1977, and the populist democratic pact between 1977 and 1987.

The new political pact that is finally emerging with the stabilization of the currency and the election of Cardoso is a social-democratic and pragmatic political pact. It is a modernization pact consequent on a broad class coalition. If it outgrows the election of a president and becomes consolidated in the next few years, it will be consistent with the interpretation of Latin America I have presented in this book. It will be a mixture of a European social-democratic and an East Asian pragmatic approach to social and economic development in which a financially recovered state will play a major role in complementing the market, coordinating the economy, and promoting welfare.

Yet this pact is not all-encompassing. Some social groups will lose because of it, particularly the bureaucrats in state-owned enterprises and the lower bureaucracy that was able to receive some privileges of the state. Acuña and Smith (1994:22) observed that "the transformations implied by this 'return to the market' are not neutral with regard to [the] prevailing structure." This is true. The economic groups that have difficulty participating in the market struggle will tend to lose income share. Yet I am not so sure that the adoption of market-oriented reforms "clearly reinforces the structural international capitalist interests and the leading sectors of the domestic entrepreneurial classes" (Acuña and Smith 1994:22). This happened, for instance, in Mexico and Argentina, where economic reforms were confidence-building-oriented. In Brazil they were more pragmatic and consistently more Brazil-oriented.

It is a serious mistake to assume—as most do—that in the good old days of national developmentalism, income distribution was more favorable to the poor or to the workers. This is simply false. The import substitution strategy was accompanied by income concentration throughout Latin America. Now with Cardoso, the social aspects of development are expected to receive special emphasis. Of course, we now know, based on the Asian experience, that export-led growth strategies are more consistent with equitable income distribution as long as the industries that are more able to export are labor-intensive. The import substitution strategy, with its capital-intensive projects, tends naturally to concentrate income, whereas a more market-oriented, internationally competitive economy will have the opposite outcome.

There are obvious obstacles to this pact, which I have discussed in this chapter. Further, we know that a development-oriented political pact only fully defines itself when economic development is already taking place. This constitutes a classic chicken-and-egg problem. The solution for this type of problem is always practical and unpredictable. In 1993 and 1994 Brazil finally experienced growth, and this growth will probably continue. There are signs that the new paradigmatic moment of interpretation of Latin America is beginning to be defined—the crisis of the state or social-democratic approach. This is probably occurring because the crisis of the 1980s is receding, and economic development is being tentatively resumed.

The positive factors that favor a new political pact are present. The Brazilian social structure underwent deep transformations during the past thirty years. As Wanderley Guilherme dos Santos (1985) noted, the four major social actors in Brazil—entrepreneurs, workers, rural workers, and the complex middle class—are very different today from what they were prior to 1964. Entrepreneurs today are represented by myriad associations parallel to the official representative system. The same has happened with workers. Rural workers underwent an enormous unionization process. The middle class—which I would rather call the bureaucratic or salaried middle class (the capitalist or traditional middle class corresponds to the lower stratum of the capitalist class)—increased in size, was proletarized, and became increasingly unionized. In a recent study, dos Santos (1993) examined the impressive increase in the number of special interest associations in Brazil. This extreme fragmentation is a basic reason for the disorder because it makes political representation difficult and complex, but it also demonstrates the vitality of civil society.

The capitalist class, as the dominant class, is ready to participate in a new political pact. It is not afraid of communism or subversion. And recent experience—since the transition to democracy was achieved in 1985—has demonstrated that it has no chance of politically running the country alone. It will either participate in a class coalition, where it will necessarily have a leading but limited role, or it will not lead. In a political vacuum only special interest groups, particularisms, and corporatisms of all sorts will prevail, as is the case today.

The working class today is much better prepared to participate in a political pact than it was before. It now boasts a political party, the PT, with three central unions—the CUT, Força Sindical, and the CGT—and an enormous number of civil associations. It has become more realistic and less demanding than it was immediately after the transition to democracy. In the first years after the new democratic regime was empowered, the representatives of the working class felt they were the creditors of an enormous social debt because of actual and presumed "salary losses." They believed the only way to get what they demanded was through a political organization. They no longer believe that. They rightfully continue to protest against low wages and poverty, but they know the economic crisis is more serious than they thought and that wage increases and income distribution will be possible only if stabilization is consolidated and growth resumed. Through the central unions they did increase their technical capacity to discuss national problems. Before the 1980s they could discuss and demand only wage increases. They had little or no capacity to discuss inflation, stabilization, fiscal adjustment, and development strategies. This situation has changed in a positive direction. They are much more inclined to participate in social and political agreements than was the case in 1985–1986, when they rarely did so. The appearance of the "unionism of outcomes" within the Força Sindical is only one indication of this fact. The changes that have occurred in the CUT and in the PT are also very clear.

The problem of the bureaucracy or salaried middle class is more complex. First, people, including intellectuals and politicians, usually insist on ignoring this class. I will not repeat my arguments on this subject.[6] The bureaucratic middle class is a large and complex social class. As the bourgeoisie or capitalist class is defined by private property or means of production—that is, by capital—the bureaucratic middle class is defined by collective property or control of bureaucratic organizations, whether private, public, or state organizations. Whereas capitalists make profits, the bureaucratic or "new" middle class receives salaries, and the workers receive wages. This class has been increasing worldwide over the last hundred years, basically as an associate of the capitalist class. At one point in the Soviet Union and the other communist countries it tried to fight and replace the bourgeoisie, but it eventually failed. In Brazil it has been on the defensive since the 1970s, not only because of its compromise with the authoritarian regime but also because the crisis of the state and the neoconservative wave were powerful factors in weakening it.

Second, the problem is complex because this emergent class usually disguises or negates itself, particularly since the mid-1970s when the upper state bureaucracy came under attack by the democratic political forces fighting the authoritarian regime. Third, to the bureaucracy the crisis of the state has meant increased instability and disorganization and decreased salaries and prestige. Thus, besieged politically and dismantled by the crisis of the state apparatus, the state bureaucracy today has difficulty participating in a new political coalition.

This last fact implies a neoliberal contradiction comparable to the classical populist contradiction. To promote growth, populists called for active state intervention but weakened the state, supporting chronic budget deficits; neoliberals, to achieve market-oriented economic reforms and efficient resource allocation, fight the state bureaucracy because it is the agent of state intervention. Only a strong state bureaucracy, however, can achieve fiscal adjustment and promote the required market-oriented reforms, which are essentially reforms of the state.[7] The state bureaucracy is not necessarily committed to state interventionism or to neoliberalism. Its commitment is to a kind of rationality, a sort of bureaucratic efficiency that case by case may have different applications.

Yet we know that in contemporary, market-oriented but bureaucratic capitalism it is impossible to have an effective class coalition without the participation of the bureaucratic middle class, particularly the state upper bureaucracy, which in Brazil had a key role in economic development between 1930 and 1980.[8] The state bureaucracy, the public nonstate, and the private bureaucracy are supposed to participate in the emergent political pact: the upper state bureaucracy directly participating in government decisions and the implementation of policies; the public nonstate bureaucracy participating in decisions through the universities and all nonprofit organizations; and the upper private bureaucracy participating through large business and consulting organizations.

What will be the content of such a political pact? It will be a social-democratic and pragmatic pact. It will dominate the political center. It will probably adopt the crisis of the state approach to explain the Brazilian and Latin American crisis. It will agree that the basic cause of the crisis is the crisis of the state, which paralyzed the state. Thus the first job is to rebuild or reform the state, restore state finances, valorize state personnel, and reform and make more flexible the state apparatus, which the 1988 Constitution left extremely rigid.

The second task will be to define a development strategy. This strategy will probably be a mixture of European social democracy, which is welfare-oriented, and East Asian pragmatism, which is industrially and technologically oriented. It will refuse narrow nationalism but adopt a consistent international policy based on the national interest—an interest that has to be defined case by case.

If the state technobureaucracy recovers part of its prestige and is able to participate in a new political pact, a problem will immediately arise: will this bureaucracy be able to pragmatically adopt a mixture of a social-democratic and East Asian approach to economic problems? Theoretically, the answer is yes. It is true that the Latin American high technobureaucracy is composed mostly of economists—many with doctorates from U.S. universities who were strongly influenced by the neoconservative ideas that dominate those universities. Thus as James Malloy (1991:27) observed, "We may be witnessing a new kind of ideological division within neo-liberal coalitions: one that sets off abstract theoretical constructions of market capitalism fashioned by macro economic technocrats from understandings of capitalism forged in the concrete experience of firms and economic sectors. . . . The central contradiction emerges from the fact that technocrats attached to governments design programs around concerns with aggregate outcomes (GNP, etc.) of a market based economic logic and not the fate of any given firm or group." This danger no doubt exists.

Yet if the state bureaucracy is strongly affected by foreign influences, its national orientation remains dominant. This has been the case in the past and remains so today. In many circumstances the state bureaucracy has been an effective guardian of the national interest in Brazil. In addition to adopting the rationality principle, which is its raison d'être, it is also strongly influenced by the dominant views of the local bourgeoisie. Given the ideological hegemony of this class, if it turns to neoliberalism bureaucrats will tend to do the same. Because a reaction against neoliberalism is already evident in the world, including in Brazil, it is reasonable to expect that the upper state bureaucracy—which is essentially flexible in ideological terms—will be a strategic partner in the social-democratic and pragmatic political pact that is emerging.

Abbreviations

❖❖

ABDIB	Associação Brasileira da Indústria de Base
ALADI	Associación Latinoamericana de Integración
ARENA	Alianca Renovadona Nacional
BNDES	Banco Nacional de Desenvolvimento Econômico e Social
BTN	Bônus do Tesouro Nacional
CGT	Confederação Geral dos Trabalhadores
CIP	Conselho Interministerial de Preços
CPA	Comissão de Política Aduaneria
CUT	Central Única dos Trabalhadores
ECLAC	Economic Commission for Latin America and the Caribbean
EU	European Union
FGV	Fundação Getúlio Vargas
FIESP	Federação das Indústrias do Estado de São Paulo
FINEP	Financiadora de Estudos e Projetos
FIPE	Fundação Instituto de Pesquisas Econômicas
G-7	Group of Seven
GATT	General Agreement on Tariffs and Trade
IBGE	Instituto Brasileiro de Geografia e Estatística
IDB	Inter-American Development Bank
IDF	International Debt Facility
IGP-DI	Índice Geral de Preços–Disponibilidade Interna (General Price Index–Domestic Available)
IGP/FGV	Índice Geral de Preços (General Price Index/Fundação Getúlio Vargas)
IMF	International Monetary Fund
INPC	Índice Nacional de Preços ao Consumidor (National Consumer Price Index)
IOF	Imposto sobre Operações Financeira (Tax on Financial Operations)
IPC	Índice de Preços ao Consumidor (Consumer Price Index, IBGE)
IPEA	Instituto de Pesquisas Econômicas Aplicadas
LDCs	less developed countries
LFTs	Letras Financeiras do Tesouro
NAFTA	North American Free Trade Agreement
OECD	Organization for Economic Cooperation and Development
PDS	Partido Democrático Social

PDT	Partido Democrático Trabalhista
PFL	Partido da Frente Liberal
PL	Partido Liberal
PMDB	Partido do Movimento Democrático Brasileiro
PNBE	Plano Nacional das Bases Empresariais
PND II	Segundo Plano Nacional de Desenvolvimento (Second National Development Plan/Brazil)
PPB	Partido Progressista Brasileira
PPR	Partido Popular Republicano
PSBR	public-sector borrowing requirements
PSDB	Partido de Social Democracia Brasileira
PT	Partido dos Trabalhadores
PTB	Partido Trabalhista Brasileiro
SEPLAN	Secretaria do Planejamento da Presidência da República do Brasil
URV	Unidade Real de Valor
USP	Universidade de São Paulo

Notes

❧❧

INTRODUCTION

1. This view should not be confused with the "development approach *from within*" proposed by Sunkel and Ramos (1993:24). They oppose both the *inward-looking* structuralist strategy and the *outward-looking* strategy now dominant, offering an intermediary alternative that Sunkel (1993:46) defines as based on an "initial creative impulse [that] gives rise to industries such as iron and steel, electrical machinery and engineering, and basic chemistry and petrochemicals, and infrastructure for energy, transportation and communications." Development always comes "from within," but today a development strategy must necessarily be export-led—that is, internationally competitive. The old concern with infrastructure is still valid, but the concern with heavy industry does not deserve the same attention national developmentalism gave it in the past.

CHAPTER 1

1. The current account deficit for Latin America was 35.0, 44.9, and 53.2 billion U.S. dollars in 1992, 1993, and 1994, respectively. The source is ECLAC, *Panorama Económico de América Latina 1994* (Santiago, Chile: Economic Commission for Latin America and the Caribbean of the United Nations).

2. My basic discussion of the interpretations of Brazil is found in "Six Interpretations of the Brazilian Social Formation" (Bresser Pereira 1984b).

3. For an analysis of recent political pacts, see Chapter 17.

4. If this chapter is compared with the Introduction, the reader will note that I eliminated two interpretations (the functional capitalist and the imperialist superexploitation) and make only a reference to the new dependency theory. The reason for this is that here I am dealing with interpretations and strategies that were put into practice. The functional capitalist and imperialist interpretations were only interpretations. The new dependency approach was more than that, but in this chapter it fell between the national-developmentalist and crisis of the state interpretations. For this reason and also because it was more an interpretation than a strategy, I decided to exclude it from the present analysis.

5. This policy was still practiced at the end of the 1980s, notwithstanding all the criticism the import substitution model was subject to. In the last half of the 1980s FINEP carried out a study to determine the sectors in which Brazilian technological development was deficient. These sectors were supposed to have priority in receiving FINEP loans. An export-oriented technological policy, such as that in Japan or Korea, would have selected those sectors in which the country had the possibility of competing for international technological leadership.

6. Rather than a theory, economic populism is a very widespread economic policy practice. Thus it is not a prerogative of the Latin American national-develop-

mentalist approach. I edited a book on the subject, *Populismo Econômico* (Bresser Pereira 1991), with chapters by Canitrot, O'Donnell, Díaz-Alejandro, Sachs, Dornbusch and Edwards, Cardoso and Helwege, Dall'Acqua, and myself.

7. PT is the leading workers' party, headed by Lula; PDT is a labor party tied to Leonel Brizolla; PMDB is the populist center-left party that commanded the transition to democracy; PSDB is the social-democratic party that split from the PMDB in 1985; PFL is a center-right populist party, splintered off of the PDS in 1985; and PDS is the right-wing party that governed with the military. In September 1995, the PPR (formerly the PDS) combined with the PL (Liberal Party) and received a new name: PPB. Originally, PDS was called ARENA, and was the party that supported the military regime between 1964 and 1984.

CHAPTER 2

1. One of the first economists to study the crisis of the state was Rogério F. Werneck. In the 1980s he wrote several articles published in book form in 1987. Probably the first political scientist to study the crisis of the state was José Luiz Fiori (1984) in his Ph.D. dissertation, "Conjuntura e Ciclo." See also Brasílio Salum, Jr. 1988. My first attempt to analyze this crisis was an article on the changing pattern of financing investment in Brazil (1987), which corresponds to Chapter 5 of this book.

2. At that time the crisis was viewed as a liquidity crisis rather than a structural crisis of the state's finances. My experience as finance minister nursed the diagnosis of the Latin American crisis as a fiscal crisis of the state. For an account of this period, see Bresser Pereira 1992a, 1993a, 1995.

3. The state in Brazil is financed internally by the overnight market. Each day, economic agents transform their deposit accounts in the banks into loans to the state with a one-day maturity. In this way, financial assets are indexed and protected from inflation, whereas the state is financed with a bond that is quasi money. The Collor Plan I (March 1990) was an attempt to cope with this problem (see Chapter 13).

4. It is important to distinguish lack of creditworthiness of the state from lack of credibility of the government. A state without credit is an institution to which economic agents feel reluctant to make loans; a government without credibility is a government that does not keep its word, making economic agents feel insecure about its economic policy. Mainstream economics—which is taught in the best universities—usually confuses these two categories.

5. We could exclude the state-owned enterprises from current revenues and expenditures. In such a case the simplest way to consider their savings (or dissavings) is to add the profits (savings) to the identity or deduct the losses (dissavings).

6. I have no knowledge of any study of public savings in Latin American countries. As for Brazil, the information exists, but, as everywhere, it excludes state-owned enterprises. See Rogério Werneck 1987 for a pioneering study of the public savings concept.

7. It is curious to observe how the expression *structural* was co-opted by neoliberalism. In the 1950s and 1960s it was used by structuralist, national-developmentalist economists who asked for structural reforms; of these, agrarian and progressive tax reforms were the most popular. In the 1980s structural reforms meant market-oriented reforms of the state.

8. See Chapter 6, where I discuss the perverse character of the present capital flows to Latin America and the vanishing motivation to effectively solve the debt crisis.

9. On the fiscal character of the crisis, see also Sachs 1987; Bresser Pereira

1987 and Part 2 of this book; Fanelli and Frenkel 1989; and Reisen and Trotsenburg 1988.

10. Economic populism has some classical contributions, including Canitrot 1975; O'Donnell 1977; and Díaz-Alejandro 1979. These works plus contributions by Sachs (1988), Dornbusch and Edwards (1989), Cardoso and Helwege (1990), and myself with Fernando Dall'Acqua (1989), were put together in a book, *Populismo Econômico* (Bresser Pereira, ed., 1991).

11. For example, an oil tax to finance road construction and oil prospecting; an electric energy tax to finance power-generating plants.

12. In Brazil most of the investments in the oil industry by Petrobrás and in the telecommunications industry by Telebrás were financed by internal profits.

13. The average income tax in Latin America in 1988 was only 23 percent of total government revenues. And this figure is inflated because of the oil producers, like Ecuador and Mexico (Cheibub 1991).

14. Williamson's qualification of the Washington consensus in his article "Democracy and the 'Washington Consensus'" (1993a) is a good demonstration of this fact.

15. As I observed to John Williamson, he identified but did not invent the Washington consensus. Once he did so, he lost control of his creature, which started to have an independent life. He may continue to specify what he understands by the consensus, as he did in his 1993 article, but the consensus itself is (or was) another thing.

16. On the loss of interest in the dependency theory in the 1980s, at exactly the time foreign influence in Latin America increased greatly, see Stallings 1991.

17. The literature on the theory of inertial inflation is already vast. It is an essential part of the crisis of the state approach because it provides the most important Latin American theoretical critique of the conventional economic theory the Washington consensus adopts. See Pazos 1972; Bresser Pereira and Nakano 1983, 1987; Arida and Resende 1984; Baer 1987; and Dornbusch, Sturzenegger, and Wolf 1990. Chapters 5 and 13–15 in this book are examples of applications of the theory.

18. This is not consensual in Washington. Recently, the World Bank has been stressing the importance of increasing taxes to balance the budget and also to finance antipoverty programs that would make fiscal adjustment and structural reforms compatible with democracy. The IMF is increasingly concerned with how to achieve stabilization with growth. See particularly Vito Tanzi's chapter (1989) in the IMF book edited by Mario Blejer and Ke-young Chu.

19. This critique was originally developed by Sachs (1987).

20. There is obviously an alternative: to finance growth with foreign savings, particularly foreign direct investment. This is in part the route presently being followed by Mexico. Foreign investment and capital repatriation permitted Mexico to overcome stagnation and begin economic recovery.

21. See, for instance, Fajnzylber 1990.

22. The populist nationalist approach shuns any type of adjustment, proposes that fiscal deficits and higher wages invigorate aggregate demand and growth, and denies that state intervention has been too extreme and that the protectionist import substitution strategy is exhausted. The number of proponents of these ideas in Latin America has been drastically reduced in recent years. The corresponding practices, however, continue to be widespread.

23. Japan, Korea, and Taiwan did not have to be particularly concerned with income distribution because the reforms imposed by the United States in these countries after World War II, particularly agrarian and tax reform, coupled with the high educational levels already existing, provided the basis for a reasonably fair income distribution.

24. Yet, a new stabilization plan, led by Finance Minister Fernando Henrique Cardoso, was under way. This plan, analyzed in Chapter 15, has competently controlled inertial inflation in Brazil.

CHAPTER 3

1. Note that I am not equating capitalists with the upper class, and technobureaucrats with the middle class. There are many middle-class capitalists and a growing number of upper-class technobureaucrats.

2. The hypothesis that the state's growth follows a cyclical pattern was originally presented at the symposium "Democratizing the Economy," Wilson Center and the University of São Paulo (1988), and was published in Portuguese in *Revista de Economia Política* 9(3), July 1989.

3. The literature concerning state intervention in Brazil is fairly extensive. See, for instance, Suzigan 1976, 1988; Martins 1985; Evans 1979; and Rezende da Silva 1972.

4. See "The Tokyo Symposium on the Present and Future of the Pacific Basin Economy—A Comparison of Asia and Latin America," sponsored by the Institute of Developing Economies, Tokyo, July 25–27, 1989. The papers were published in Fukuchi and Kagami 1990.

5. Actually, some were competent theoretical economists.

6. On this point see, among others, Naya 1989.

7. This attack on the technobureaucracy was part of the long Brazilian transition to democracy. The alliance between the bourgeoisie and the military and civilian technobureaucrats was first broken in Brazil in the mid-1970s. In my book *O Colapso de uma Aliança de Classes* (1978), I analyzed this political process.

CHAPTER 4

1. I discussed the first two variables in an earlier work (Bresser Pereira 1986).

2. Joseph Schumpeter (1911) felt finance had a decisive role in the investment decision. Kalecki (1933) and Keynes (1937) also thought the financial system played a crucial role in the increase of investment. A recent debate among post-Keynesian economists (Asimakopulos 1983, 1986; Kregel 1984–1985, 1986; and Davidson 1986) follows the same line. For underdeveloped countries, the role of external finance has been recognized since the first studies of development economics were conducted in the 1940s. In this chapter I am taking for granted the role of finance and am emphasizing the role of primitive accumulation and forced saving in the early stages of development.

3. At this time Antonio Delfim Netto, who created the CIP in the late 1960s, assumed the Planning Ministry.

CHAPTER 5

1. The original articles on the fiscal crisis of the state in Brazil are Werneck 1983, 1985, 1986, 1987; and Bresser Pereira 1987. Werneck's work on the fiscal crisis was pioneering. My contribution was to define, first in an article and then through

the Macroeconomic Control Plan (Ministério da Fazenda 1987), the fiscal crisis of the state as the basic cause of the Brazilian crisis in the 1980s. Chapter 4 essentially corresponds to this 1987 article, which was presented at a seminar in Cambridge shortly before I took office as finance minister (April 29, 1987).

2. A populist developmentalist economic policy adopted by the rightist authoritarian government during these two years achieved GDP growth rates above 8 percent, whereas the external debt increased from $38 to $60 billion. Populism may be distributivist when its origin is in the left or developmentalist when its origin is in the right. Its results are little different in terms of internal and external unadjustment.

3. Between 1980 and 1984 state expenditures on personnel were reduced from 6.18 to 5.59 percent of GDP; in 1988, however, total government expenditures on personnel were back to 7.80 percent of GDP. It is interesting to note that a considerable part of the reduction was reached at the municipal and state levels. At these levels the expenditure decreased from 2.71 to 2.39 percent of GDP between 1980 and 1984 and increased to 3.30 percent of GDP in 1988.

4. Brazilian economists realized this in early 1985. See Arida 1984 and Neto and Resende 1985.

5. On the validating character of the money supply in Brazilian inflation, see Rangel 1963 and Bresser Pereira and Nakano 1983. It is interesting to observe the pioneering character of Rangel's contribution, which was published seven years before Kaldor's well-known article (1970).

6. After and as a result of the 1981–1983 recession, the public deficit was not eliminated, but it achieved its lowest level of the decade—2.7 percent of GDP—in 1984 (see Table 5.2).

7. The positive change in 1990 was a consequence of the extraordinary measures involved in the Collor Plan I (March 1990), including the freeze of almost 70 percent of financial assets in Brazil (see Chapter 13).

8. The interest rate did not necessarily increase because of the trade-off with maturities. In 1986 the creation of the Letras do Banco Central, which had a very short maturity (practically one day), was a recognition that with very large rates of inflation it was impossible to have long-term financing for the Brazilian state, but it was also a form of controlling speculation and reducing the interest rate to nearly zero in open market operations.

9. Bacha (1989) showed that the real transfer of resources from Latin America was the main factor in the drop of the gross formation of capital in the region from 23.4 percent of GDP in 1979 to 18.8 percent in 1986 because internal savings remained almost constant in this period.

10. Real transactions include the trade balance plus real services minus interests.

11. For a general presentation of this theory, including a survey of the main initial contributions to it, see Bresser Pereira and Nakano 1987.

12. The term *inertial* is not the best to define this high and chronic type of inflation. In Nakano's and my first articles on the subject, we used the expression *autonomous* inflation.

13. For an interesting analysis of the endogenous acceleration of inflation based on a rational expectations (but not monetarist) approach, see Antonio Kandir 1988:170: "In conditions of financial fragility of the public sector, the expectational dimension of prices, which usually has a fundamental role, becomes dominant in the process of acceleration of inflation."

14. For a very interesting critique of this view, see Baer and Beckerman 1989.

15. These equations were originally developed in Phillip Cagan's classic arti-

cle on hyperinflation (1956). But he did not conclude from these relations that the character of the money supply was essentially endogenous.

16. The rate of inflation, p', can also be expressed as dp/p. If we define real seigniorage as dM/p, we have

$$dM/p = (dM/M)(M/p) = d(M/p) + p' M/p$$
$$p' M/p = dM/p - d(M/p)$$

See the application of these concepts to the Brazilian economy in Cardoso 1988a and Dall'Acqua 1989.

17. It is relevant to note that one of the outstanding Brazilian economists who helped to formulate the industrialization strategy through protection and state investment, Ignácio Rangel, has become a supporter of privatization of public services to promote needed investments in this area since he wrote the Postface of the third edition of *A Inflação Brasileira* (1978).

18. Figures on capital flight are always imprecise, but according to estimates made in the Brazilian financial market, capital flight, around $1 billion in the 1970s, increased to around $3 billion when the debt crisis became evident in 1983; in 1988 it doubled, and in 1989 it was over $10 billion. According to World Financial Markets (December 1988), the accumulated flight of capital assets from Brazil was $6, $8, and $31 billion in 1980, 1982, and 1987, respectively. From a relatively low level, it was growing at a faster pace than, for instance, was the case in Mexico, whose respective figures were $19, $44, and $84 billion. In 1980 accumulated capital flight was more than three times higher in Mexico; in 1987 it was 2.7 times higher. In both countries the relationship between capital flight and the internal crisis that followed the debt crisis is fairly clear.

19. The capital-output ratio, around 3 in the 1970s, averaged 5.5 in the 1980s if we take the investment rate in constant prices.

CHAPTER 6

1. William Cline, who in the 1980s insisted that the debt crisis was only a liquidity crisis (1984), recently published a book (1994) and an essay in *The Economist* (1995) in which he aknowledged that the 1980s debt crisis eventually became not a liquidity problem but a solvency crisis. He stressed that this crisis is over because the net debt relative to exports for the seventeen highly indebted Baker countries (most in Latin America), which in 1986 was 384 percent, had fallen to 225 percent in 1993. Yet he insisted that the December 1994 Mexican crisis was really only a liquidity crisis. Let us hope Cline is now being realistic. Washington economists tend to be optimists when policies are originated in the developed countries, whereas they are pessimists whenever decisions arise in developing countries.

2. Estimates of the reduction achieved by Mexico vary from 11 to 18 percent, according to the method used.

3. Dornbusch (1989:350), examining the data on the debt and on the U.S. balance of payments, observed that "it is quite apparent that the large size of the U.S. external deficit is at least to some extent a counterpart of the ability of debtor countries to service their debt by noninterest surpluses."

4. These two ideas were the core of the Brazilian strategy for dealing with the foreign debt in 1987, when I was finance minister. After a "nonstarter" from Secretary Baker (September 1987), the two ideas received wide acceptance. See Bresser Pereira 1992a, 1993a, 1995.

5. At the beginning of September 1987, when, speaking for Brazil, I proposed the securitization of part of the Brazilian debt and received a "nonstarter" from Secretary Brady, the only support I received came from Kiichi Miyazawa, then finance minister of Japan, who said "he felt attracted by the idea of converting the old debt into new securities as proposed by Brazil [and] suggested that an international financial agency—such as the World Bank, through the IFC [International Finance Corporation]—present a precise project on the subject" (*Gazeta Mercantil,* September 15, 1991, reproducing a *Financial Times* report). At the 1988 IMF–World Bank meeting in Toronto, Miyazawa presented a plan for debt reduction that was a direct antecedent to the Brady Plan.

6. The exposure of the nine top U.S. banks in Latin America, as a percentage of primary capital, was reduced from 179.8 percent in June 1982 to 74.9 percent in September 1989 (ECLAC 1990:43).

7. On the self-defeating character of fiscal adjustment for the highly indebted countries, see Chapter 5.

8. It cannot be said that a straightforward relationship exists between debt and inflation because there are some highly indebted countries with low inflation. The trend, however, is clear. Highly indebted countries tend to suffer high inflation. According to the IMF (1990:61), among the net debtor developing countries that had high inflation between 1983 and 1989, 89 percent had debt-servicing difficulties.

9. For an original overview of the theory of inertial inflation, see Bresser Pereira and Nakano 1987. The complete original statements on the theory are found in Bresser Pereira and Nakano 1983, Resende and Arida 1984, and Lopes 1984. On the need for combining orthodox and heterodox policies to control this type of inflation, see also Ramos 1986, Bacha 1988, Kiguel and Liviatan 1988, Beckerman 1991, and Bruno 1991.

10. The failed coup d'état in Venezuela in February 1992 is a good example of the political instability associated with tight fiscal and monetary policies while foreign creditors are spared the adjustment burden. There is a large body of literature on the relationship between stabilization policies and the consolidation of democracy. A partial survey of this literature is found in Bresser Pereira, Maravall, and Przeworski 1993.

11. On the limits of the Brady Plan, see Bacha 1989, 1991; Bresser Pereira 1989b; Devlin 1989b; and Sachs 1989b.

12. The view of the banks, which evolved toward voluntary debt reduction beginning in September 1987, is well described in the December 1988 issue of *World Financial Markets,* published by Morgan Guaranty ("LDC Debt Reduction: A Critical Appraisal").

13. This section was originally written with Jeffrey Sachs.

14. The IDDC was the name of the debt facility proposed in a pioneering way by Peter Kenen (1983), when the discount in the secondary market did not yet exist. Felix Rohatyn (1983) made a similar proposal at that time based on the financial strategy he had used to solve New York City's debt crisis. James Robinson III, chair of the American Express Bank, made a similar and very detailed proposal (1988).

CHAPTER 7

This chapter was written with Yoshiaki Nakano.

1. Transference of real resources is equal to the current account minus factor payments (interest and dividends), or it is equal to the real transaction surplus: the surplus in the trade account plus the balance in the real services account.

2. We exclude the Bresser Plan from these consequences because it was an emergency plan enacted to control the deep crisis ensuant on the Cruzado Plan's failure. It did not intend to end inflation but only to halt it for a time. It did not include monetary reform, the deindexation of the economy, or the freeze of the exchange rate, unlike the other plans. Launched in June 1987 it assumed that by December of that year inflation would reach 10 percent; in reality, it reached 14 percent (Bresser Pereira 1993a).

3. In Table 7.3 we use the IGP/FGV because it is an index with a long and consistent series, whereas the official consumer price index IPC/IBGE—which we often use in the text, was subjected to methodological changes (vectors) during the 1986, 1987, and 1989 freezes.

4. In fact, this spread varied greatly during the year, as successive speculative attacks against the novo cruzado raised it. The government responded with its only and self-defeating weapon: increased interest rates.

CHAPTER 8

1. The term *left* in Latin America is often confused with the extreme left. In this work I am speaking only of the left and the right, without using the concepts of moderate left and moderate right. I am also not using the idea of "center," which is generally a euphemism for the right to hide behind. In this chapter the left extends from the far left to the centrist left.

2. The left intends to have its base among the workers, the proletariat, but to a greater or lesser extent, intellectuals or, in a broader sense, technobureaucrats always constitute the base and the leadership of the left.

3. I make the assumption that the state develops through a cyclical process similar to long economic cycles. The state and the market are complementary agents in coordinating the economy. Faced with the limitations of the market, the state tends to increase its intervention in the economy. This intervention is initially successful, but distortions later emerge that ultimately produce fiscal crisis and the necessity to again reduce the role played by the state.

4. This is just the opposite of what occurred with the left, which often tended to be nationalistic based on the fact that the imperialist countries are also capitalist. Ultimately, this nationalism became anti–North Americanism, just as the right's "selling out" or cosmopolitan position was a way for it to identify with the capitalism of the countries of the center.

5. In the United States the term *left* applies only to the Marxist or neo-Marxist left. The moderate or progressist left is called *liberal*. I prefer to use progressive or social-democratic to avoid confusion with the European meanings of *liberal* and *liberalism*. A liberal in the U.S. sense is a democratic social reformist who opposes the conservatives—the European and Latin American liberals. Galbraith is the ultimate U.S. liberal. President Franklin D. Roosevelt is the prototype of the U.S. liberal politician. To avoid misunderstanding, the English, who are placed between the United States and Europe, very appropriately began to use the term *neoliberal* to define today's radical liberals in the European meaning. They may also be called neoconservative. B. Schneider gets confused and calls neoliberals the "new liberals"—that is, the new progressive politicians who appeared in the Democratic Party beginning in the 1970s, stressing market coordination of the economy, as opposed to the "old liberals" in the Roosevelt-Galbraith tradition.

6. This began with the speech I gave when I took office (April 1987) in the midst of the crisis caused by the Cruzado Plan. I was called "conservative" when I

spoke of the necessity to make adjustments in the Brazilian economy and to increase exports. From that day on, it became clear to me that one of the Latin American left's important tasks was to define progressive thought and economic policy.

CHAPTER 9

1. The inefficiency or incompetence of economic reforms—not only because they are populist but also because they are orthodox, ignoring the specificities of the Latin American countries and particularly the abnormal times the region underwent in the 1980s—is a basic assumption this book adopts. The theme is discussed especially in Chapter 12.

2. On populist literature, see Weffort 1965, 1980; Di Tella 1966; Ianni 1968; Bresser Pereira 1984; Erickson 1975; and Touraine 1988.

3. The original version of this chapter was presented at the seminar "L'Internationalization de la Démocratie Politique," University of Montreal, September 1988. In the same year in Venice, Jeffrey Sachs presented an excellent paper on economic populism, "Social Conflict and Populist Policies in Latin America" (1988). Three years later, Dornbusch and Edwards (1991) and Bresser Pereira (1991), in the United States and Brazil, respectively, edited similar books on economic populism.

4. See the first Brazilian editions of Bresser Pereira 1984.

5. I further developed this new interpretation of Latin America, which would later be called the dependency theory, in Bresser Pereira 1984. Chapter 4 in this book describes the collapse of the populist pact as some of its tenets were being refuted. The most important tenet was the belief that multinationals would oppose Brazil's industrialization. The imperialist interpretation took this view for granted; the new dependency theory challenged it. Investments coming from the multinationals could distort the economy and the distribution of income, but they had indeed been realized in the manufacturing industry since the early 1950s.

6. Alexandre Barbosa Lima Sobrinho (1963:11, 19) said "the substance of nationalism is an antagonism of interests or ideals." And adds, quoting Boyd C. Shafer (*Nationalism: Myth and Reality*), "the true nationalism is also *anti* something foreign to the nation."

7. Developmentalism and economic populism were later also an attitude and a practice adopted by the right, as the economic policies of the military regime (1964–1984) demonstrate. The National Plan of Development II (1974) is an example of developmentalism, and the 1979–1980 attempt to produce a new economic miracle rather than adjusting, an example of economic populism.

8. The 1989 Summer Plan was a typical attempt to control inflation by adopting a very orthodox monetary policy. The resulting high interest rates were a major cause of the subsequent hyperinflation. In May–December 1990 the second phase of the Collor Plan—the Eris Plan—was a fully monetarist attempt to control inflation.

9. The last edition of Samuelson and Nordhaus's classical introductory textbook on economics has a full section on inertial inflation.

CHAPTER 10

1. I use "legitimacy" in the Weberian sense, which has nothing to do with legality. A government that has legitimacy is one that is supported by civil society.

Civil society is the complement of the state in a nation-state or a country. It is the society operating in the market and in politics, made up of classes, groups, and individuals with differentiated political powers depending on their organization, their control of the economic means, and their intellectual competence.

2. Marcílio Marques Moreira adopted a conventional or orthodox plan to fight Brazilian inflation. The plan received formal IMF approval but obviously failed. I analyze this failure in Chapter 14.

3. See Cardoso 1991.

4. This political pact is analyzed in Chapter 17.

5. Collor borrowed the concept of social liberalism from an outstanding Brazilian political thinker, José Guilherme Merquior. Merquior's source was probably Norberto Bobbio, who has debated this contradictory concept in his books. The idea was initially proposed in Italy at the beginning of the century. For a survey, see Bobbio 1990.

6. On the new neoliberal right, see Bosanquet 1983, Levitas, ed., 1986, Dunleavy and O'Leary 1987, and Barry 1987.

7. For example, Andrés Perez in Venezuela, de la Madrid and Salinas in Mexico, Fujimori in Peru, and Menem in Argentina.

8. President Collor's popularity, measured nationally by Datafolha, consistently declined. In April 1990, after its first month in government, 67 percent of the population evaluated the Collor administration as very good or good. After one year in office this rate fell to 16 percent. Two years later it fell to 10 percent. In April 1992, after he changed his cabinet, the percentage of the population viewing Collor's administration as good or very good increased to 12 percent. Two months later, after the new political crisis, this rate remained at 12 percent, but the percentage of the population considering the administration bad or very bad reached an all-time high of 65 percent. After one year in office this percentage was 42 percent, and after two years it was 58 percent (*Folha de S. Paulo,* June 25, 1992).

9. I am indebted to the collaboration of Philippe Faucher on this section.

10. On the net costs of adjustment and reform, see Bresser Pereira 1993c, Abud 1992, and Bresser Pereira and Abud 1994.

CHAPTER 11

1. I am well aware that many people who call themselves social democrats and who are members of social-democratic political parties are, in fact, liberal democrats.

2. Note that I always use the term *liberal* in the European sense.

3. See World Bank, *World Development Report* 1991.

4. The sources for these figures are the Instituto Brasileiro de Geografia e Estatística (IBGE) and the World Bank, *World Development Report* 1991.

5. The poverty line in these studies, in terms of monthly dollar income, varies according to the cost of living in each region or city. The poverty line was $54 in the urban north and center-west, $35 in the urban northeast, $48 in the urban southeast, and $39 in the urban south.

6. I developed this theme in the book *Estado e Subdesenvolvimento Industrializado* (1977: Chapter 2). This theory was one of the assumptions I used to predict the transition to democracy in Brazil as an outcome of the bourgeoisie's decision to quit its political alliance with the military (Bresser Pereira 1977).

7. This problem could be solved or circumvented by a minimum-income social program, based on the idea of the negative income tax, as Senator Eduardo

Matarazzo Suplicy proposed in Congress (see Suplicy and Cury 1994). The effectiveness of such propositions, however, is limited, and they fail to address the fiscal crisis of the state.

CHAPTER 12

1. The Soviet Union was the extreme case of a dominantly statist social formation. I wrote extensively on this subject in the 1970s: the statist or technobureaucratic mode of production, the bureaucratic organization as the correspondent relationship of production, the bureaucratic class as the collective owner of the means of production, high direct and indirect salaries as the form of appropriation of the surplus, and so on. See Bresser Pereira 1980.

CHAPTER 13

This chapter was written with Yoshiaki Nakano.

1. This consensus was held by everyone except a few populist economists, who either insisted that a budget deficit was acceptable when there was no full employment (actually, Brazil was near full employment in 1989) or said that reducing the stock of public debt was more effective in stabilizing the economy than cutting the budget deficit, which was essentially a financial or structural deficit.

2. The real interest rate on Treasury bills was high between 1981 and 1984 and in 1988 and 1989, when monetarist policies prevailed. It was low or negative in 1985–1986 for populist reasons. At the end of 1986, with the creation of a new system of Treasury bills whose rate of interest was defined daily (the Letras do Banco Central and Letras Financeiras do Tesouro, which replaced the Obrigações do Tesouro Nacional), it was possible to limit speculation and to reduce the rate of interest on the overnight market. In 1987 the government was able to pay low interest rates while maintaining a positive interest rate in the financial market. The trade-off was that the money supply became additionally endogenous.

3. The figures in Table 13.1 overestimate the interest on the internal debt and the public deficit. They were calculated by the Central Bank using as a deflator the IPC of the month, t. The acceleration of inflation was very strong in 1989, and so this methodology is unacceptable. Since the IPC measures inflation with a lag of about one month, an alternative deflator ($t + 1$ IPC) can be used. According to this more correct methodology, the interest on the domestic debt will probably fall to 4.3 percent of GDP in 1989; for the other years it will likely turn negative. The public deficit in 1989 should fall to 7.2 percent of GDP.

4. In the German monetary reform of June 1948, for instance, the conversion factor between reichsmarks and deutsche marks was 10 to 1. Thus 90 percent of the old reichsmarks were confiscated, whereas in Brazil the novos cruzados (the old money) have only been blocked.

5. M4 was NCz $4.2 trillion (US$100 billion, considering the official exchange rate on March 16 of 42.3 cruzeiros per dollar). Around US$33 billion was converted in cruzeiros; thus initially US$77 billion in novos cruzados was blocked.

6. There are no official figures for the operational deficit in 1989, but the estimates are around 7 percent. Part of this increase can be explained by the extraordinary acceleration of inflation and the active interest policy adopted by the former government.

7. For financial asset holders who made their investments at the end of February, this did not represent a loss because the rate of inflation "point to point"—from February 28 to March 31—was around 40 percent. Investors who bought assets earlier, however, may have suffered a loss (that is, the government won a debt reduction) because an underestimation of inflation would be compensated for by the official rate of inflation of 84 percent in March.

8. See Rangel 1963, Kaldor 1970, Merkin 1982, Bresser Pereira and Nakano 1983, and Davidson 1984. Merkin's chapter includes a survey on the subject.

9. I am considering a GDP of US$365 billion.

10. The stabilization plan did not change the rules of the financial market regarding overnight deposits. It continued to be possible to transfer part of the cash deposits to overnight deposits every afternoon (until 1 P.M.) and have them be automatically transformed to cash deposits the next morning. Thus the increase of $M1$ and the reduction of the overnight deposits were smaller than would have been the case if the government had established a minimum maturity of one week for Treasury bills. Doing something in this direction would have reduced the confusion about what is money and what is not, although confusion would not have been eliminated.

11. The real interest rate immediately following the plan was very high. It went down because the nominal interest rate was lowered by the authorities (or by monetary policy). In early May it was still very high. In June, as inflation accelerated and the Central Bank did not acknowledge this fact, the real interest rate became increasingly lower and finally negative.

12. The consumer price index in March, utilizing the traditional methodology of comparing the average prices for the month against average prices in the previous month, was 84 percent.

13. Average real wages decreased 22.6 percent from February 1989 to February 1990, according to the FIESP index of real wages (indexed by inflation of the next month $[t + 1]$ because the consumer price index [IPC/IBGE] has a lag of one month). In March the real wage reduction had fallen to 10 percent. In June, given the pressure of unions, the pressing public issue related to the plan was the "recovery of losses" suffered by workers.

14. Regular price indices are inadequate to measure inflation after a freeze. They include a heavy inflation residuum because they compare the present month's average prices against the last month's average prices. As a consequence, it takes some time for the index to reflect the end of the inflationary process. Thus end-to-end is a more realistic measure of inflation following a shock because it eliminates the carryover embodied in regular price indices that work with monthly averages.

15. Based on the previous wage law, which indexed wages according to the inflation (IPC/IBGE) of the previous month, workers demanded a wage increase of 84 percent for April and 44 percent for May (a total of 166 percent), whereas actual inflation, calculated according to the end-of-the-month/end-of-the-month methodology rather than the average-of-the-month methodology, was 3.3 percent in April and 6.2 percent in May.

CHAPTER 14

1. It should be noted that John Williamson (1993b), who coined the expression "Washington consensus," feels strongly that in addition to political support, successful economic reforms require a competent and stable economic team and a comprehensive economic program.

2. In this chapter a "heterodox" stabilization policy is one that acts directly over prices, wages, or the exchange rate, whereas an "orthodox" one acts indirectly

over prices through fiscal and monetary policies that affect demand, change expectations, or both. According to this definition, income policy is a heterodox policy.

3. A shock may be heterodox (a price freeze combined with a social agreement) or may be based on a nominal anchor (usually the exchange rate, which will be fixated and made convertible). The alternative to shock therapy is gradualism, which may be orthodox (based on fiscal and monetary policies or on guidelines) or heterodox (also based on guidelines and on an income policy).

4. Given the high interest rates, only the state, the state-owned enterprises, and a few bankrupt firms are highly indebted in Brazil today.

5. The first opportunity was lost with the inauguration of the new administration in March 1990, when the Collor Plan I was implemented and failed to stabilize the economy.

6. Hélio Jaguaribe became the secretary of science and technology, Celso Lafer of foreign affairs, Adib Jatene of the Ministry of Health, Elieser Batista of special economic development projects, and José Goldemberg became the minister of education; all had been in the government since March 1990. Marcílio Marques Moreira had been in the government since April 1991.

7. In fact, even with small or moderate inflation the money supply is relatively endogenous. See Rangel 1963 and Kaldor 1970.

8. The explanation for the acceleration of previous inflation is found in Chapter 13.

9. For more on this, see Tokeshi 1991. In this work he looks for the "microfoundations" of inertial inflation.

10. The distinction between expectations and decisions can be illustrated by the views of a rich Brazilian rice merchant, who once actually said to me, "Money is a serious matter. One should not play with it." "Money" to him means profit. To "play with profit" is to make decisions according to volatile, unreliable expectations.

11. I owe this distinction between price decisions in the real sector and those in the financial sector to Fernando Hollanda Barbosa.

12. On my personal experience in the Finance Ministry, see Bresser Pereira 1992a, 1993a, 1995.

13. In a previous article on which this chapter is partially based (Bresser Pereira 1992b), I referred to eleven rather than twelve plans. The reason for this difference is that I decided to recognize the second phase of the Collor Plan I as a distinct stabilization plan—the Eris Plan, after the Central Bank governor Ibrahim Eris.

14. I developed this idea in Bresser Pereira 1989a.

15. According to Ffrench-Davis and Devlin (1993:4), "The Brady agreements represented a modest foreign cash flow relief, inferior to 1 percent of the GDP (it varied from 0.2 to 0.8 percent)."

16. I originally developed the concept of net transitional costs in Bresser Pereira 1993c. For further development of the concept, see Abud 1992 and Bresser Pereira and Abud 1994.

17. This last case was analyzed and formalized by Przeworski (1991) and Alesina and Drazen (1991).

18. From May to October 1992 the Marcílio Plan was the victim of the political crisis that led President Fernando Collor to resign. Yet the political crisis does not explain the failure of the stabilization program, which was already clear in April.

CHAPTER 15

1. The insufficient discount the Brady Plan provided was immediately signaled by Devlin (1989b), Sachs (1989b), and Bresser Pereira (1989b). Recently a Ph.D.

candidate at the Getúlio Vargas Foundation (Jairo Abud) critically evaluated Mexico's debt agreement and, more generally, its macroeconomic policy. According to Abud (1994:35), between July 1989 and December 1993 the average reduction in interest disbursements was 5.6 percent of the debt (equivalent to US$759 million), which is smaller than the expected reduction for one year.

2. The best-known example of an orthodox, gradual stabilization of high inflation is the case of Chile (1973–1979). The social costs, however, were extremely high, compatible only with a fierce dictatorship like that of General Pinochet. Also in Chile, although inflation was high, it did not become inertial or have an informal indexation.

3. See, for example, Dornbusch and Fischer 1986; Kiguel and Liviatan 1988; and Bruno 1989, 1991.

4. Bresser Pereira and Nakano (1984) and Lopes (1984) were the first to propose a price freeze. Arida (1983, 1984) and Lara Resende (1984), individually and together (Arida and Resende 1984), were the first and only authors to propose the index money (Arida) or the second money (Resende) as a means to neutralize inertia.

CHAPTER 16

1. On the "anti" character of nationalism, see Lima Sobrinho 1963.

2. See Bresser Pereira and Thorstensen 1992; and Thorstensen, Nakano, Faria Lima, and Sato 1994.

3. This testimony is published in Bresser Pereira 1991.

4. This expression was used by Uruguay's president, Júlio Maria Sanguinetti, in his speech in Cancún, Mexico, in November 1987, when eight Latin American presidents met to discuss the debt crisis.

CHAPTER 17

1. I am not using the term *government* as synonymous with the state, as is usual in the Anglo-Saxon tradition, but as the people who direct the state in the executive, legislative, and judicial branches. Government here is the top of the state.

2. I analyzed the political pacts in Brazil in three books (Bresser Pereira 1978, 1984, 1985).

3. Bolívar Lamounier (1989, 1990) emphasized the 1974 election as the turning point in the transition, whereas I, although not ignoring the significance of that election, maintain that the bureaucractic-authoritarian coalition actually began to break down in 1977. I first developed this explanation for Brazil's transition to democracy in Bresser Pereira 1978. See also Bresser Pereira 1983, in which I analyzed the process of democratization within civil society, and Bresser Pereira 1984: Chapter 9, in which I discussed the dialectic of redemocratization—demanded by society—and *abertura,* an authoritarian strategy to postpone or limit the democratization process. Bresser Pereira 1985 is a collection of articles on the theme of political pacts and the transition to democracy.

4. See, among others, Martins 1983, O'Donnell and Schmitter 1986, Selcher 1986, and Mainwaring 1992. O'Donnell and Schmitter (1986:19), whose work was extremely influential, say "there is no transition whose beginning is not the consequence—direct or indirect—of important divisions within the authoritarian regime

itself, principally along the fluctuating cleavage between hard-liners and soft-liners. Brazil and Spain are cases of such a direct causality." Stepan (1986:19) originally adopted the same stand. Yet in the English version of his book, which was published later, fully revised, as *Rethinking Military Politics* (1988), he gave more relevance to civil society.

5. In April 1977 President Geisel closed Congress when it did not approve a law to reform the judicial system. The authoritarianism and gratuitousness of this act provoked national indignation that set off the transition to democracy because it broke down the political alliance between the bourgeoisie and the civil and military bureaucracy controlling the government. See Bresser Pereira 1978.

6. See Bresser Pereira 1977, 1978, 1980.

7. On the neoliberal paradox, see Haggard and Kaufman 1991; and Sola 1993.

8. For an analysis of the Brazilian state bureaucracy, see, among others, Martins 1976, 1985; Abranches 1978; Nunes 1984; Schneider 1991; and Gouvêa 1994.

References

Abranches, Sérgio H. (1978) "The Divided Leviathan: The State and Policy Formation in Authoritarian Brazil." Ph.D. diss., Department of Political Science, Cornell University Ithaca, N.Y.

——— (1990) "O Dilema Político-institucional Brasileiro." In João Paulo dos Reis Velloso, ed., *A Crise Brasileira.*

——— (1993) "Do Possível ao Desejável: Lógicas de Ação Coletiva e Modelos de Desenvolvimento." Paper presented to the Fifth Fórum Nacional, May 3–6, São Paulo.

Abud, Jairo (1992) "Interpretação Gráfica dos Custos de Programas de Ajustamento." *Revista de Economia Política* 11(4), October.

——— (1994) "Dívida Externa, Estabilização Econômica, Abertura de Capital, Fluxos de Capitais Externos e Baixo Crescimento Econômico: México 1989–1993." Ph.D. diss., Department of Economics, Fundação Getúlio Vargas, São Paulo.

Acuña, C., and W. Smith (1994) "The Political Economy of Structural Adjustment: The Logic of Support and Opposition to Neoliberal Reform." In W. Smith, C. Acuña, and E. Gamarra, eds., *Latin American Political Economy in the Age of Neoliberal Reform.* New Brunswick and Miami: Transactions Publishers and North-South Center.

Alesina, A., and A. Drazden (1991) "Why Are Stabilizations Delayed?" *American Economic Review* 81(5), December.

Alesina, A., and S. Edwards (1989) "External Debt, Capital Flight and Political Risk." *Journal of International Economics* 27(3–4), November.

Alesina, A., and G. Tabellini (1988) "Credibility and Politics." *European Economic Review* 32.

Arida, Pérsio (1983) "Neutralizar a Inflação, uma Idéia Promissora." *Economia e Perspectiva* (Conselho Regional de Economia de São Paulo), July.

——— (1984) "A ORTN Serve Apenas para Zerar a Inflação Inercial." *Gazeta Mercantil,* October 19.

——— (1985) "O Déficit Público: um Modelo Simples." *Revista de Economia Política* 5(4), October.

Arida, P., and A. L. Resende (1984) "Inertial Inflation and Monetary Reform." In J. Williamson, ed., *Inflation and Indexation* (1985). Originally a paper presented at a seminar, Institute of International Economics, Washington, D.C., November 1984.

Asimakopulos, A. (1983) "Kalecki and Keynes on Finance, Investment and Saving." *Cambridge Journal of Economics* 7.

——— (1986) "Finance, Liquidity, Saving and Investment." *Journal of Post-Keynesian Economics* 9(1), Fall.

Bacha, Edmar L. (1988) "Moeda, inércia e conflito: reflexões sobre as políticas de estabilização no Brasil." *Pesquisa e Planejamento Econômico* 18(1), April.

——— (1989) "Crise da dívida, transferências externas e taxa de crescimento dos países em desenvolvimento." *Revista de Economia Brasileira* 44(3):437–456,

July 1990. Paper presented to the conference Economic Reconstruction of Latin America, Fundação Getúlio Vargas, Rio de Janeiro, August 1989.

——— (1991) "The Brady Plan and Beyond: New Debt Management Options for Latin America." Working Paper no. 257. Department of Economics of the Catholic University (PUC), Rio de Janeiro, May.

Baer, W., and P. Beckerman (1989) "The Decline and Fall of Brazil's Cruzado." *Latin American Research Review* 24(1).

Baer, Werner (1987) "The Resurgence of Inflation in Brazil: 1974–1986." *World Development* 15(8), August.

Barry, Norman P. (1987) *The New Right*. London: Croom Helm.

Batista, Jorge Chami (1987) "A estratégia de ajustamento externo do Segundo Plano Nacional de Desenvolvimento." *Revista de Economia Política* 7(2), April.

Batista, Paulo N., Jr. (1987) "Formação de capital e transferência de recursos ao exterior." *Revista de Economia Política* 7(1), January.

Beckerman, Paul (1990) "Recent 'Heterodox' Stabilization Experience." In Baer, Petry, and Simpson, eds., *Latin America: The Crisis of the 80s and the Opportunities of the 90s*. Bureau of Economic and Business Research, University of Illinois, 1991.

Blejer, M., and K. Chu, eds. (1989) *Fiscal Policy, Stabilization and Growth in Developing Countries*. Washington, D.C.: International Monetary Fund.

Blejer, M., and N. Liviatan (1987) "Fighting Hyperinflation: Stabilization Strategies in Argentina and Israel, 1985–86." *Staff Papers* (International Monetary Fund) (3), September.

Bobbio, Norberto (1990) *Profilo Ideologico del '900*. Milan: Gazanti.

Bosanquet, Nick (1983) *After the New Right*. London: Heinemann.

Bradford, Colin I., Jr. (1991) "New Theories on Old Issues: Perspectives on the Prospects for Restoring Economic Growth in Latin America in the Nineties." In L. Emmerij and H. Iglesias, eds., *Restoring Financial Flows to Latin America*.

Bresser Pereira, Luiz Carlos (1963) "O Empresário Industrial e a Revolução Brasileira." *Revista de Administração de Empresas* 2(8), June. Also in Luiz Carlos Bresser Pereira, *Empresários e Administradores no Brasil*, São Paulo: Brasiliense, 1974.

——— (1977) *Estado e Subdesenvolvimento Industrializado*. São Paulo: Brasiliense.

——— (1978) *O Colapso de uma Aliança de Classes*. São Paulo: Brasiliense.

——— (1980) *A Sociedade Estatal e a Tecnoburocracia*. São Paulo: Brasiliense.

——— (1983) "Os Limites da 'Abertura' e a Sociedade Civil." *Revista de Administração de Empresas* 23(4), October. Republished in Luiz Carlos Bresser Pereira, *Pactos Políticos*, São Paulo: Brasiliense, 1985.

——— (1984a) *Development and Crisis in Brazil: 1930–1983*. Boulder: Westview Press.

——— (1984b) "Six Interpretations on the Brazilian Social Formation." *Latin American Perspectives* 11(1), Winter.

——— (1985) *Pactos Políticos*. São Paulo: Brasiliense.

——— (1986) *Lucro, Acumulação e Crise*. São Paulo: Brasiliense.

——— (1987) "Changing Patterns of Financing Investment in Brazil." *Bulletin of Latin American Research* (Glasgow: University of Glasgow) 7(2).

——— (1989a) "The Perverse Macroeconomics of Debt, Deficit, and Inflation in Brazil." In T. Fukuchi and M. Kagami, *Perspectives on the Pacific Basin Economy: A Comparison of Asia and Latin America*. Tóquio: Institute of Developing Economies, 1990.

——— (1989b) "Os Limites do Plano Brady." *Exame,* May 3.

——— (1991) *Os Tempos Heróicos de Collor e Zélia: Aventura da Modernidade, Desventura da Ortodoxia*. São Paulo: Nobel.

———— (1992a) "Contra a Corrente: A Experiência no Ministério da Fazenda." *Revista Brasileira de Ciências Sociais* 19, July. Testimony to the Instituto Universitário de Pesquisas do Rio de Janeiro (presented in September 1988 and revised in 1991). Not available in English. In French: "Experiences d'un Gouvernment." *Problèmes d'Amérique Latine* 93, 3d quarter 1989.

———— (1992b) "1992—A Estabilização Necessária." *Revista de Economia Política* 12(3), July.

———— (1993a) "Brazil." In John Williamson, ed., *The Political Economy of Policy Reform*. Originally a paper presented to the conference The Political Economy of Policy Reform, Washington, D.C., January 14–16, 1993.

———— (1993b) "The Failure to Stabilize." In *Brazil: The Struggle for Modernization*. London: Institute of Latin American Studies of the University of London.

———— (1993c) "Efficiency and Politics of Economic Reforms in Latin America." In L. Bresser Pereira, A. Przeworski, and J. M. Maravall, *Economic Reforms in New Democracies*. Cambridge: Cambridge University Press.

———— (1993d) "Economic Reforms and the Cycles of the State." *World Development* 21(8), August. Based on a paper presented at the conference Democratizing the Economy, University of São Paulo and the Wilson Center, São Paulo, July 1988. Published in Portuguese: *Revista de Economia Política* 9(3), July 1989.

———— (1995a) "A Turning Point in the Debt Crisis." Working Paper no. 4. São Paulo: Instituto Sul-Norte, January.

———— (1995b) "A Turning Point in the Debt Crisis." Working Paper no. 45. São Paulo: Department of Economics, Getúlio Vargas Foundation, May 1995.

Bresser Pereira, Luiz Carlos, ed. (1991) *Populismo Econômico*. São Paulo: Nobel.

Bresser Pereira, L., and J. Abud (1994) "Net and Total Transition Costs: The Timing of Adjustment." Working Paper no. 41. São Paulo: Department of Economics, Fundação Getúlio Vargas, November.

Bresser Pereira, L., and F. Dall'Acqua (1991) "Economic Populism x Keynes: Reinterpreting Budget Deficit in Latin America." *Journal of Post-Keynesian Economics* 14(1), Fall.

Bresser Pereira, L., A. Przeworski, and J. M. Maravall (1993) *Economic Reforms in New Democracies*. Cambridge: Cambridge University Press.

Bresser Pereira, L., and Y. Nakano (1983) "The Theory of Inertial or Autonomous Inflation." In Bresser Pereira and Nakano, *The Theory of Inertial Inflation*. Originally published in Portuguese in 1983.

———— (1984) "Administrative Policy: Gradualism or Shock." In Bresser Pereira and Nakano, *The Theory of Inertial Inflation*. Originally published in Portuguese in 1984.

———— (1987) *The Theory of Inertial Inflation*. Boulder: Lynne Rienner Publishers.

———— (1991) "Hyperinflation and Stabilization in Brazil: The First Collor Plan." In Paul Davidson and Jan Kregel, eds., *Economic Problems of the 1990s*. London: Edward Elgar.

Bresser Pereira, L., and Vera Thorstensen (1992) "From Mercosul to American Integration." Paper presented to the Inter-American Development Bank and the ECLAC Project on Trade in the Western Hemisphere, Washington, D.C., September 28. Working Paper IDB/ECLAC, WP-TWH–14, November. Published in Portuguese, *Política Externa* 1(3), December.

Bresser Pereira, Sylvio (1990) "O Erro Básico do Plano Collor." *Folha de S. Paulo,* April 4.

Bruno, Michael (1989) "Econometrics and Design of Economic Reform." *Econométrica* 57(2), March.

———— (1991) "Introduction and Overview." In M. Bruno et al., eds., *Lessons of Economic Stabilization*.

Bruno, M., et al., eds. (1991) *Lessons of Economic Stabilization and its Aftermath*. Cambridge, Mass.: The MIT Press.

Cagan, Phillip (1956) "The Monetary Dynamics of Hyperinflation." In Milton Friedman, ed., *Studies in the Quantity Theory of Money*.

Camargo, Aspásia (1990) "As Duas Faces de Janus: Os Paradoxos da Modernidade Incompleta." In João Paulo dos Reis Velloso, ed., *A Crise Brasileira*.

Camargo, J. M., and F. Giambiagi, eds. (1991) *Distribuição de Renda no Brasil*. São Paulo: Paz e Terra.

Camargo, José Márcio (1993) "Os miseráveis." *Folha de S. Paulo,* March 28.

Canitrot, Adolfo (1975) "La experiencia populista de redistribucion de ingresos." *Desarrollo Económico* 15(59), October.

Cardoso, Eliana (1988a) "O processo inflacionário no Brasil e suas relações com o déficit e a dívida do setor público." *Revista de Economia Política* 8(2), April.

———— (1988b) "Seigniorage and Repression: Monetary Rhythms of Latin America." Paper presented at the Fourteenth International Congress of the Latin American Studies Association, New Orleans, March.

Cardoso, E., and A. Helwege (1990) "Populism, Profligacy and Redistribution." In Cardoso and Helwege, *Latin America's Economy*. Boston: The MIT Press, 1992. Published as a working paper, 1990.

Cardoso, Fernando Henrique (1976) "The Consumption of the Dependency Theory in the United States." Paper presented at the Latin American Studies Association Congress, Atlanta, March.

———— (1991) "A Crise Brasileira." Speech in the Brazilian Senate, September 5.

Cardoso, F. H., and E. Faletto (1969) *Dependency and Development in Latin America*. Berkeley: University of California Press, 1979. First Spanish edition, 1969.

Castro, A. B. de, and F. Pires de Souza (1985) *A Economia Brasileira em Marcha Forçada*. Rio de Janeiro: Paz e Terra.

Central Bank of Brazil. *Brazil Economic Program* (several issues). Brasília: Banco Central do Brasil.

Cheibub, José Antônio (1991) "Taxation in Latin America: A Preliminary Report." Department of Political Science, University of Chicago, July. (This report developed into Cheibub's Ph.D. dissertation.)

Cline, William R. (1984) *International Debt: System Risk and Policy Response*. Washington, D.C.: Institute for International Economics.

———— (1988). "International Debt: Progress and Strategy." *Finance and Development* (International Monetary Fund and World Bank, Washington, D.C.) 8(2), June.

———— (1994) *International Debt Reexamined*. Washington, D.C.: Institute for International Economics.

———— (1995) "Managing International Debt—How One Big Battle Was Won." *Economist,* February 18.

Cline, W., and S. Weintraub, eds. (1981) *Economic Stabilization in Developing Countries*. Washington, D.C.: The Brookings Institution.

Corbo, V., A. Krueger, and F. Ossa, eds. (1985) *Export Oriented Development Strategies*. Boulder: Westview Press.

Dall'Acqua, Fernando M. (1989) "Imposto inflacionário: uma análise para a economia brasileira." *Revista de Economia Política* 9(3), July.

Dall'Acqua, F., and L. Bresser Pereira (1987) "A composição financeira do déficit público." *Revista de Economia Política* 7(2), April.

Davidson, Paul (1984) "Endogenous Money Supply, the Production Process and Inflation Analysis." *Economie Apliqué* 16(1), 1988. Paper presented in Ottawa, October 1984.

―――― (1986) "Finance, Funding, Saving and Investment." *Journal of Post-Keynesian Economics* 9(1), Fall.

Devlin, Robert (1989a) *Debt and Crisis in Latin America*. Princeton: Princeton University Press.

―――― (1989b) "From Baker to Brady: A New Debt Plan That Can Work If . . ." Santiago, Chile: Economic Commission for Latin America and the Caribbean, May.

Díaz-Alejandro, Carlos (1979) "Southern Cone Stabilization Plans." In W. Cline and S. Weintraub, eds., *Economic Stabilization in Developing Countries* (1981).

Di Tella, Torquato (1965) "Populism and Reform in Latin America." In C. Véliz, *Obstacles to Change in Latin America*. New York: Oxford University Press.

Dornbusch, Rudiger (1989) "Debt Problems and the World Economy." In J. D. Sachs, ed., *Developing Country Debt and the World Economy*.

―――― (1990) "Policies to Move from Stabilization to Growth." Proceedings of the World Bank Annual Conference on Development Economics, 1990 (supplement to the *World Bank Economic Review*).

Dornbusch, R., and S. Edwards (1989) "The Macroeconomics of Populism." *Journal of Development Economics* 32(2), April 1990. Originally a paper presented in Bogotá, March 30–April 1, 1989.

Dornbusch, R., and S. Edwards, eds. (1991) *The Macroeconomics of Populism in Latin America*. Chicago: University of Chicago Press.

Dornbusch, R., and S. Fischer (1986) "Stopping Hyperinflation: Past and Present." *Weltwirschaftliches Archiv* 22, January.

Dornbusch, R., F. Sturzenegger, and H. Wolf (1990) "Extreme Inflation: Dynamics and Stabilization." *Brookings Papers on Economic Activity* 2.

Dunleavy, P., and B. O'Leary (1987) *Theories of the State*. New York: Meredith Press.

ECLAC (Economic Commission for Latin America and the Caribbean) (1990) *Panorama Económico de América Latina 1990*. Santiago de Chile: ECLAC.

―――― (1991) *Panorama Económico de América Latina 1991*. Santiago de Chile: ECLAC.

Edwards, S., and G. Tabellini (1990) "Explaining Fiscal Policies and Inflation in Developing Countries." Cambridge, NBER Working Paper no. 3,493, October.

Emmerij, L., and Iglesias, H. (1991) *Restoring Financial Flows to Latin America*. Paris and Washington: OECD and Inter-American Development Bank.

Erickson, Kenneth (1975) "Populism and Political Control of the Working Class." *Proceedings of the Pacific Coast Council of Latin American Studies* 4.

Escudé, Carlos (1991) "Relaciones Internacionales de Argentina." *América Latina/Internacional* (FLACSO) 8(27), January.

Ethier, Diane, ed. (1990) *Democratic Transition and Consolidation in Southern Europe, Latin America and Southeast Asia*. London: Macmillan.

Evans, Peter (1979) *The Alliance of Multinational, State and Local Capital in Brazil*. Princeton: Princeton University Press.

Fajnzylber, Fernando (1989). "Sobre la Imposterable Transformacion Productiva de América Latina." *Pensamiento Iberoamericano* 16, July–December.

―――― , coord. (1990) *Changing Production Patterns with Social Equity*. Santiago, Chile: ECLAC.

Fanelli, J., and R. Frenkel (1989) "Desequilibrios, Políticas de Estabilización e Hyperinflación en Argentina." CEDES Working Paper, November.

Fanelli, J., R. Frenkel, and G. Rozenwurcel (1990) "Growth and Structural Reform in Latin America: Where We Stand." Report prepared for UNCTAD. Buenos Aires: CEDES, October.

Faro, Clovis, ed. (1990) *Plano Collor: Avaliações e Perspectivas.* Rio de Janeiro: Livros Técnicos e Científicos Editora.

Feldman, G., C. Holtfreisch, G. Ritter, and P. Witt, eds. (1982) *The German Inflation.* Berlin: Walter de Guyter.

Ffrench-Davis, R., and R. Devlin (1993) "Diez Años de Crisis de la Deuda Latinoamericana. *Comercio Exterior* 43(1) January.

FGV. *Conjuntura Econômica* (several issues). Rio de Janeiro: Fundação Getúlio Vargas.

Fiori, José Luiz (1984) "Conjuntura e Ciclo na Dinámica de um Estado Periférico." Ph.D. thesis. Instituto de Economia Industrial da Universidade do Rio de Janeiro.

Fischer, Stanley (1989) "Resolving the International Debt Crisis." In J. D. Sachs, ed., *Developing Country Debt and the World Economy.*

Fishlow, Albert (1991) Review of *Handbook of Development Economics. Journal of Economic Literature* 29(4), December.

Fraga Neto, A., and A. Lara Resende (1985) Déficit, Dívida e Ajustamento: Uma Nota sobre o Caso Brasileiro. *Revista de Economia Política* 5(4), October.

Friedman, Milton, ed. (1956) *Studies in the Quantity Theory of Money.* Chicago: University of Chicago Press.

Fritsch, W., and G. Franco (1993) "The Political Economy of Trade and Industrial Policy Reform in Brazil in the 1990s." *Série Reformas de Política Pública* 6. Santiago, Chile: ECLAC.

Fukuchi, T., and M. Kagami (1990) *Perspectives on the Pacific Basin Economy: A Comparison of Asia and Latin America.* Tokyo: Institute of Developing Economies.

Furtado, Celso (1950) "Características Gerais da Economia Brasileira." *Revista de Economia Brasileira* 4(1), March.

——— (1964) *Dialectica do Desenvolvimento.* Rio de Janeiro: Editora Fondo de Cultura.

——— (1992) *Brasil: A Construção Interrompida.* São Paulo: Paz e Terra.

Gouvêa, Gilda Portugal (1994) *Burocracia e Elites Dominantes do País.* São Paulo: Paulicéia.

Haggard, S., and R. Kaufman (1991) "The State in the Initiation and Consolidation of Market Oriented Reform." Paper presented at a seminar sponsored by the University of São Paulo (USP), July. USP, Working paper of the Instituto de Estudos Avançados. Published in Portuguese in Lourdes Sola, ed., *Estado, Mercado, Democracia* (1993).

Helpman, E. (1988) "Macroeconomic Effects of Price Controls: The Role of Market Structure." *Economic Journal* 98(391), June.

——— (1989) "Voluntary Debt Reduction: Incentives and Welfare." NBER Working Paper Series no. 2,692, August.

Hirschman, Albert (1974) "Policymaking and Policy Analysis in Latin America—A Return Journey." In *Essays in Trespassing: Economics to Politics and Beyond.* Cambridge: Cambridge University Press, 1981. Originally presented to a conference in 1974.

——— (1982) *Shifting Involvements.* Princeton: Princeton University Press.

——— (1989) "Duzentos Anos de Retórica Reacionária: O Caso do Efeito Perverso." *Novos Estudos CEBRAP* 23, March.

——— (1991) *The Rhetoric of Reaction.* Cambridge: Harvard University Press.

Husain, I., and I. Diwan, eds. (1989) *Dealing wih the Debt Crisis.* Washington, D.C.: The World Bank.

Ianni, Octavio (1968) *O Colapso do Populismo no Brasil.* Rio de Janeiro: Civilização Brasileira.

IBGE. *Anuário Estatístico* (several issues). Rio de Janeiro: Instituto Brasileiro de Geografia e Estatística.

IDB (1990) *Economic and Social Progress in Latin America.* Washington, D.C.: Inter-American Development Bank.

IMF. *World Economic Outlook* (several issues). Washington, D.C.: International Monetary Fund.

——— (1990) *World Economic Outlook.* Washington, D.C.: International Monetary Fund, May.

Jaguaribe, Hélio (1990) "O PSDB Ante a Presente Situação do Brasil." Rio de Janeiro: Instituto de Estudos Políticos e Sociais, November. Mimeo.

Kagami, Mitsuhiro (1990) "A Fiscal Comparison of Asia and Latin America." In T. Fukuchi and M. Kagami, eds., *Perspectives on the Pacific Basin Economy.*

Kaldor, Nicholas (1970) "The New Monetarism." *Lloyds Bank Review,* July.

Kalecki, Michael (1933) "Outline of a Theory of the Business Cycle." In Kalecki, M., *Select Essays on the Dynamics of Capitalist Economy.* Cambridge: Cambridge University Press, 1971. Originally published in Polish in 1933.

Kandir, Antonio (1988) "A Dinâmica da Inflação." Ph.D. diss., State University of Campinas.

Kenen, Peter (1983) "A Bail-Out for the Banks." *New York Times,* March 6.

Keynes, John M. (1937) "The 'Ex-Ante' Theory of the Rate of Interest." In *The General Theory and After. Part II: Defense and Development.* Vol. 14 of *The Collected Writing of Keynes.* London: Macmillan (1973). Originally published in *Economic Journal,* December 1937.

Kiguel, M. A., and N. Liviatan (1988) "Inflationary Rigidities and Orthodox Stabilization Policies: Lessons from Latin America." *World Bank Economic Review* 2(3), September.

——— (1992) "When Do Heterodox Stabilization Programs Work? Lessons from Experience." *World Bank Research Observer* 7(1), January.

Kregel, Jan (1984–1985) "Constraints on the Expansion of Output and Employment: Real or Monetary." *Journal of Post-Keynesian Economics* 7(2), Winter.

——— (1986) "A Note on Finance, Liquidity, Saving, and Investment." *Journal of Post-Keynesian Economics* 9(1), Fall.

Krueger, Anne O. (1985) "The Experience and Lesson of Asia's Super Exporters." In V. Corbo, A. Krueger, and F. Ossa, eds., *Export Oriented Development Strategies.*

Lamounier, Bolívar (1988) "Authoritarian Brazil Revisited: The Impact of Election in Abertura." In Alfred Stepan, ed., *Rethinking Military Politics.* Princeton: Princeton University Press, 1988.

——— (1990) "Brazil: Inequality Against Democracy." In L. Diamond, J. Linz, and S. M. Lipset, eds., *Democracy in Developing Countries.* Vol. 4, *Latin America.* Boulder: Lynne Rienner.

Lara Resende, A., and P. Arida (1984) "Inertial Inflation and Monetary Reform." In John Williamson, org., *Inflation and Indexation: Argentina, Brazil and Israel.* Cambridge, Mass.: MIT Press, 1985.

Lara Resende, André (1984) "A Moeda Indexada: Uma Proposta para Eliminar a Inflação Inercial." *Gazeta Mercantil,* September 26–28.

——— (1988) "Da Inflação Crônica à Hiperinflação: Observações sobre o Quadro Atual." *Revista de Economia Política* 9(1), January. Paper presented to First Fórum Nacional, Rio de Janeiro, November 1988.

——— (1992) "O Conselho da Moeda: Um Órgão Emissor Independente." *Revista de Economia Política* 12(4), October.

Levitas, Ruth, ed. (1986) *The Ideology of the New Right.* Cambridge: Polity Press.

Lima Sobrinho, Alexandre Barbosa (1963) *Desde Quando Somos Nacionalistas*. Rio de Janeiro: Editora Civilização Brasileira.

Little, Ian M.D. (1982) *Economic Development: Theory, Policy and International Relations*. New York: Basic Books.

Lopes, Francisco L. (1984) "Só um Choque Heterodoxo Pode Derrubar a Inflação." *Economia em Perspectiva* (Conselho Regional de Economia de São Paulo), August.

Lopes, Juarez Brandão (1993) "Brasil: 1989: Um Estudo Sócio-econômico da Indigência e da Pobreza Urbanas." Working Paper no. 25, July. Universidade Estadual de Campinas, Núcleo de Estudos de Políticas Públicas.

Mainwaring, S., G. O'Donnell, and J. S. Valenzuela, eds. (1992) *Issues in Democratric Consolidation*. Notre Dame: Notre Dame University Press.

Mainwaring, Scott (1992) "Transitions to Democracy and Democratic Transition: Theoretical and Comparative Issues." In S. Mainwaring, G. O'Donnell, and J. S. Valenzuela, eds., *Issues in Democratic Consolidation*.

Malloy, James (1991) "Economic Policymaking and the Problem of Democratic Governance in the Central Andes." Paper presented at the seminar sponsored by the University of São Paulo, July. Working paper of the Instituto de Estudos Avançados. Published in Portuguese in Lourdes Sola, ed., *Estado Mercado, Democracia*.

Martins, Luciano (1976) *Pouvoir et Développement Economique*. Paris: Editions Anthropos.

——— (1983) "Le Regime Autoritaire Brésilien et la Liberalization Politique." *Problemes d'Amerique Latine* 65, 3d quarter. Also published in G. O'Donnell, P. Schmitter, and L. Whitehead, eds., *Transitions from Authoritarian Rule*.

——— (1985) *Estado Capitalista e Burocracia no Brasil Pós-64*. Rio de Janeiro: Paz e Terra.

——— (1993) "Projeto de Desenvolvimento, Sistema Político e Crise do Estado-nação." São Paulo: Universidade Estadual de Campinas, July. Mimeo.

Marx, Karl (1867) *Capital*. Vol. 1, English translation. London: Penguin Books, 1976. First German edition, 1867.

Merkin, Gerald (1982) "Towards a Theory of the German Inflation." In G. Feldman, C. Holtfreisch, G. Ritter, and P. Witt, eds., *The German Inflation*.

Ministério da Fazenda (1987) *Plano de Controle Macroeconômico*. Brasília: Ministério da Fazenda.

Moisés, José Álvaro (1993) "Democratization, Mass Political Culture and Political Legitimacy in Brazil." Working Paper 1993/44, February. Madrid: Instituto Juan March de Estudios e Investigaciones.

Moura da Silva, Adroaldo, et al. (1983) *FMI x Brasil: A Armadilha da Recessão*. São Paulo: Fórum Gazeta Mercantil.

Nakano, Yoshiaki (1989) "Da Inércia Inflacionária à Hiperinflação." In J. M. Rego, ed., *A Aceleração Recente da Inflação*.

——— (1990) "As Fragilidades do Plano Collor de Estabilização." In Clovis de Faro, ed., *Plano Collor*.

Nassif, Luís (1995) "O Anacronismo do BNDES." *Folha de S. Paulo*, March.

Nassuno, Mariane (1995) "Pressão Externa e Abertura Comercial." Master's thesis. Fundação Getúlio Vargas, São Paulo.

Naya, Seiji (1989) "Economic Performance: NIEs and Beyond." In T. Fukuchi and M. Kagami, eds., *Perspectives on the Pacific Basin Economy*.

Nunes, Edson de Oliveira (1984) "Bureaucratic Insulation and Clientelism in Contemporary Brazil: Uneven State Building and the Taming of Modernity." Ph.D. diss., Department of Political Science, University of California, Berkeley.

O'Connor, James (1973) *The Fiscal Crisis of the State.* New York: St. Martin Press.

O'Donnell, Guillermo (1977) "Estado y Alianzas de Classe en Argentina, 1956–1976." *Desarrollo Económico* 16(64), January.

——— (1988) "Hiatos, Instituições e Perspectivas Democráticas." In F. Wanderley Reis and G. O'Donnell, eds., *A Democracia no Brasil.*

——— (1991) "Democracia Delegativa?" *Novos Estudos CEBRAP* 31, October.

O'Donnell, G., P. Schmitter, and L. Whitehead, eds. (1986) *Transitions from Authoritarian Rule: Comparative Perspectives.* Baltimore: Johns Hopkins University Press.

Pastore, Affonso Celso (1990) "A Reforma Monetária do Plano Collor." In Clovis de Faro, ed., *Plano Collor.*

——— (1994) "Reforma Monetária, Inércia e Estabilização." Departamento de Economia, Universidade de São Paulo, May. Mimeo.

Payer, Cheryl (1991) *Lent and Lost.* London: Zed Books.

Pazos, Felipe (1972) *Chronic Inflation in Latin America.* New York: Praeger Publishers.

Piedra, Matilde (1988) "El Componente Social del Ajuste Económico en América Latina." Santiago de Chile: ILDES, UN/ECLA, June.

Prebisch, Raúl (1949) "O Desenvolvimento Econômico da América Latina e seus Principais Problemas." *Revista Brasileira de Economia* 3(4), December. In Spanish: "El Desarrollo Latino-americano y sus Principales Problemas." *Boletín Económico de América Latina* 7(1), February 1962.

Przeworski, Adam (1990) "East-South System Transformation." Chicago: University of Chicago, February. Mimeo.

——— (1991) *Democracy and the Market.* Cambridge: Cambridge University Press.

Ramos, Joseph (1986) "Políticas de Estabilización." In Cortázar, R., ed., *Políticas macro-económicas: una perspectiva latinoamericana.* Santiago de Chile: CIEPLAN.

Rangel, Ignácio (1963) *A Inflação Brasileira.* Rio de Janeiro: Tempo Brasileiro.

——— (1978) Postface to the 3d edition of *A Inflação Brasileira.* São Paulo: Brasiliense.

Rego, J. M., org. (1989) *A Aceleração Recente da Inflação.* São Paulo: Editora Bienal.

Reisen, H., and A. Trotsenburg (1988) *Developing Country Debt: The Budgetary and Transfer Problem.* Paris: Development Centre of the OECD.

Rezende da Silva, Fernando (1972) *Avaliação do Setor Público na Economia Brasileira.* Rio de Janeiro: IPEA/INPES.

Ritter, G., and P. Witt, eds. (1982) *The German Inflation.* Berlin: Walter de Guyter.

Robinson, James D., III (1988) "A Comprehensive Agenda for an Institute of International Debt and Development." *AMEX Bank Review* 13, March.

Rocha, Sônia (1991) "Pobreza Metropolitana e os Ciclos de Curto Prazo: Um Balanço dos Anos 80." *IPEA: Boletim de Conjuntura* 12, January.

Rodrigues, Miguel Urbano (1988) "O cruel 'milagre' chileno." *Folha de S. Paulo,* September 14.

Roemer, John (1990) "Laissez-Faire Capitalism, Trade Union Capitalism, Social-Democratic Capitalism and Market Socialism." Working Paper no. 4. Department of Political Science, University of Chicago. *East-South System Transformations Project,* October.

Rohatyn, Felix (1983) "A Plan for Stretching Out Global Debt." *Business Week,* February 28.

Romão, Maurício Costa (1991) "Distribuição de Renda, Pobreza e Desigualdades

Regionais no Brasil." In J. M. Camargo and F. Gambiagi, eds., *Distribuição de Renda no Brasil*.

Sachs, Jeffrey D. (1987) "Trade and Exchange Rate Policies in Growth-Oriented Adjustment Programs." In V. Corbo, M. Goldstein, and M. Khan, eds., *Growth-Oriented Adjustment Programs*. Washington, D.C.: International Monetary Fund and the World Bank.

———— (1988) "Social Conflict and Populist Policies in Latin America." In R. Brunetta and C. Dell-Aringa, eds., *Labor Relations and Economic Performance*. London: Macmillan.

———— (1989a) "Efficient Debt Reduction." In I. Husain and I. Diwan, eds., *Dealing with the Debt Crisis*. Originally prepared for the World Bank Symposium, Dealing with the Debt Crisis, January 26–27, Washington, D.C.

———— (1989b) "Making the Brady Plan Work." *Foreign Affairs* 68(3), Summer.

Sachs, Jeffrey D., ed. (1989c) *Developing Country Debt and the World Economy*. Chicago: University of Chicago Press and the National Bureau of Economic Research.

Salama, Pierre (1989) *Dollarisation*. Paris: Editions La Découverte.

Salum, Brasílio, Jr. (1988) "Por Que Não Tem Dado Certo: Notas Sobre a Transição Política Brasileira." In Lourdes Sola, ed., *O Estado da Transição: Política e Economia na Nova República*. São Paulo: Vértice.

Santos, Wanderley Guilherme dos (1985) "A Pós-revolução Brasileira." In Hélio Jaguaribe, et al., *Brasil, Sociedade Democrática*. Rio de Janeiro: José Olympio Editora, 1985.

———— (1993) *As Razões da Desordem*. Rio de Janeiro: Editora Rocco.

Schneider, Ben Ross (1991) *Bureaucracy and Industrial Policy in Brazil*. Pittsburgh: Pittsburgh University Press.

Schneider, William (1990) "JFK's Children: The Class of '74." *Atlantic Monthly* 263(3), March.

Schumpeter, Joseph (1911) *The Theory of Economic Development*. Cambridge: Harvard University Press, 1962. First German edition, 1911.

Selcher, Wayne A. (1986) "Introduction." In Wayne A. Selcher, ed., *Political Liberalization in Brazil*. Boulder: Westview Press.

Sheahan, John (1986) "Economic Policies and the Prospects for Successful Transition from Authoritarian Rule in Latin America." In G. O'Donnell, P. Schmitter, and L. Whitehead, eds., *Transitions from Authoritarian Rule*.

Sola, Lourdes, ed. (1993) *Estado, Mercado, Democracia—Política e Economia Comparadas*. São Paulo: Paz e Terra.

Stallings, Barbara (1991) "International Influence on Economic Policy, Debt, Stabilization and Structural Reforms." In S. Haggard and R. Kaufman, eds., *The Politics of Economic Adjustment: International Constraints, Distributive Policies, and the State*. Princeton: Princeton University Press.

Stallings, Barbara, and Robert Kaufman, eds. (1989) *Debt and Democracy in Latin America*. Boulder: Westview Press.

Stepan, Alfred (1986) *Os Militares: da Abertura à Nova República*. Rio de Janeiro: Paz e Terra.

Sunkel, O., and J. Ramos (1993) "Toward a Neostructuralist Synthesis." In Osvaldo Sunkel, ed., *Development from Within*.

Sunkel, Osvaldo (1993) "From Inward-Looking Development to Development from Within." In Osvaldo Sunkel, ed., *Development from Within: Toward a Neostructuralist Approach for Latin America*. Boulder: Lynne Rienner Publishers.

Suplicy, E. M., and Cury, S. (1994) "A renda Mínima Garantida como Proposta para Remover a Pobreza no Brasil." *Revista de Economia Política,* vol. 14, 1(53), January–March.

Suzigan, Wilson (1976) "As Empresas do Governo e o Papel do Estado na Economia Brasileira." In *Aspectos da Participação do Governo na Economia.* Rio de Janeiro: IPEA/INPES.

——— (1988) "Estado e industrialização no Brasil." *Revista de Economia Política* 8(4), October.

Tanzi, Vito (1989) "Fiscal Policy, Stabilization and Growth." In M. Blejer and K. Chu, eds., *Fiscal Policy, Stabilization, and Growth in Developing Countries.*

Thorstensen, V., Y. Nakano, C. Faria Lima, and C. Sato (1994) *O Brasil Frente a um Mundo Dividido em Blocos.* São Paulo: Nobel and Instituto Sul-Norte.

Tokeshi, Hélcio (1991) "Indexação Informal, Probabilidade e Comportamento Convencional." Master's thesis, Economic Institute of the State University of Campinas, Campinas.

Toledo, Joaquim Elói (1990) "Plano Collor em Zona de Perigo." *Jornal do Economista* (Conselho Regional de Economia de São Paulo) 25, May.

Touraine, Alain (1988) *La Parole et le Sang: Politique et Societé en Amérique Latine.* Paris: Editions Odile Jacob.

Velloso, João Paulo dos Reis (1990) "Um país sem projeto: a crise brasileira e a modernização da sociedade—primeiras idéias." In João Paulo dos Reis Velloso, ed., *A Crise Brasileira.*

Velloso, João Paulo dos Reis, ed. (1990) *A Crise Brasileira e a Modernização da Sociedade.* Rio de Janeiro: José Olympio Editora.

Wanderley Reis, Fábio (1988) "Consolidação Democrática e Construção do Estado." In F. Wanderley Reis and G. O'Donnell, eds., *A Democracia no Brasil.*

Wanderley Reis, F., and G. O'Donnell, eds. (1988) *A Democracia no Brasil: Dilemas e Perspectivas.* São Paulo: Revista dos Tribunais.

Weffort, Francisco (1965) "State and Mass in Latin America." In Horowitz, ed., *Masses in Latin America.* New York: Oxford University Press (1970). Originally published as "Política de Massas," in Octavio Ianni, et al., *Política e Revolução Social no Brasil* (1965).

——— (1980) *O Populismo na Política Brasileira.* Rio de Janeiro: Paz e Terra.

——— (1989) "A Construção da Democracia e a Crise da Comunidade Nacional." In Universidade Estadual de São Paulo (UNESP), *O Desenvolvimento Ameaçado: Perspectivas e Soluções.* São Paulo, Editora UNESP.

——— (1992) *Qual Democracia?* São Paulo: Companhia das Letras.

Werneck, Rogério F. (1983) "A Armadilha Financeira do Setor Público e as Empresas Estatais." In Adroaldo Moura da Silva et al., eds., *FMI x Brasil.*

——— (1985) "Uma Análise do Financiamento e dos Investimentos das Empresas Estatais Federais no Brasil, 1980–83." *Revista Brasileira de Economia* 39(1), January.

——— (1986) "Retomada do Crescimento e Esforço de Poupança: Limitações e Possibilidades." Working Paper no. 133, July. Rio de Janeiro: Department of Economics, Catholic University.

——— (1987) *Empresas Estatais e Política Macroeconômica.* Rio de Janeiro: Campus.

Williamson, John (1990) "What Washington Means by Policy Reform" and "The Progress of Policy Reform in Latin America." In John Williamson, ed., *Latin American Adjustment.*

——— (1993a) "Democracy and the 'Washington Consensus.'" *World Development* 21(8), August.

———— (1993b) "In Search of a Manual for Technopols." In John Williamson, ed., *The Political Economy of Policy Reform.*

Williamson, John, ed. (1985) *Inflation and Indexation: Argentina, Brazil and Israel.* Cambridge: MIT Press.

———— (1990) *Latin American Adjustment.* Washington, D.C.: Institute of International Economics.

———— (1993) *The Political Economy of Policy Reform.* Washington, D.C.: Institute for International Economics.

World Bank (1984a) *Brazil: Economic Memorandum.* Washington, D.C.: The World Bank.

———— (1984b) *Brazil: Financial Systems Review.* Washington, D.C.: The World Bank.

———— *World Development Report* (several years). Washington, D.C.: The World Bank.

Yeager, Leland B., et al. (1981) *Experiences with Stopping Inflation.* Washington, D.C.: American Enterprise Institute for Public Policy Research.

Index

❖❖

About the Book

This is a book about the economic crisis that seized Brazil and the rest of Latin America in the 1980s, its political consequences, and the economic reforms that were begun in the mid-1980s but that remain incomplete a decade later.

From his vantage point as both an academic economist and a political insider, Bresser Pereira explains Brazil's—and more generally, Latin America's—economic problems in terms of a crisis of the state. Finding the paradigms of structuralism and dependency no longer useful in the face of the issues of the 1980s and 1990s, and rejecting neoliberalism as a solution, his crisis of the state approach seeks a new synthesis, advocating a pragmatic, social-democratic strategy for reform.

Fiscal adjustment and structural reforms, argues Bresser Pereira, should not be seen as attempts to minimize state intervention, but instead as reforms *of* the state, with the ultimate goal of rebuilding it.

LUIZ CARLOS BRESSER PEREIRA is Brazil's minister of federal administration and state reform and is professor of economics at the Getúlio Vargas Foundation (Brazil). Founding editor of the *Revista de Economia Política,* he has published widely (in both Portuguese and English) in the areas of political economy, development economics, and inflation theory. After Brazil's democratization, he occupied several government positions: from 1983 to 1987 he was chairman of the State Bank of São Paulo, chief of staff of the Government of São Paulo, secretary of science and technology of São Paulo, and, in 1987, finance minister of Brazil. He has been a member of Brazil's Social-Democratic Party since its founding in 1988.